Blood on the Tracks

volume 2

Shuzo Oshimi

CHAPTER 8 A Mother's Back

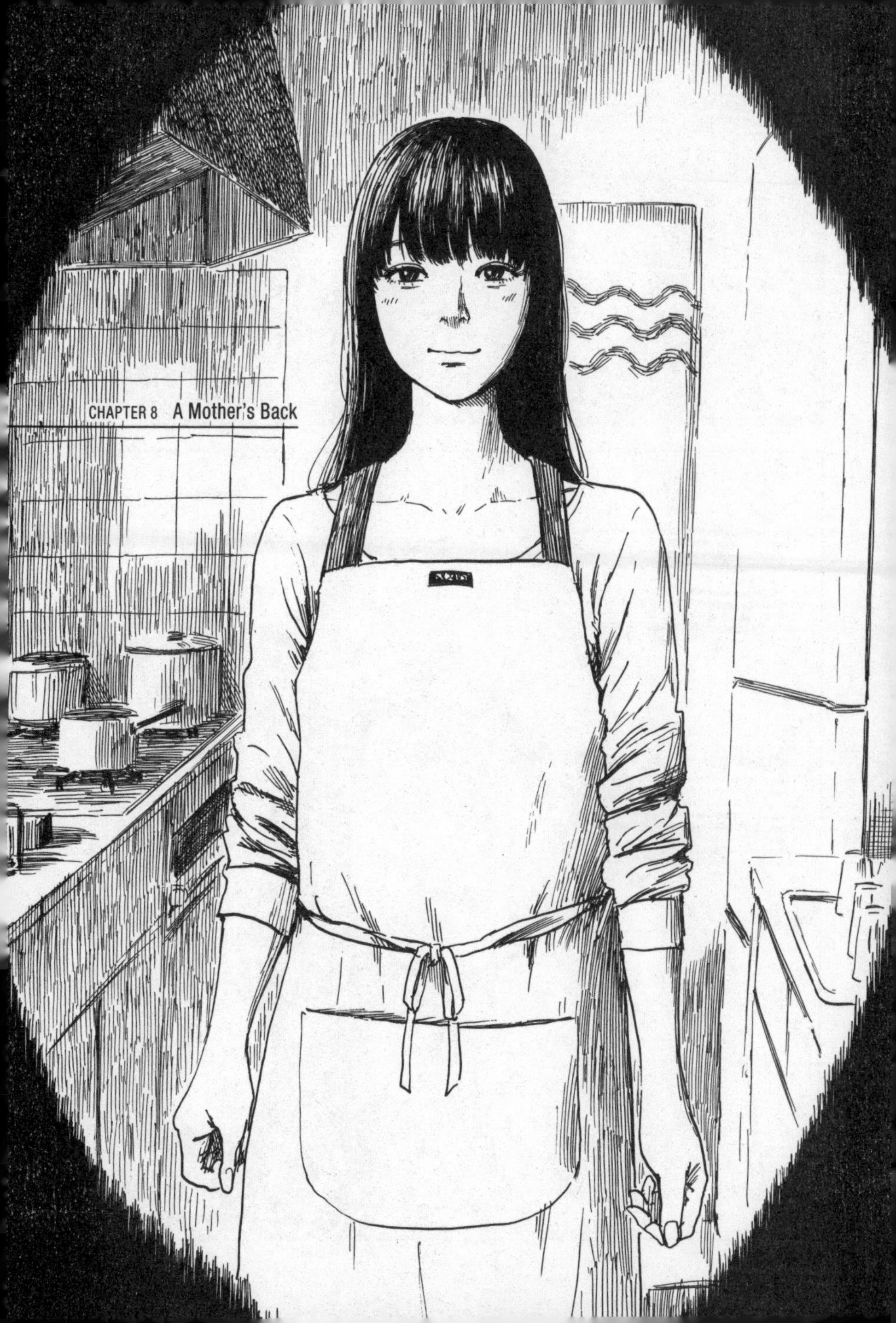

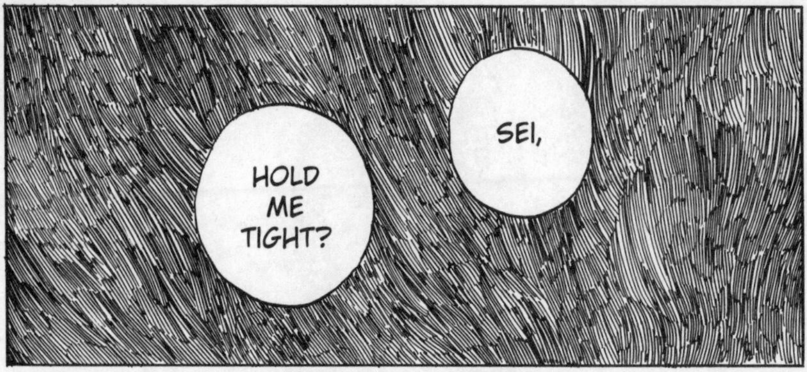
SEI,
HOLD ME TIGHT?
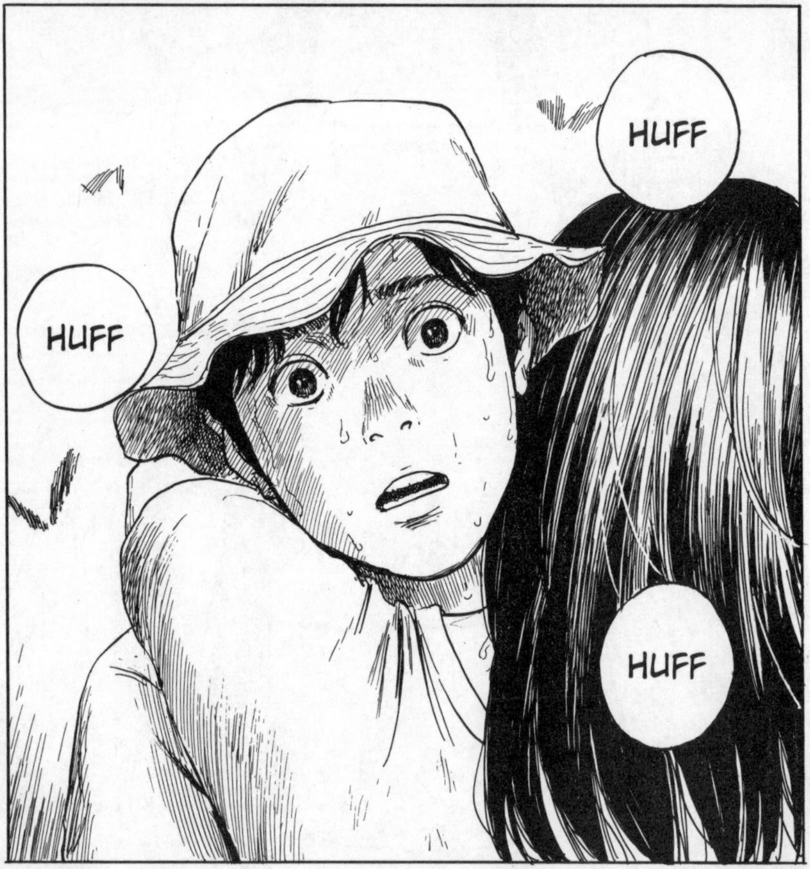
HUFF
HUFF
HUFF

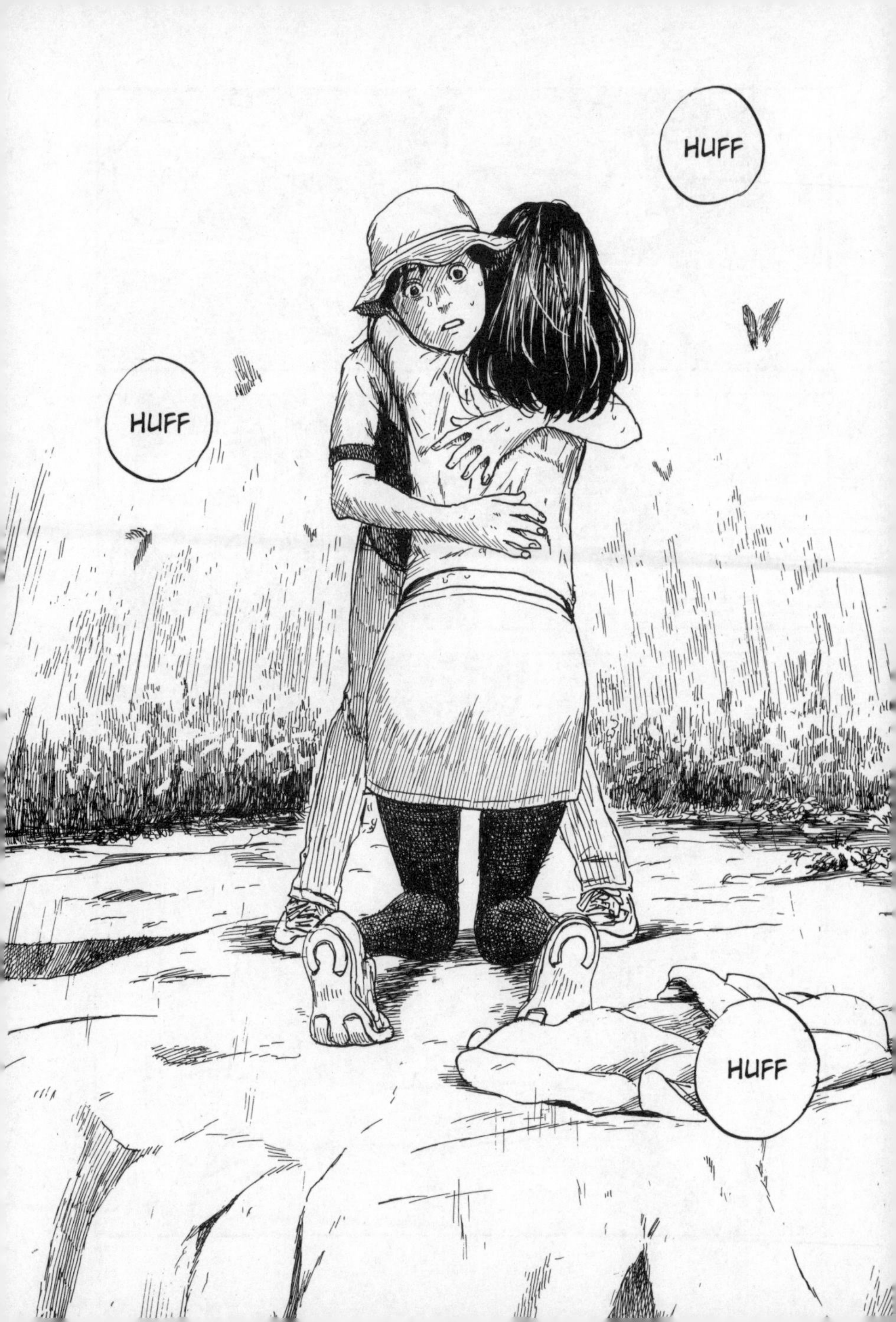
HUFF
HUFF
HUFF

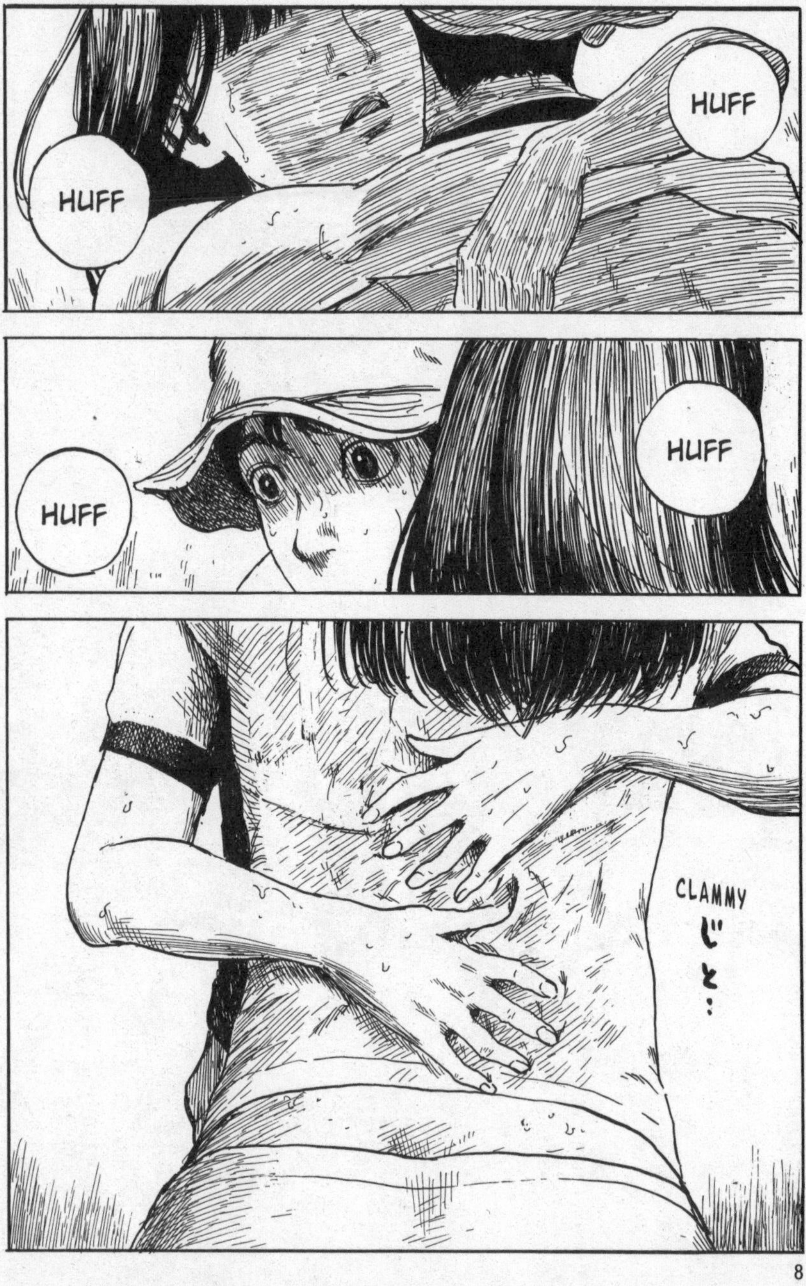
HUFF
HUFF
HUFF
HUFF
CLAMMY
じと…

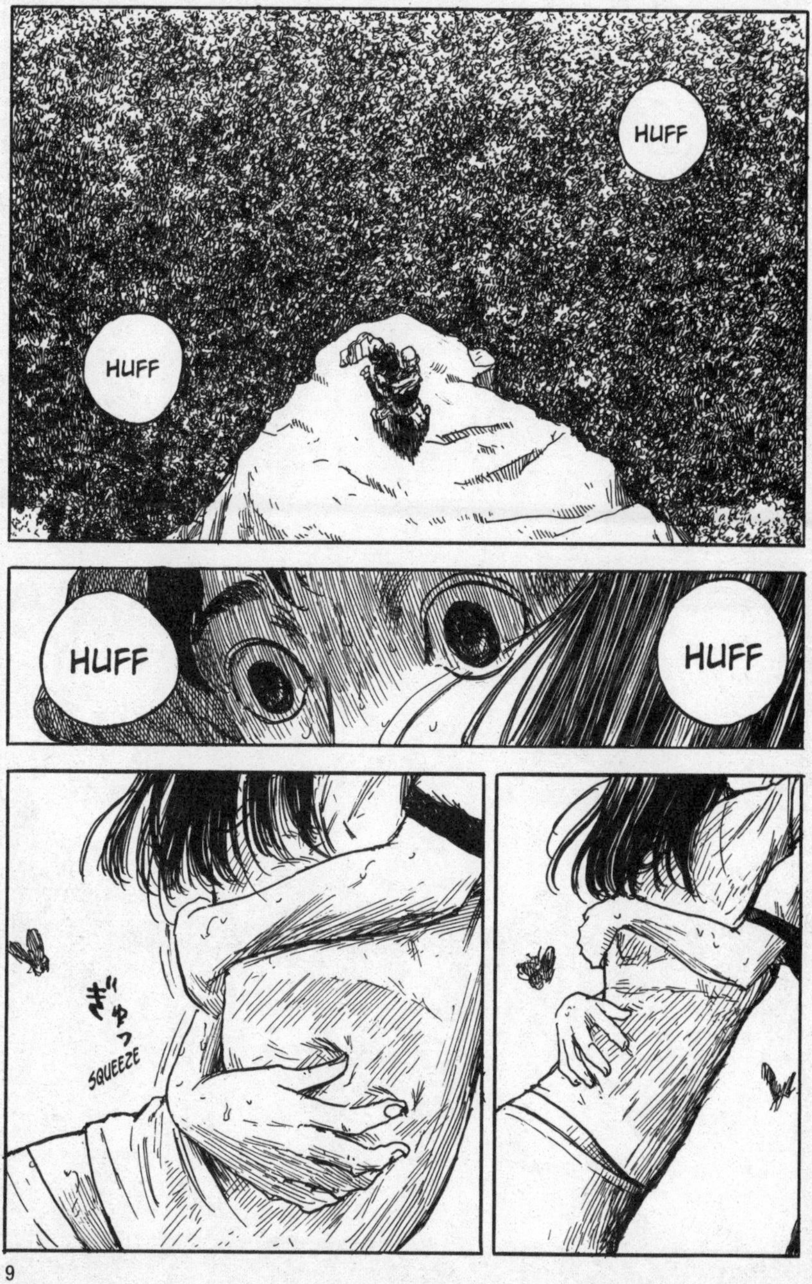
HUFF
HUFF
HUFF
HUFF
ぎゅっ
SQUEEZE

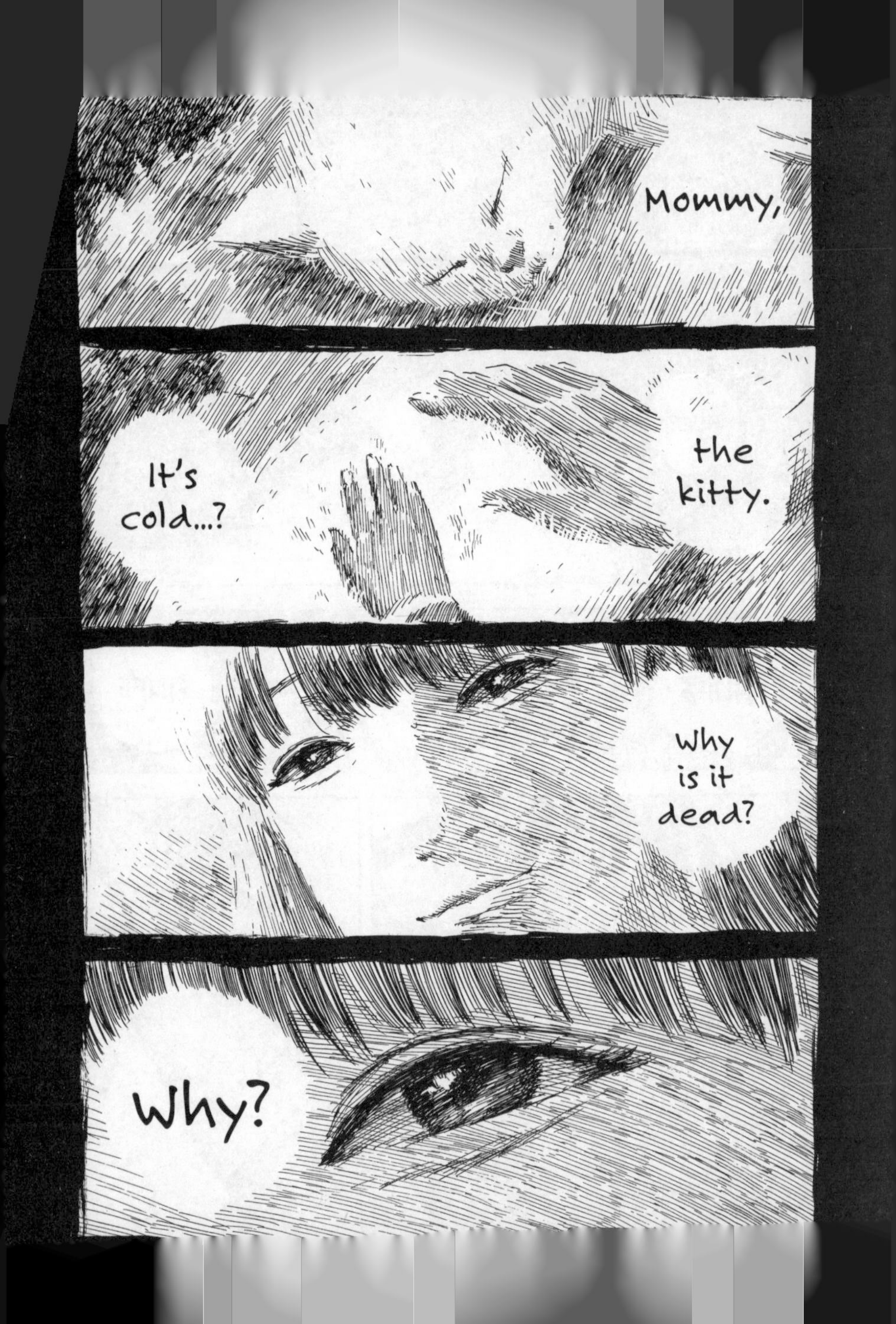
Mommy,
the kitty.
It's cold...?
Why is it dead?
Why?

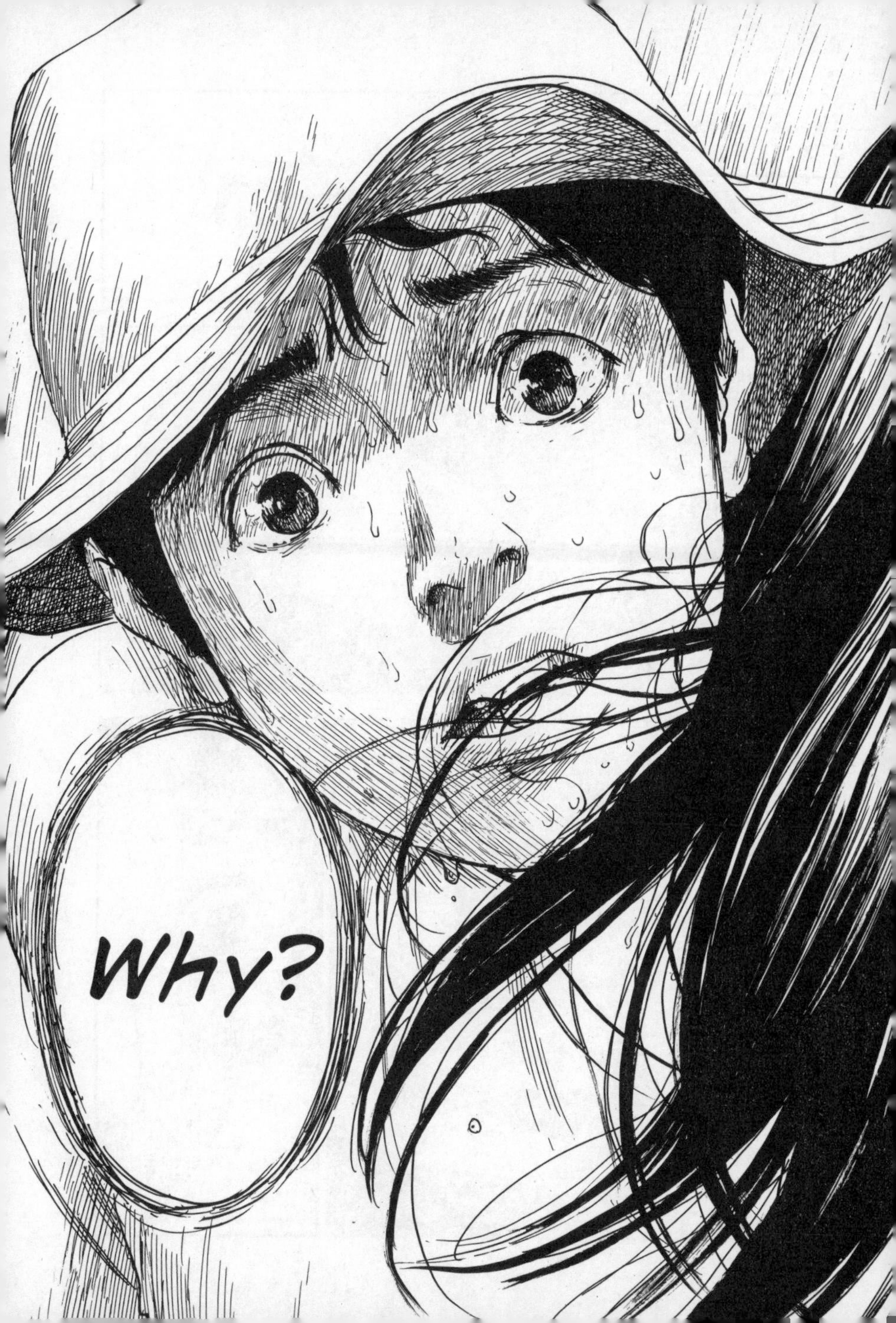
Why?

SEI.
LET GO.
GRP

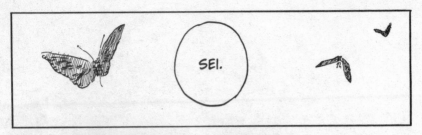

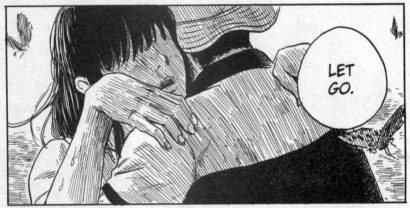

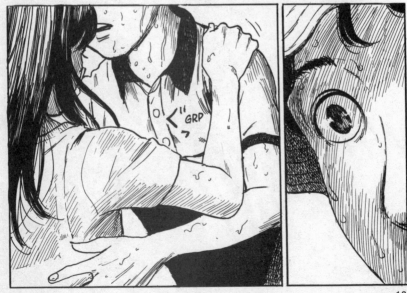

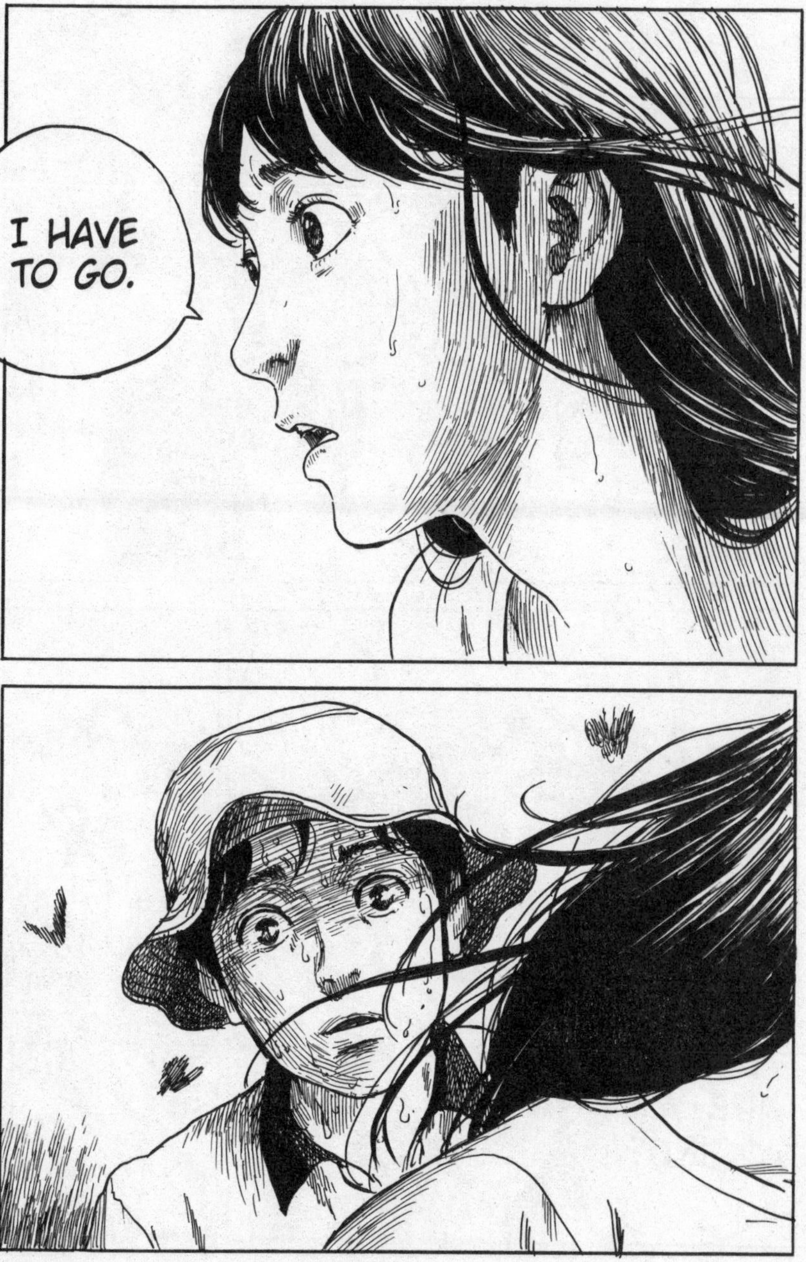
I HAVE TO GO.

WOBBLE

WH—

WHERE...
WHERE
ARE YOU
GOING?!

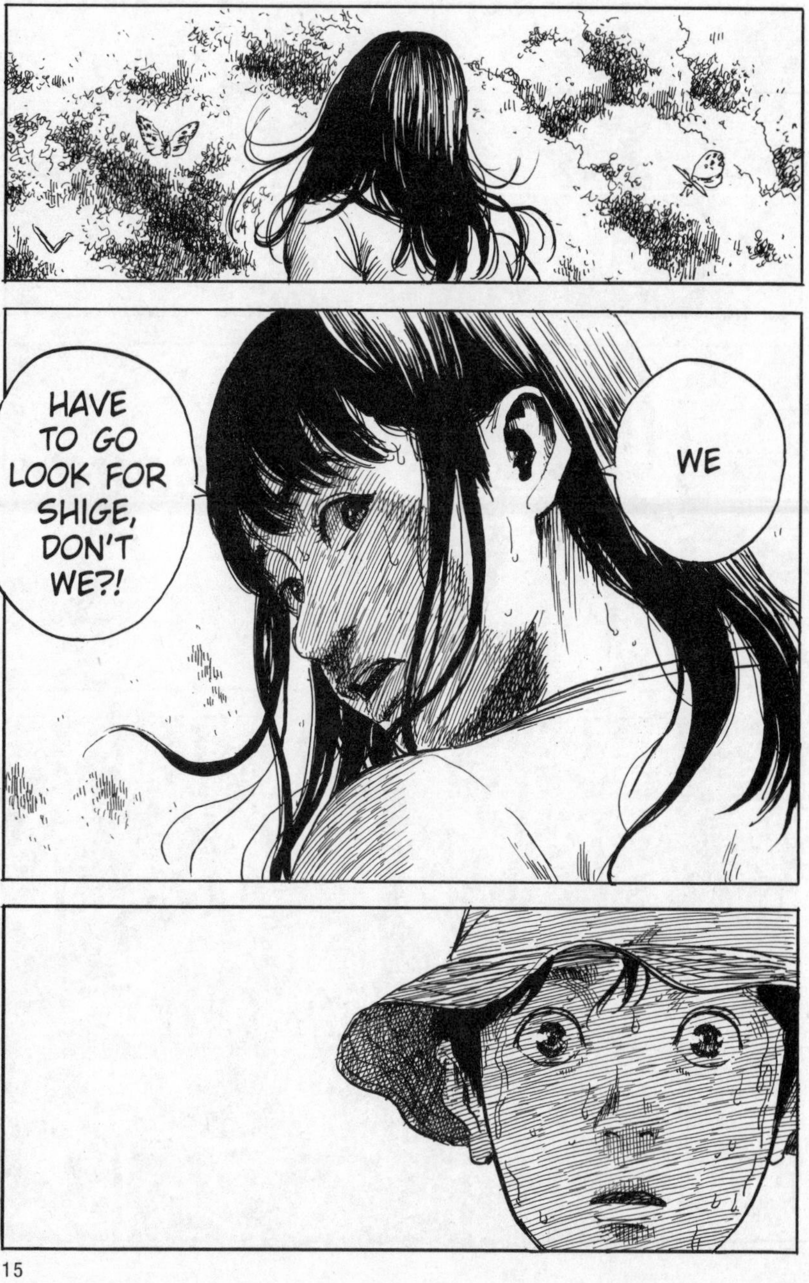
WE
HAVE TO GO LOOK FOR SHIGE, DON'T WE?!

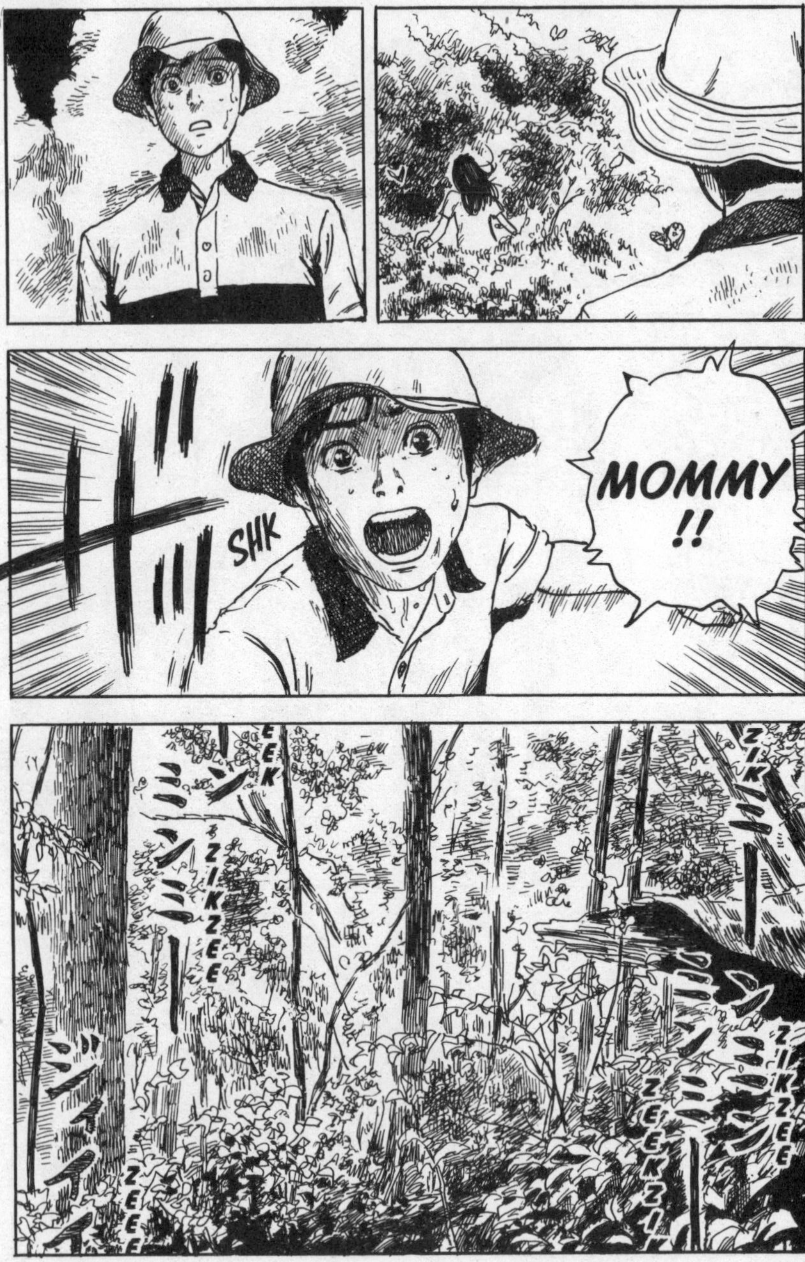
MOMMY !!
SHK
ZIK
ZIKZEE
ZEEKZI
EEK
ZIKZEE
ZEEE

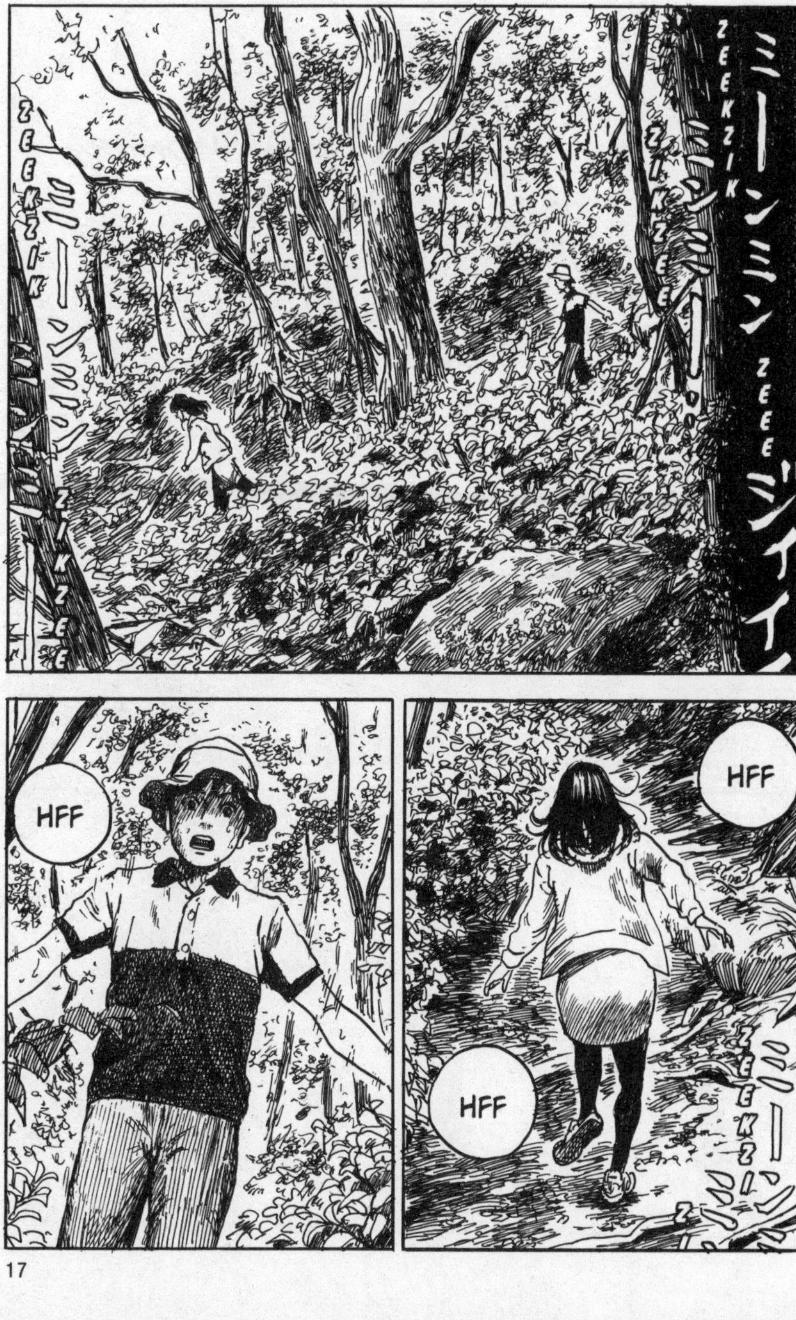
ミーンミン
ZEEE
ジイン
ZEEKZIK
ミンミー
ZIKZEEE
ZEEKZIK
ミーンミンミー
ZIKZEEE
HFF
HFF
ミーン
ZEEKZI
HFF

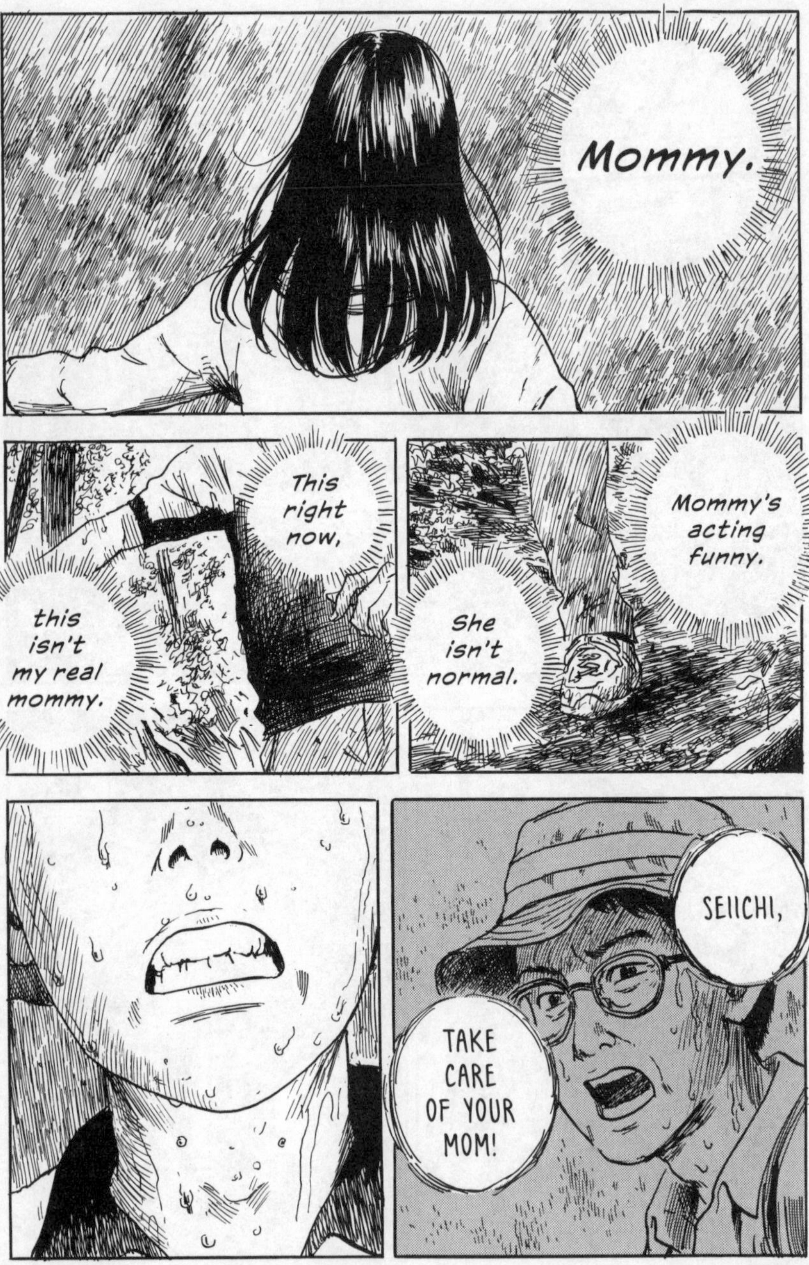
Mommy.
Mommy's acting funny.
She isn't normal.
This right now,
this isn't my real mommy.
SEIICHI,
TAKE CARE OF YOUR MOM!

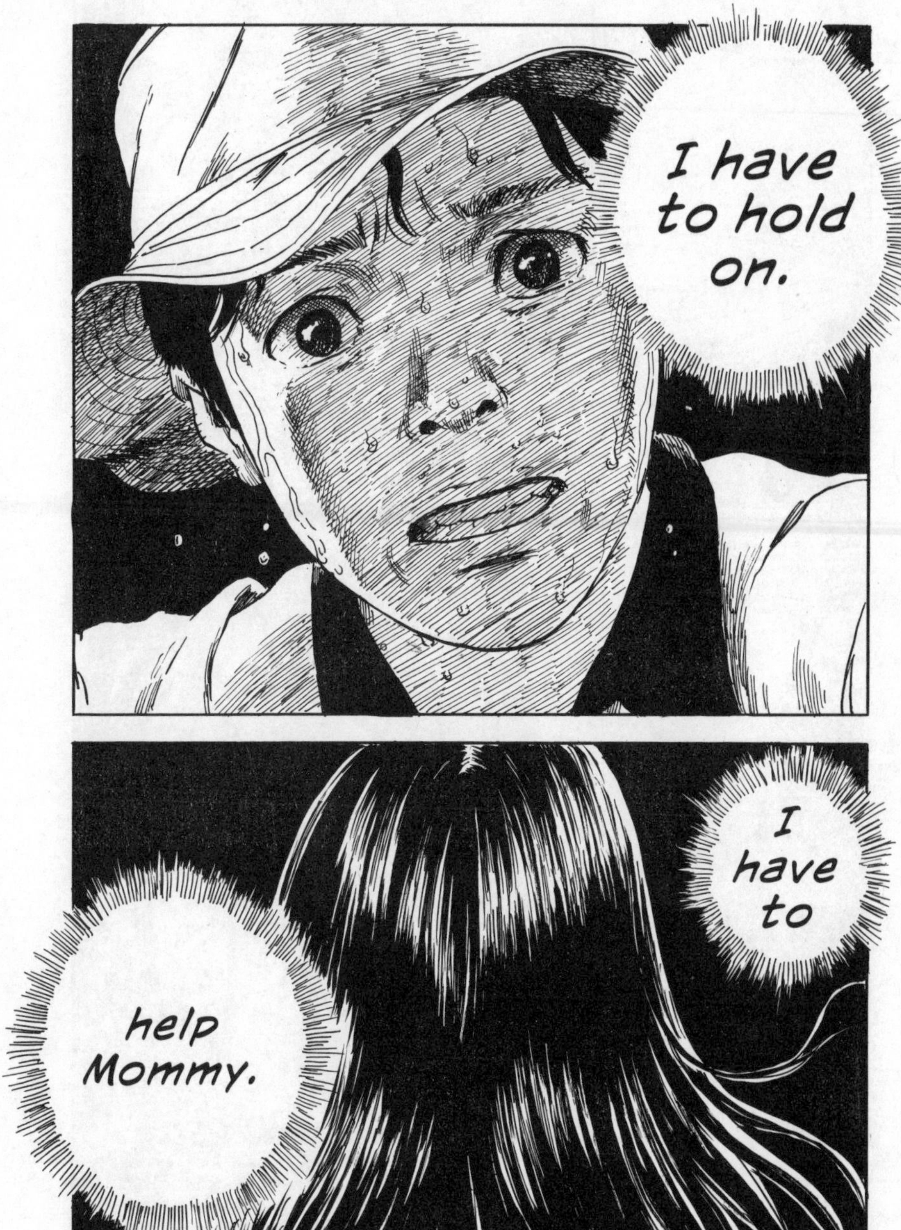
I have to hold on.
I have to
help Mommy.

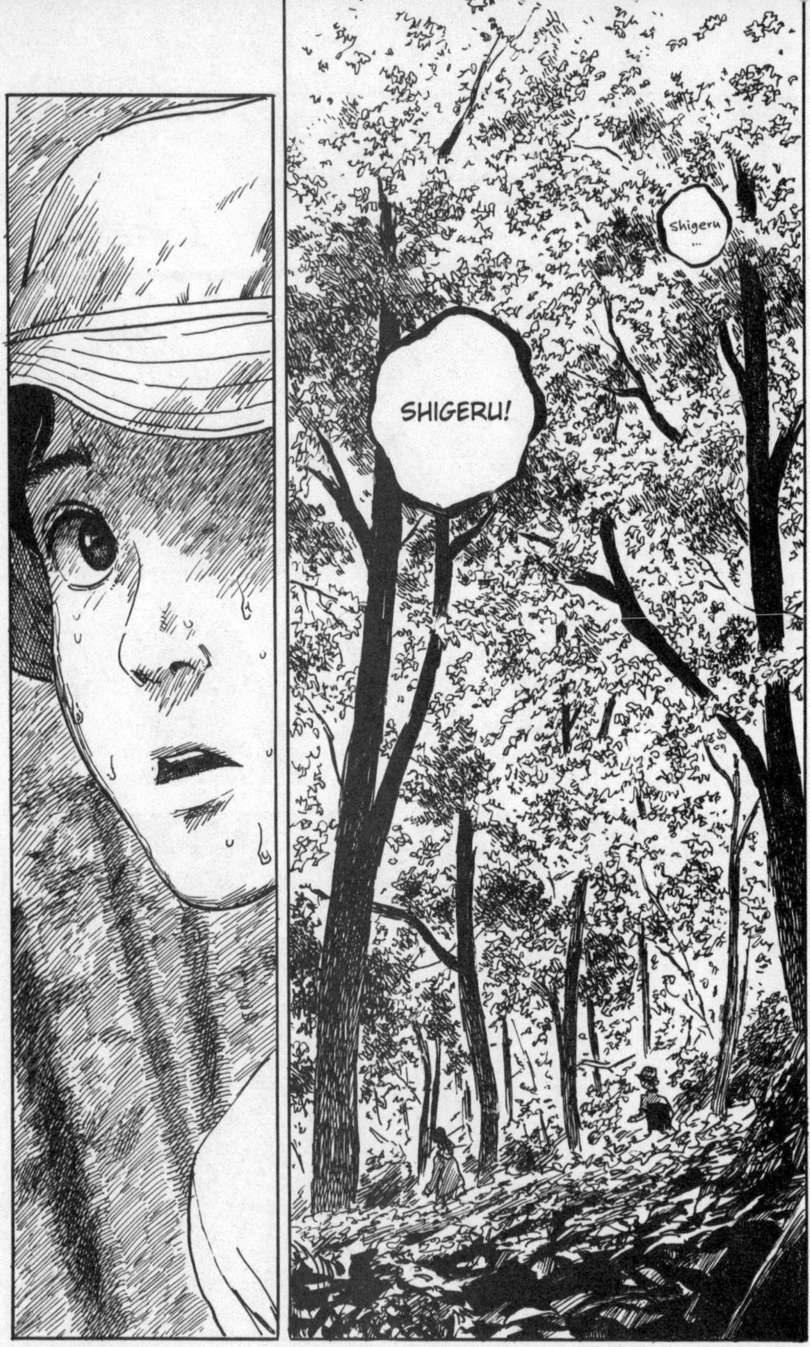
Shigeru ...
SHIGERU!

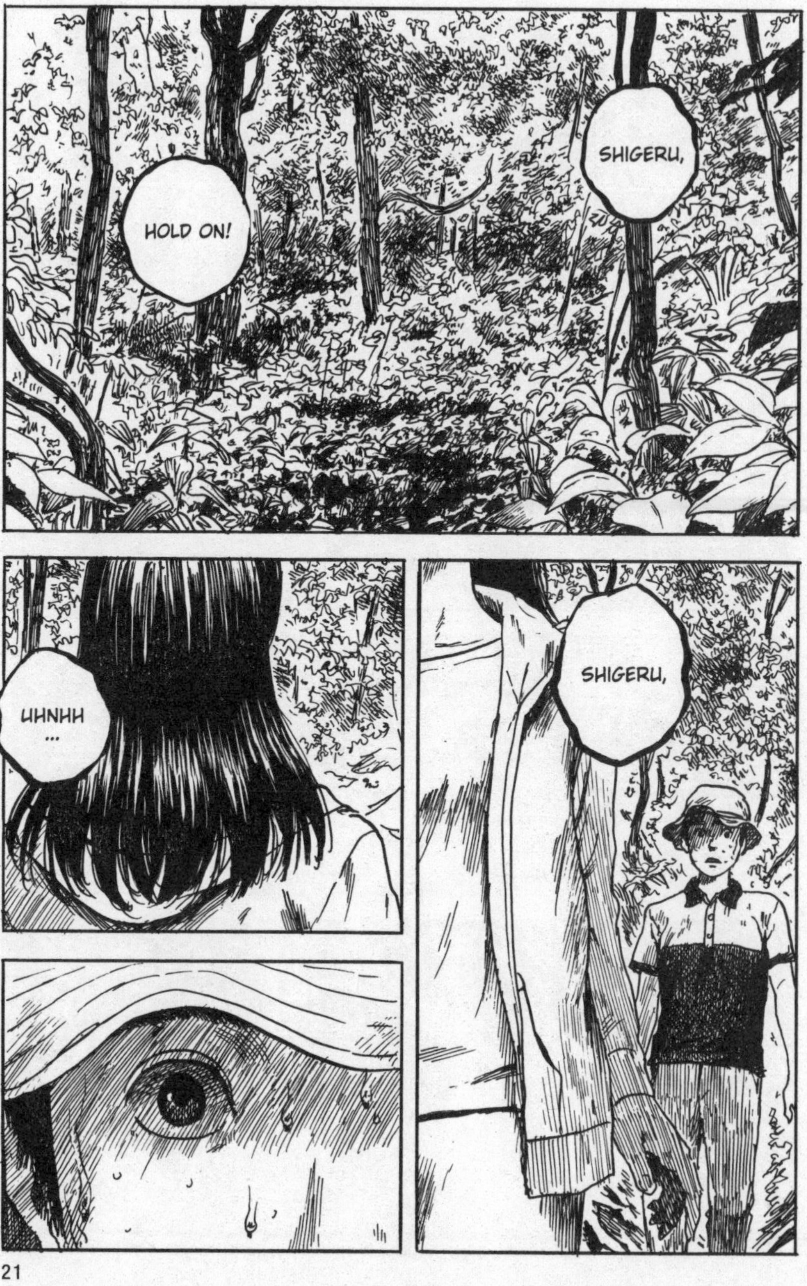
SHIGERU,
HOLD ON!
SHIGERU,
UHNHH ...

SHIGERU...

SHIGERU!

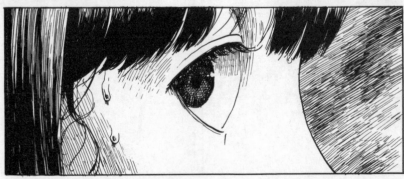

22

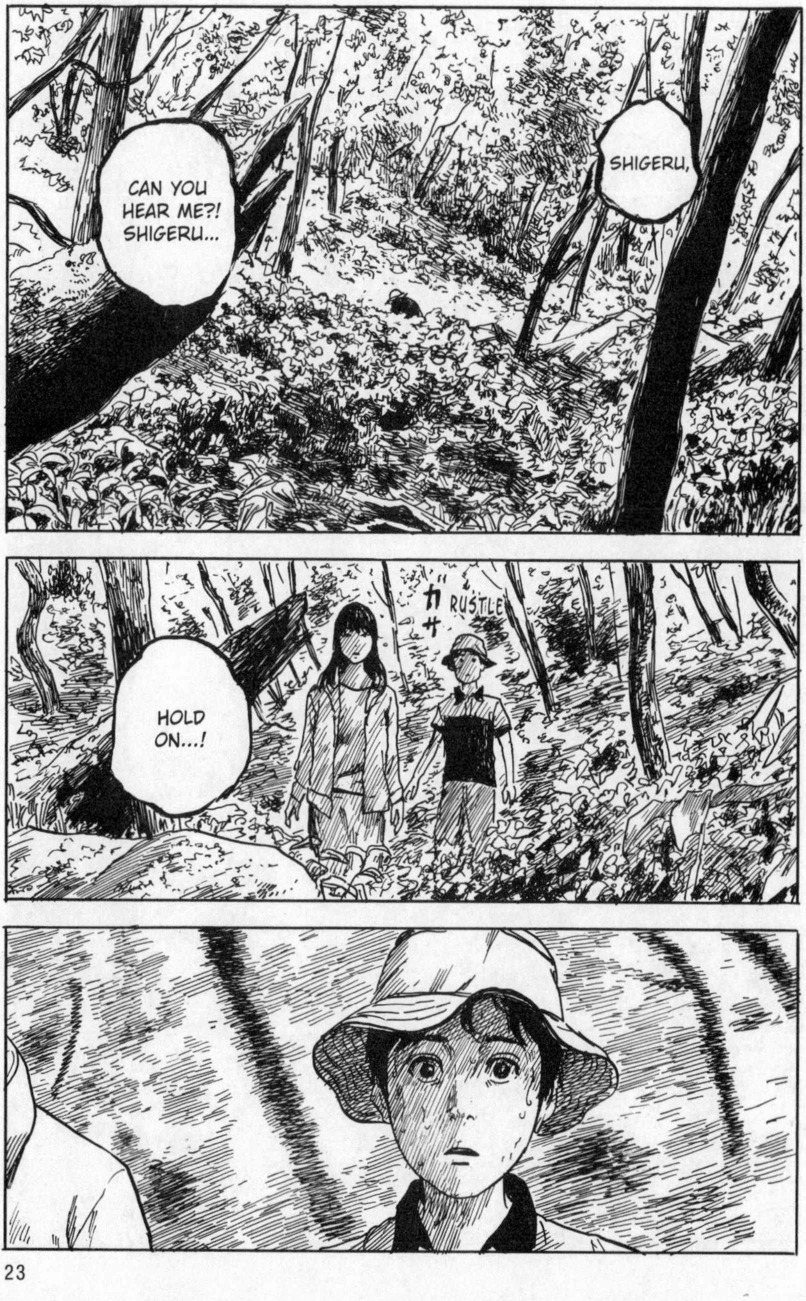
SHIGERU,
CAN YOU HEAR ME?! SHIGERU...
カサ
RUSTLE
HOLD ON...!

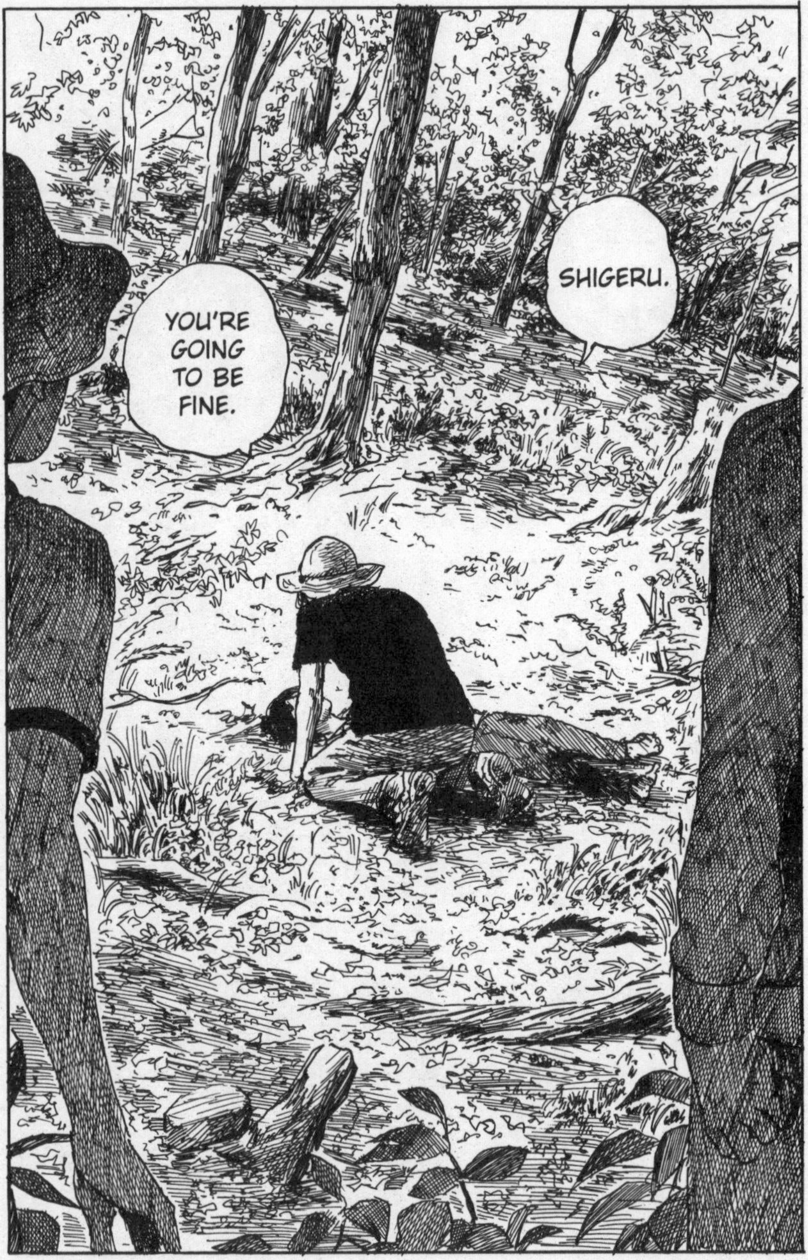
SHIGERU.
YOU'RE GOING TO BE FINE.

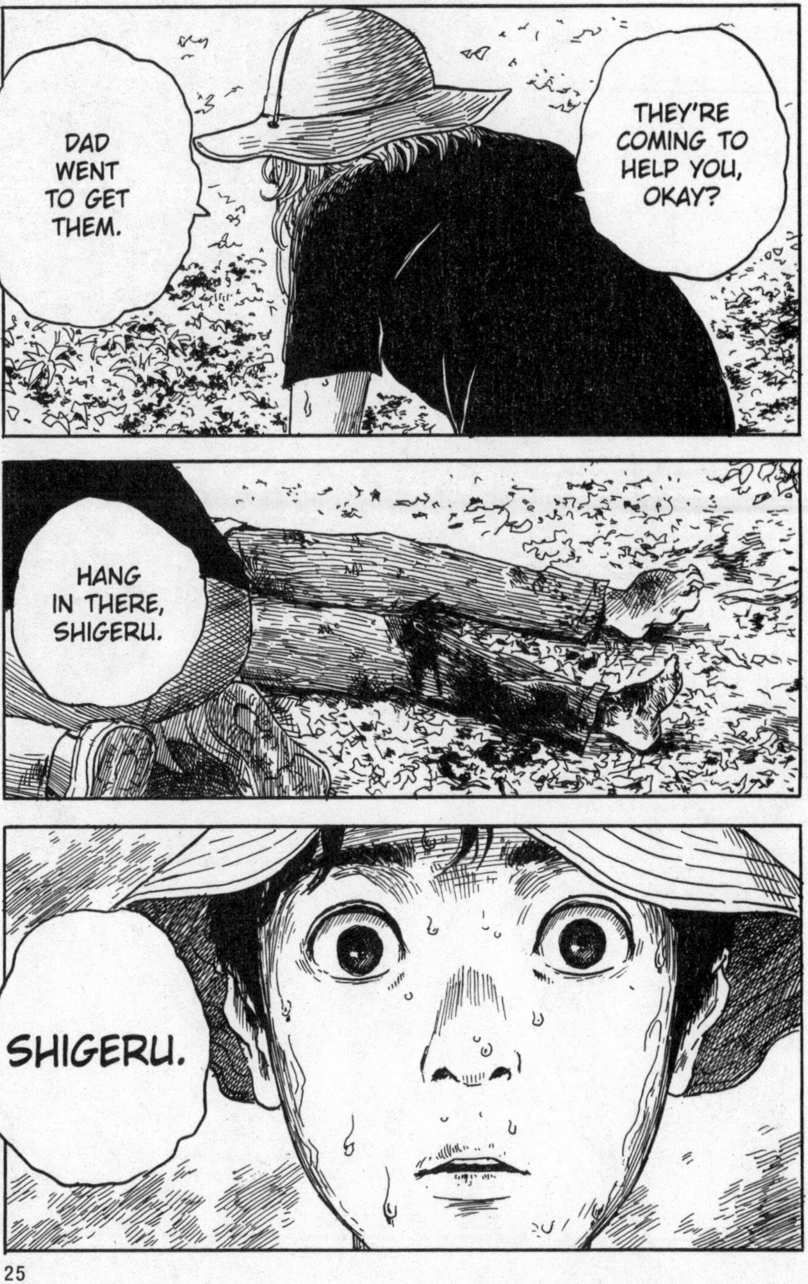
THEY'RE COMING TO HELP YOU, OKAY?
DAD WENT TO GET THEM.
HANG IN THERE, SHIGERU.
SHIGERU.

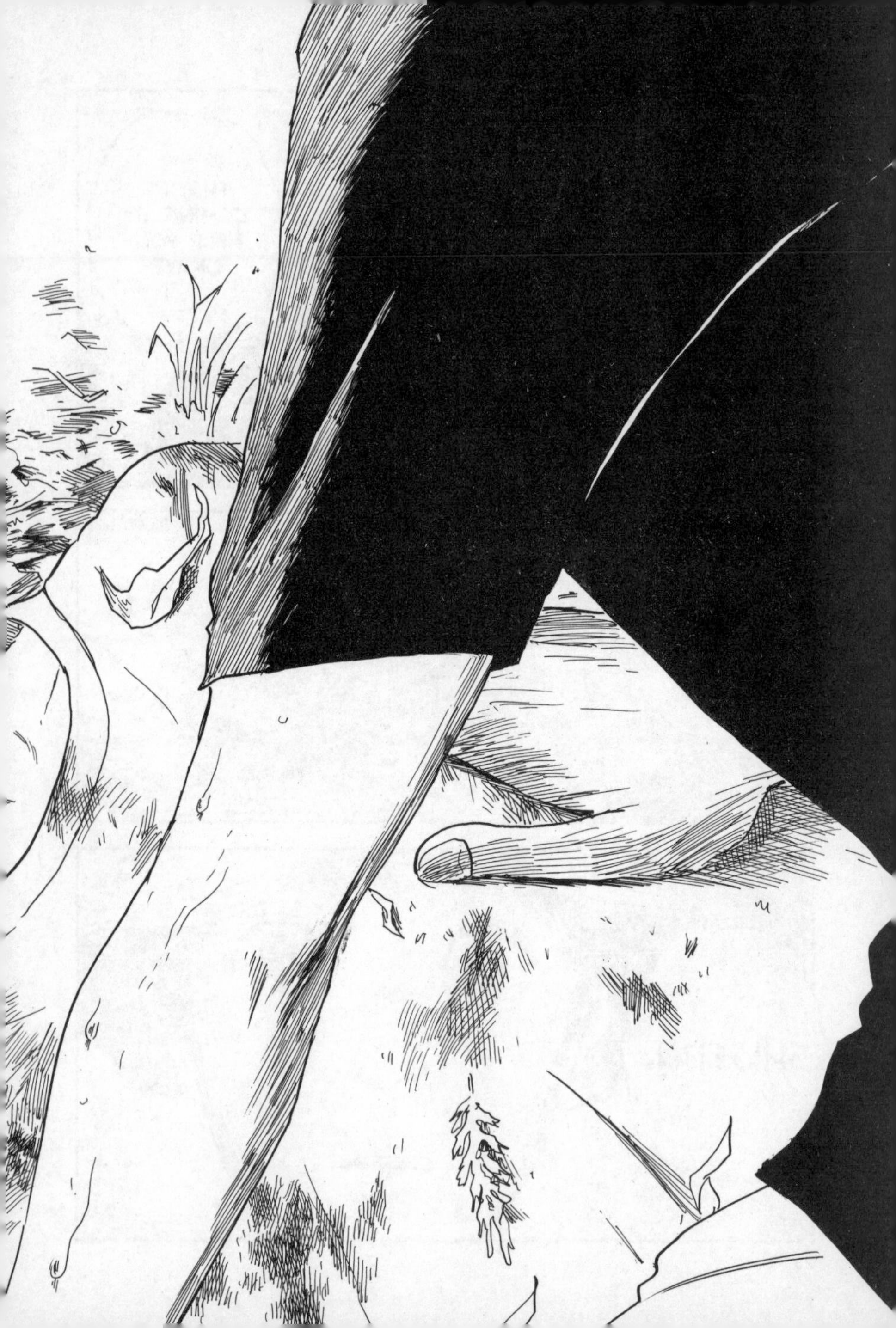

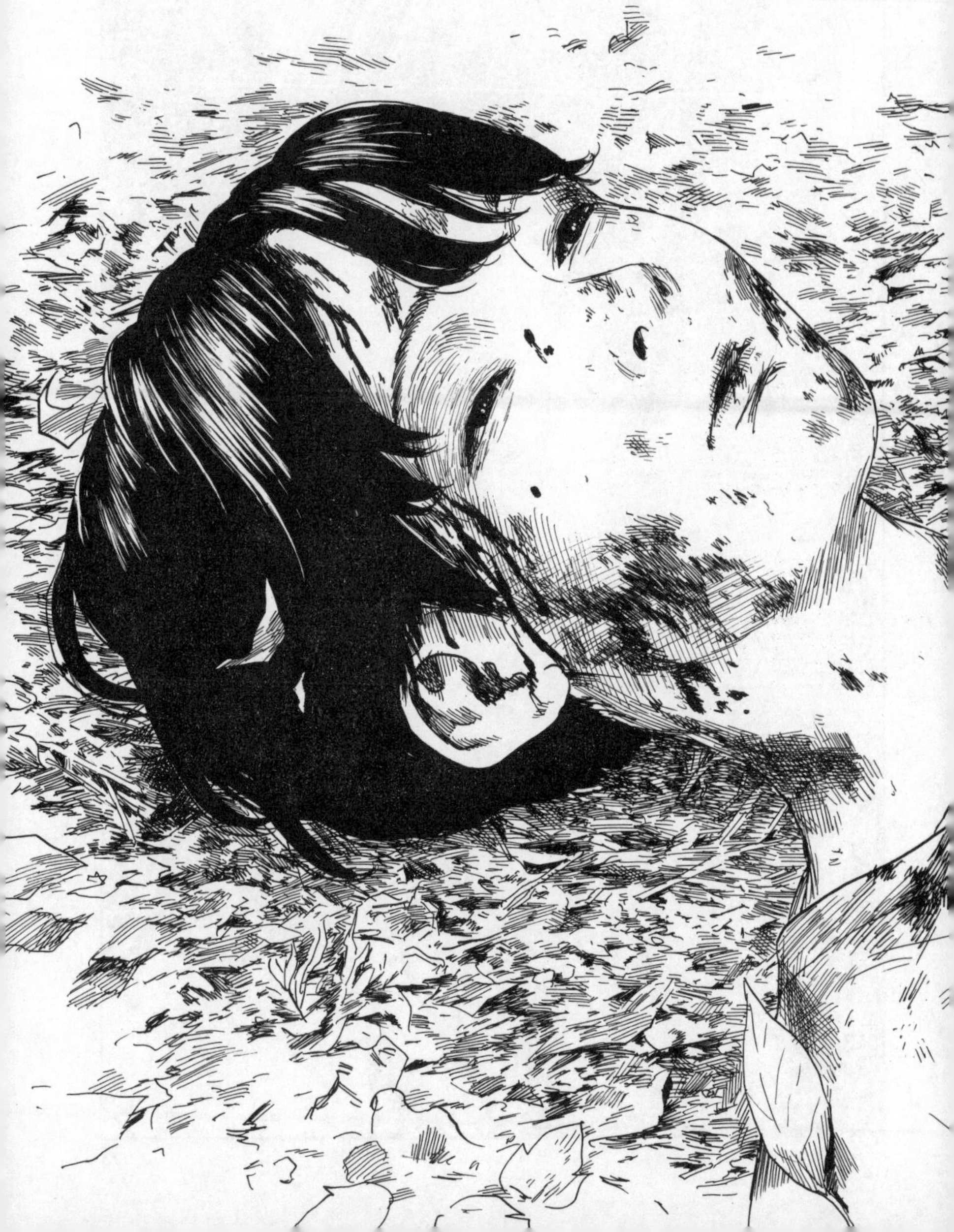

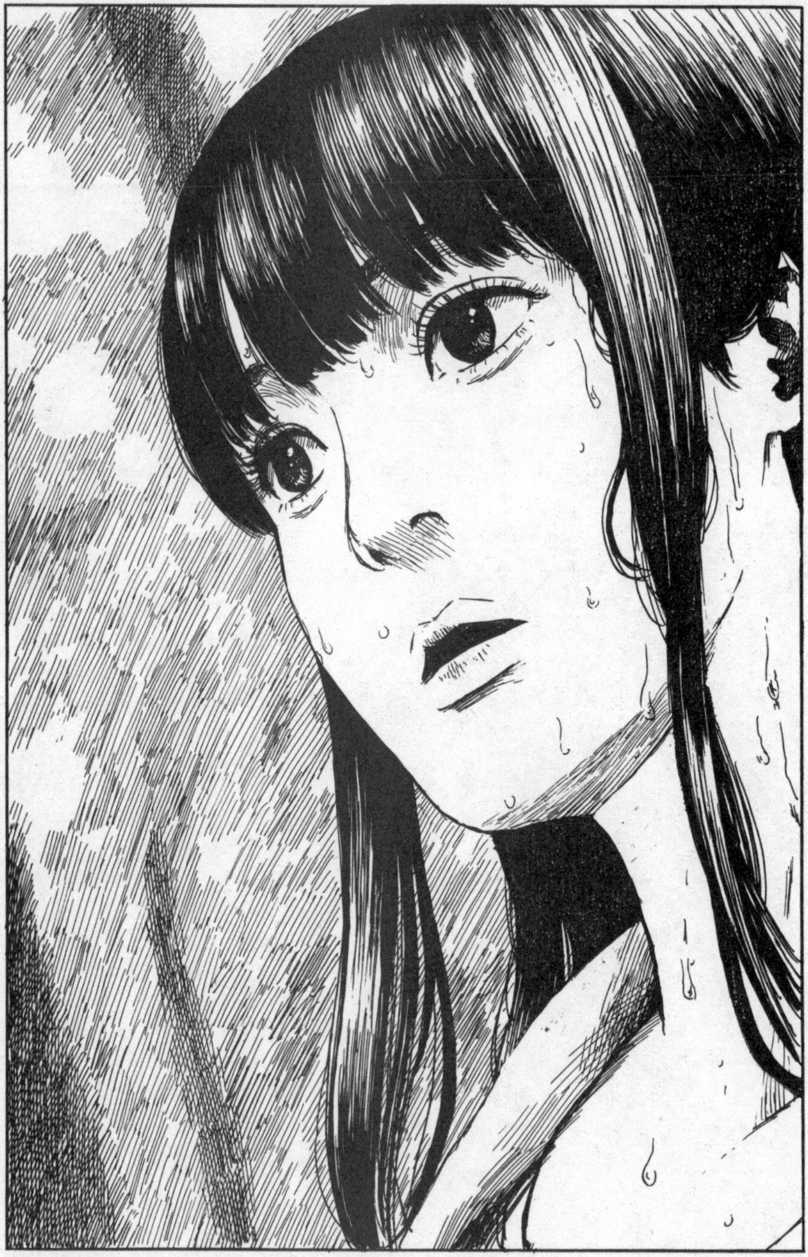

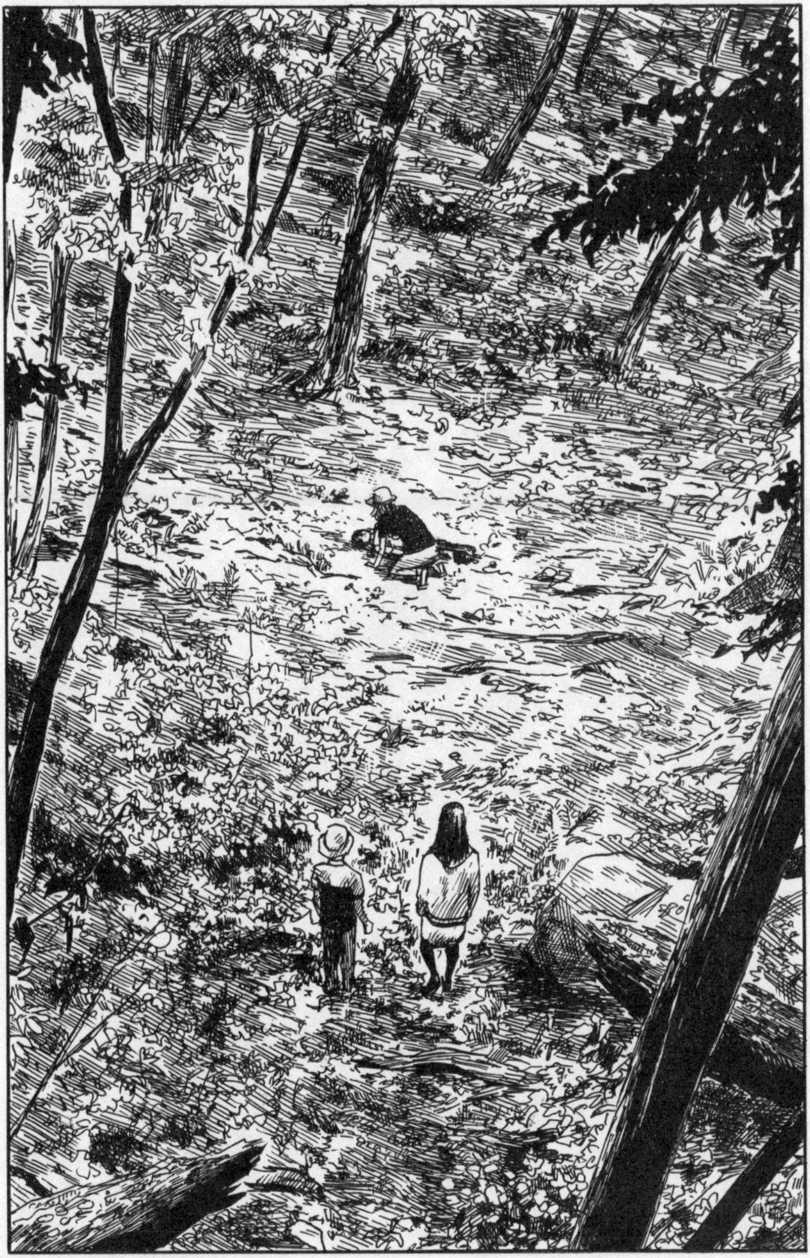

CHAPTER 9 Eye Contact

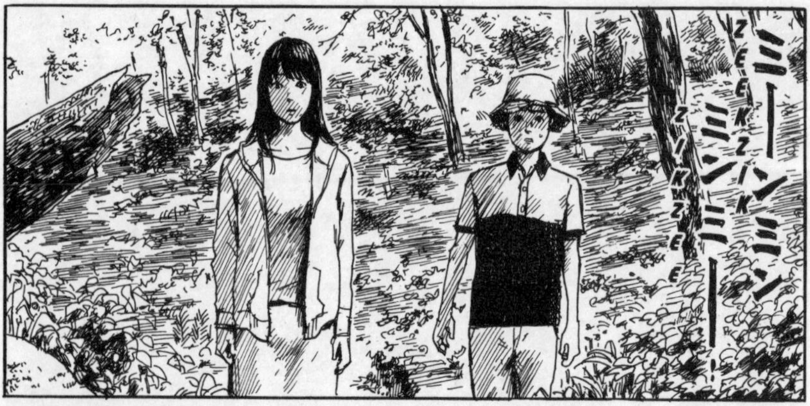
ミーンミンミンミー!
ZEEK ZIK ZIKZEE

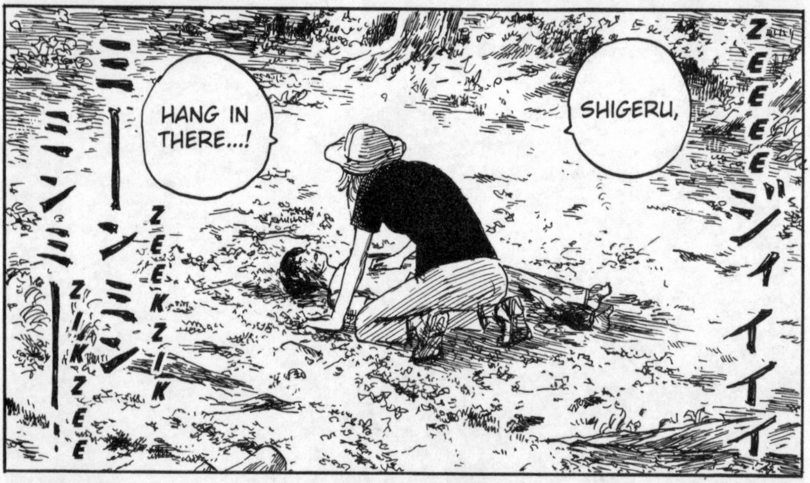
ZEEEEEE
ジーイイイー
SHIGERU,
HANG IN THERE...!
ZEEK ZIK ZIKZEE
ミーンミンミンミー!

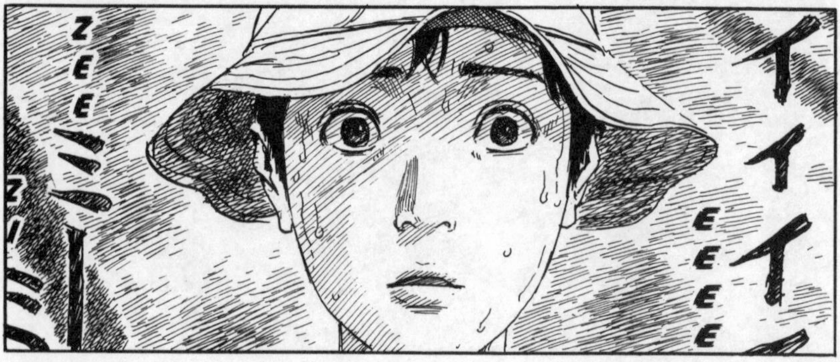
イイイ
EEEE
ZEEE

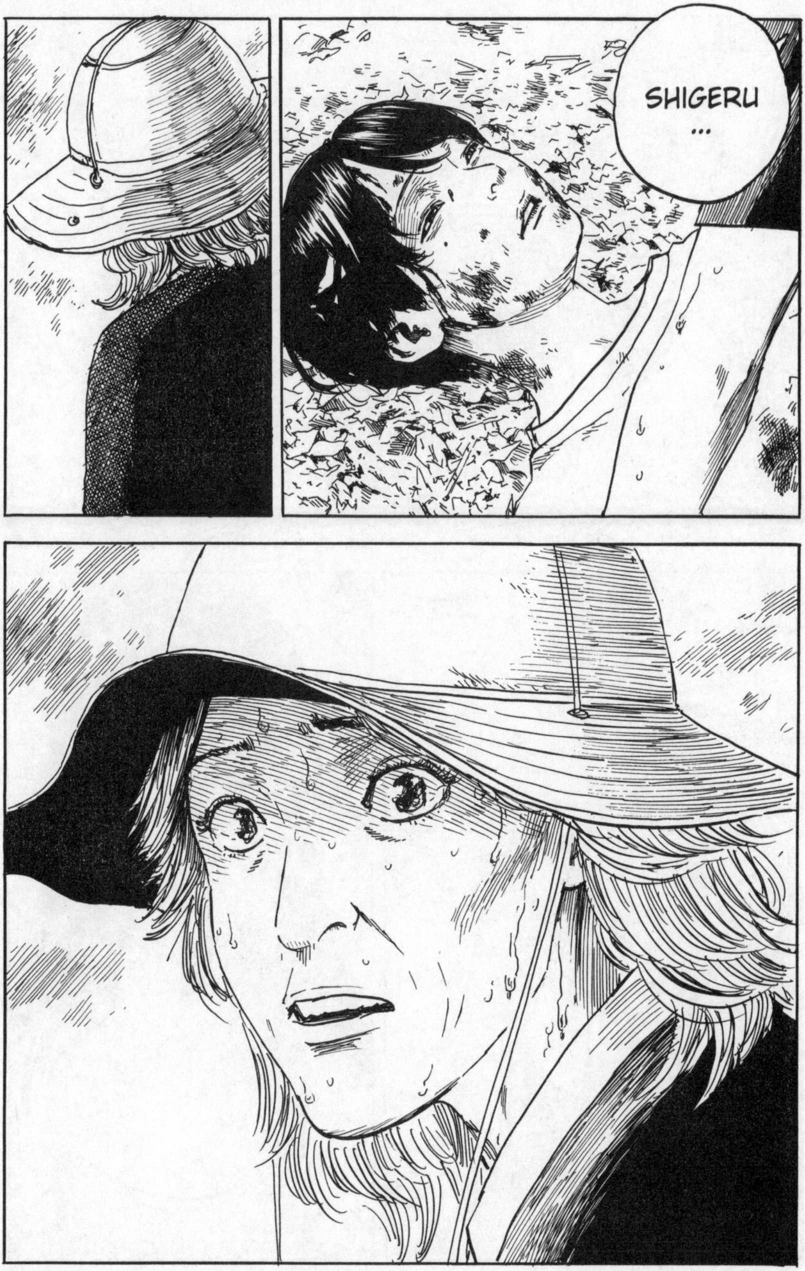
SHIGERU
...

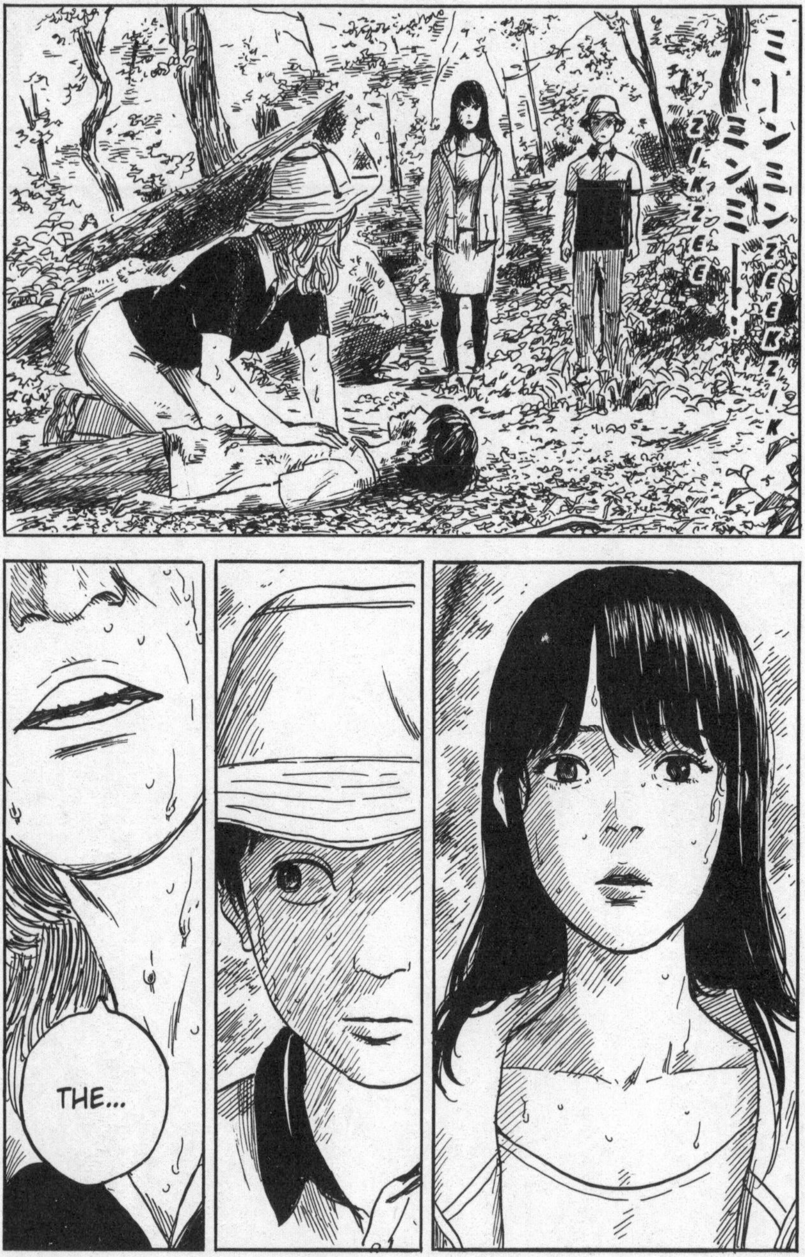
ミーンミンミンミー…!
ZEEKZIK
ZIKZEE
THE...

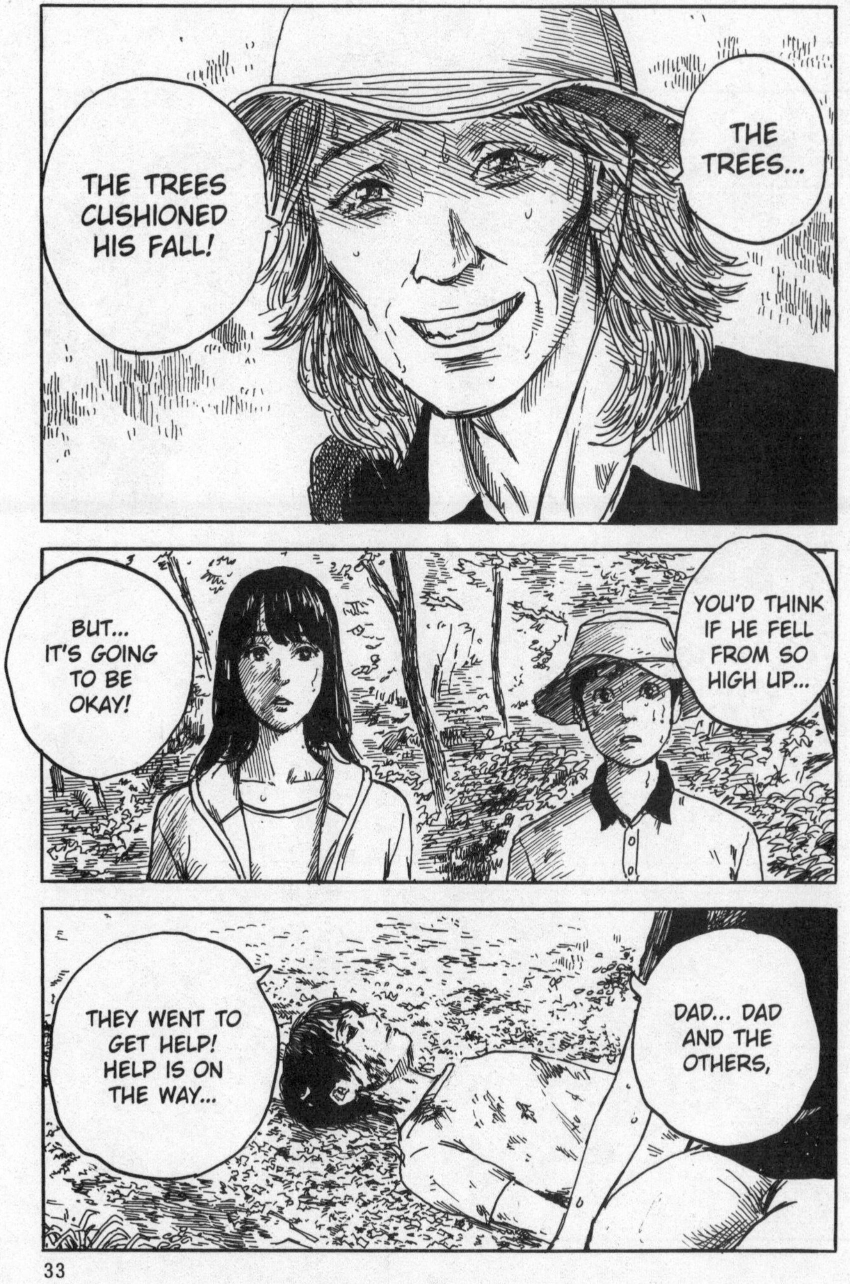
THE TREES...
THE TREES CUSHIONED HIS FALL!
YOU'D THINK IF HE FELL FROM SO HIGH UP...
BUT... IT'S GOING TO BE OKAY!
DAD... DAD AND THE OTHERS,
THEY WENT TO GET HELP! HELP IS ON THE WAY...

OKAY, SHIGERU?

THEY'RE COMING TO TAKE YOU TO THE HOSPITAL, OKAY?

YOU'RE GONNA PLAY WITH SEI AGAIN, OKAY?

OKAY?

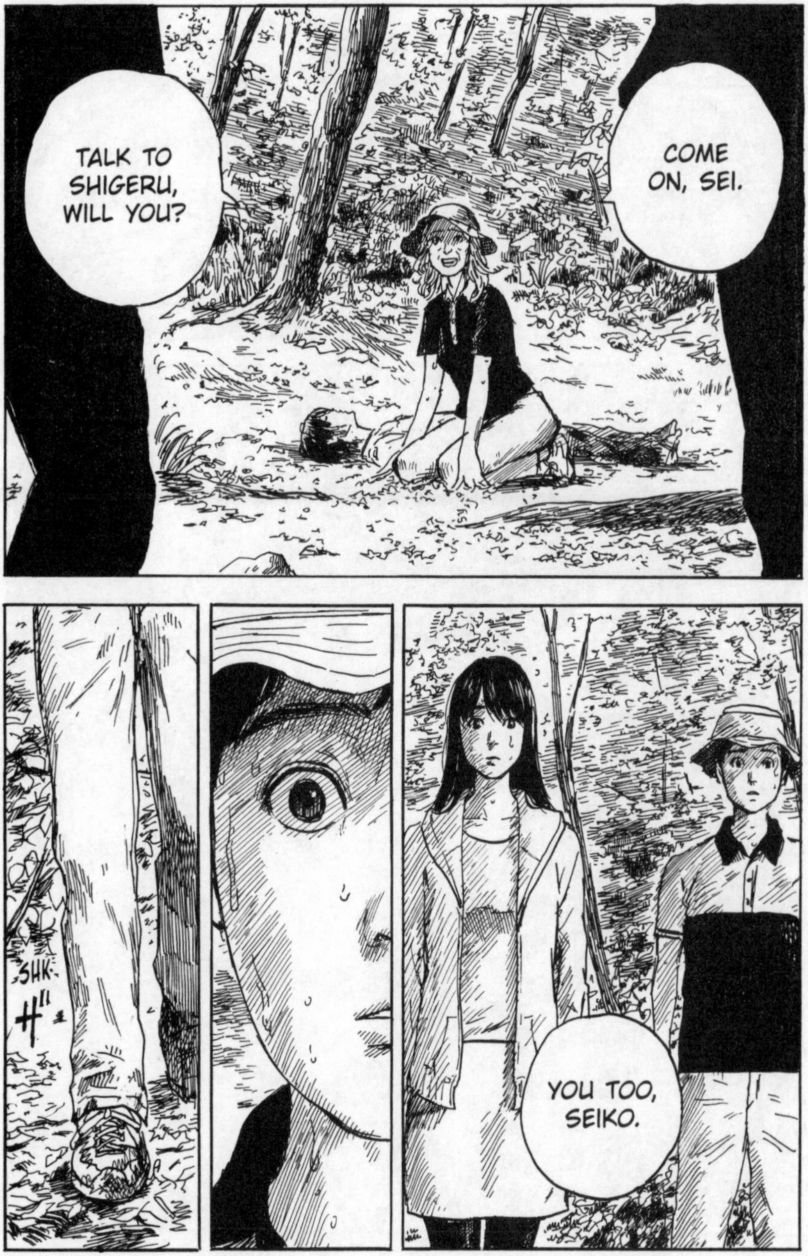
COME ON, SEI.
TALK TO SHIGERU, WILL YOU?
YOU TOO, SEIKO.
SHK-

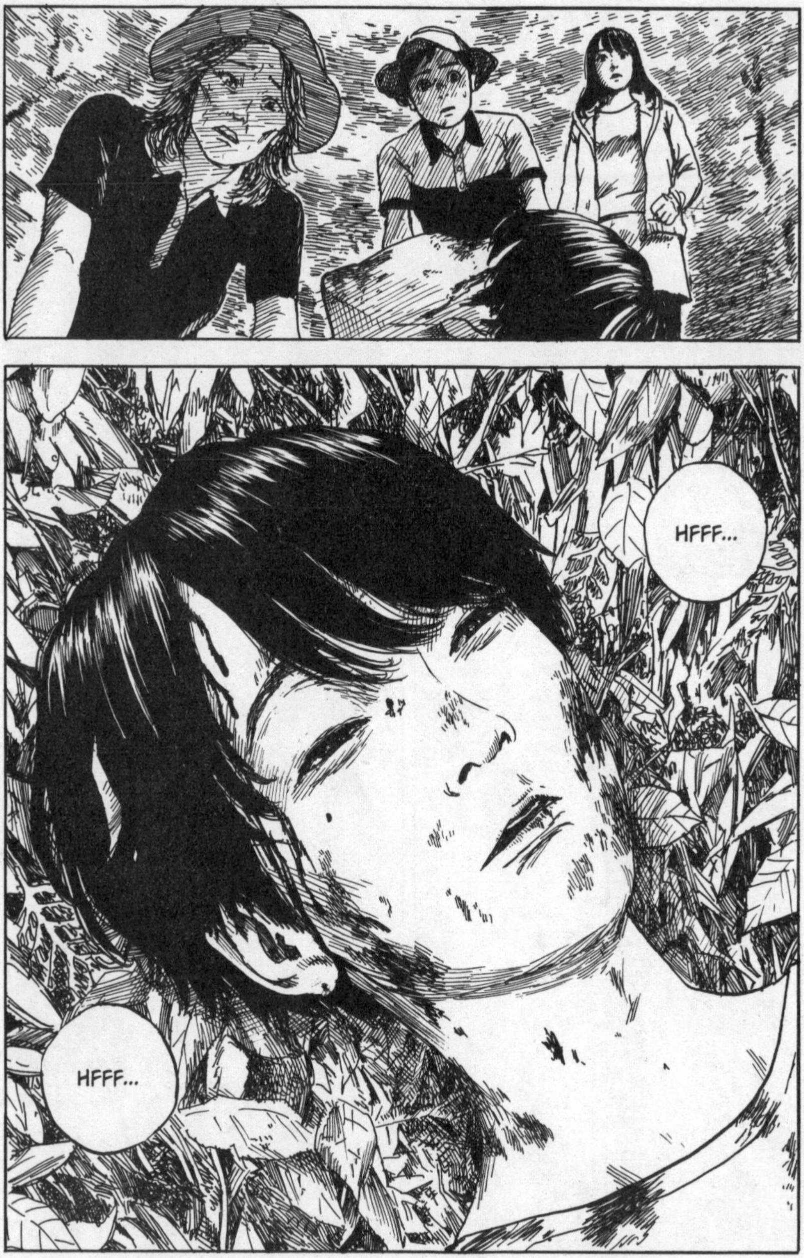
HFFF...
HFFF...

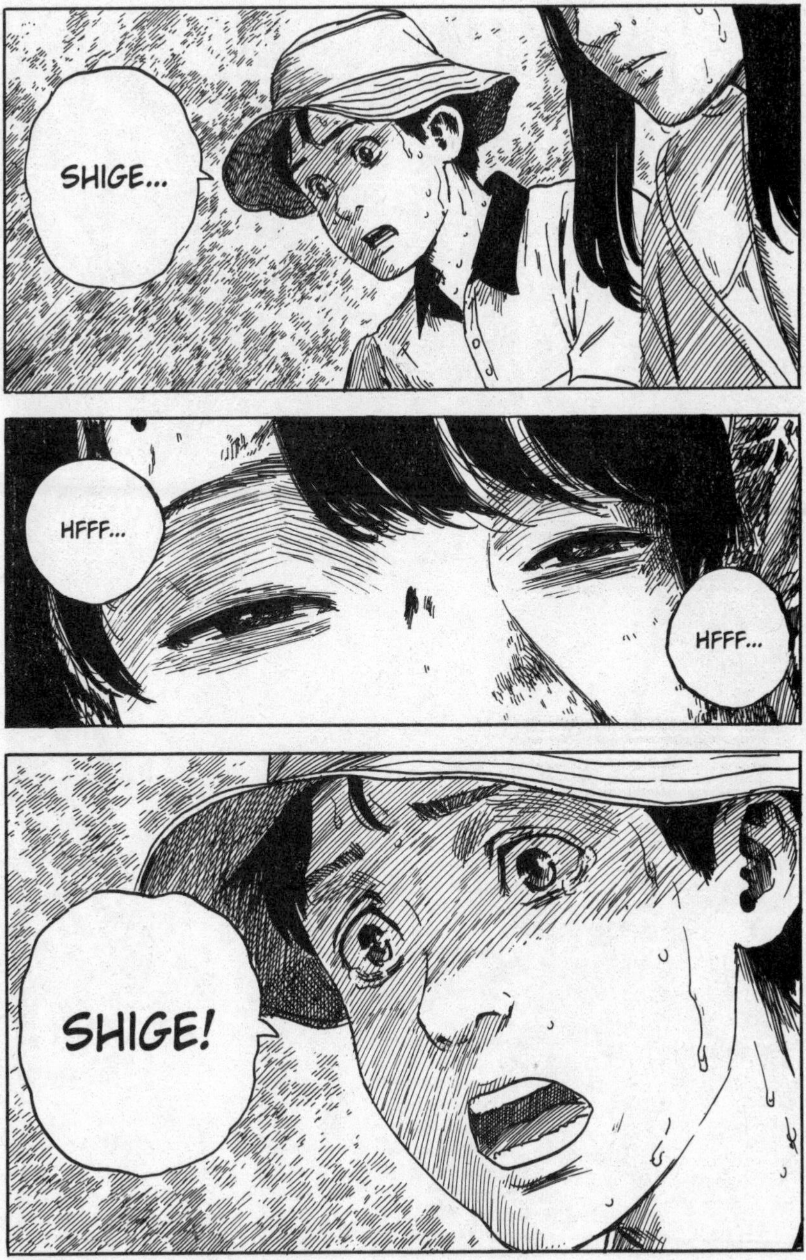
SHIGE...
HFFF...
HFFF...
SHIGE!

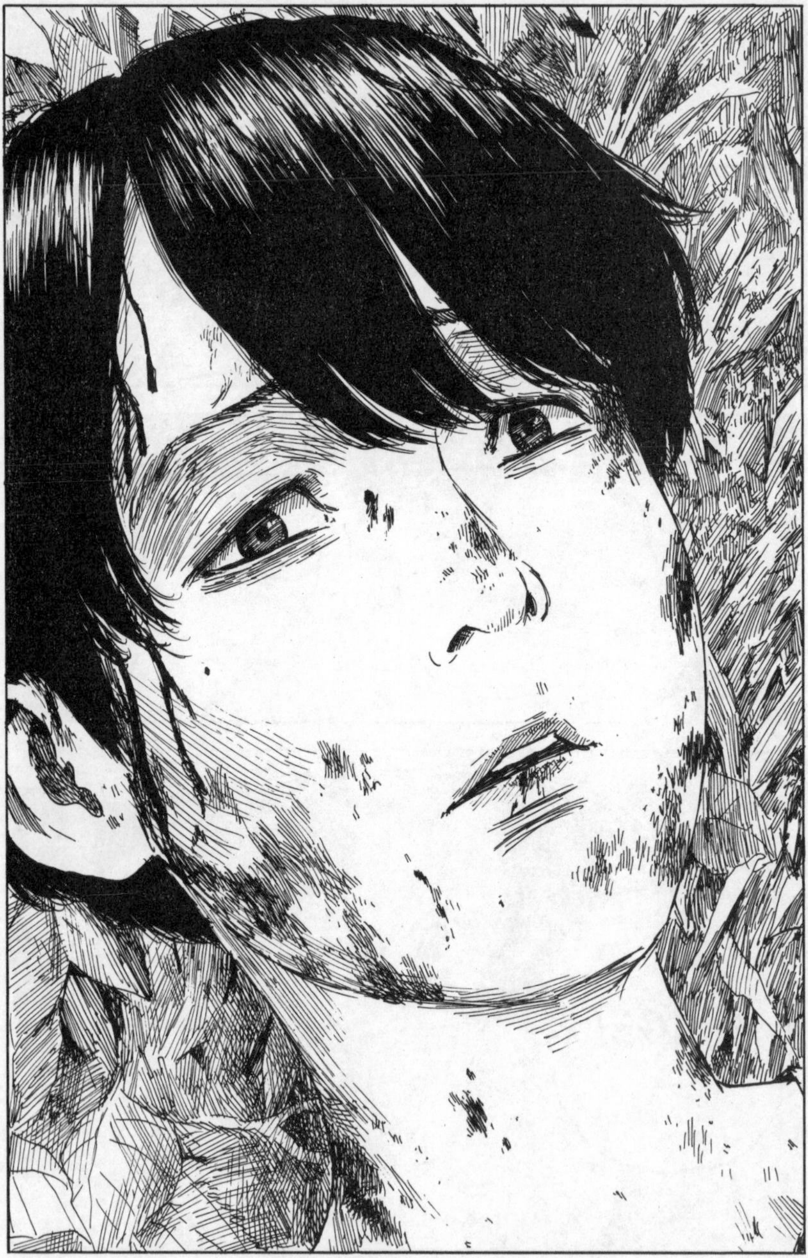

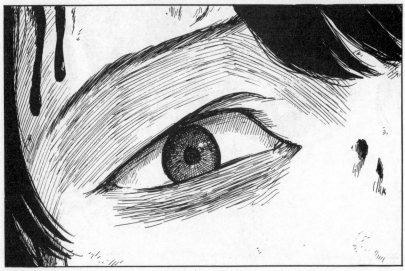

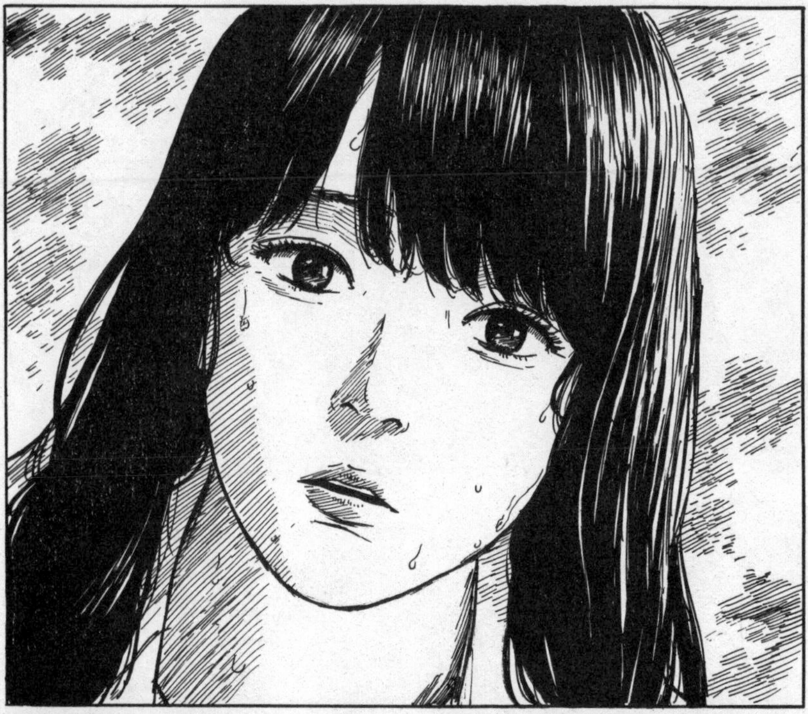
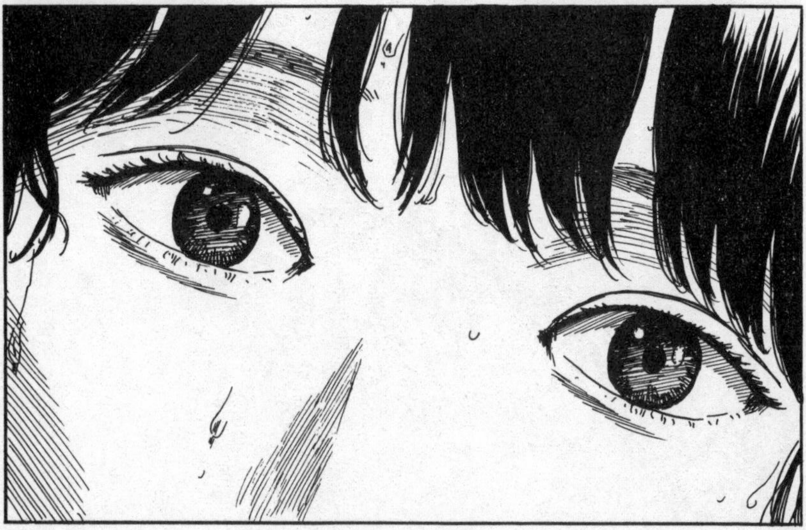

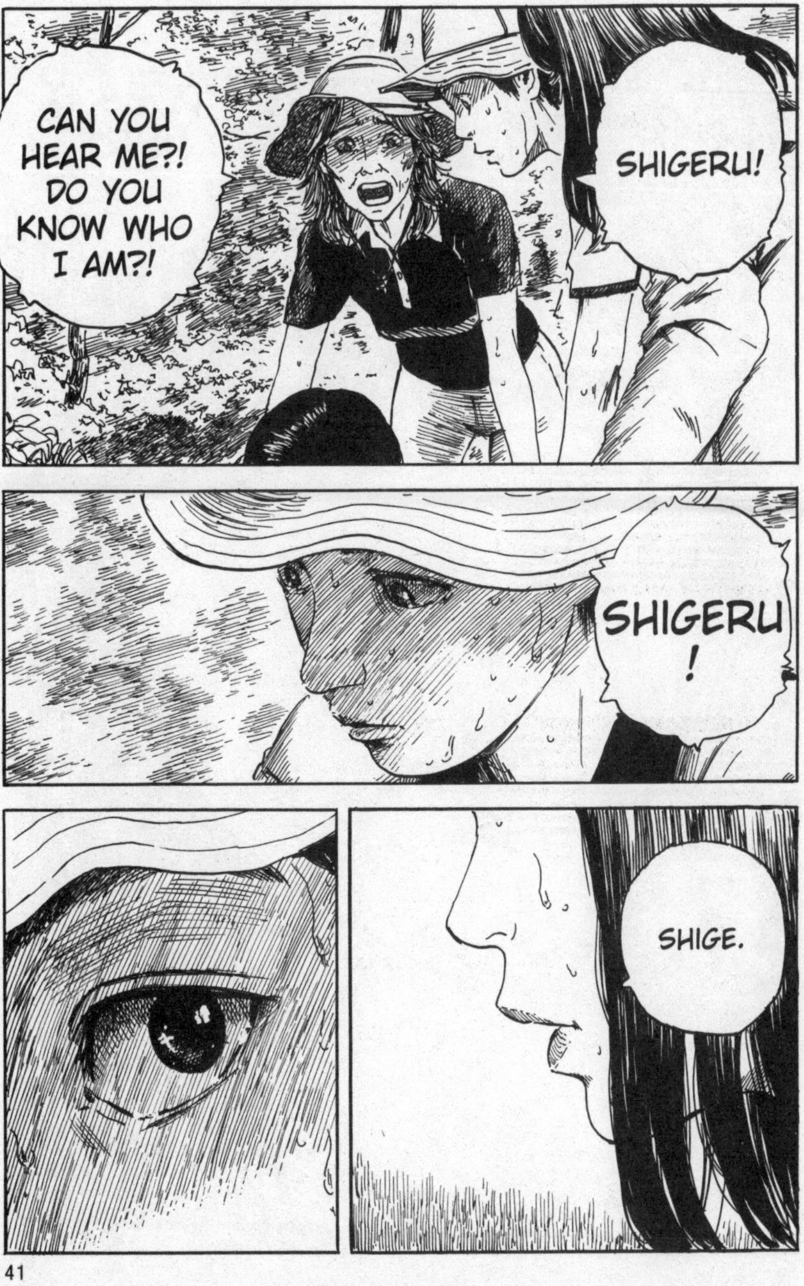
SHIGERU!
CAN YOU HEAR ME?! DO YOU KNOW WHO I AM?!
SHIGERU!
SHIGE.

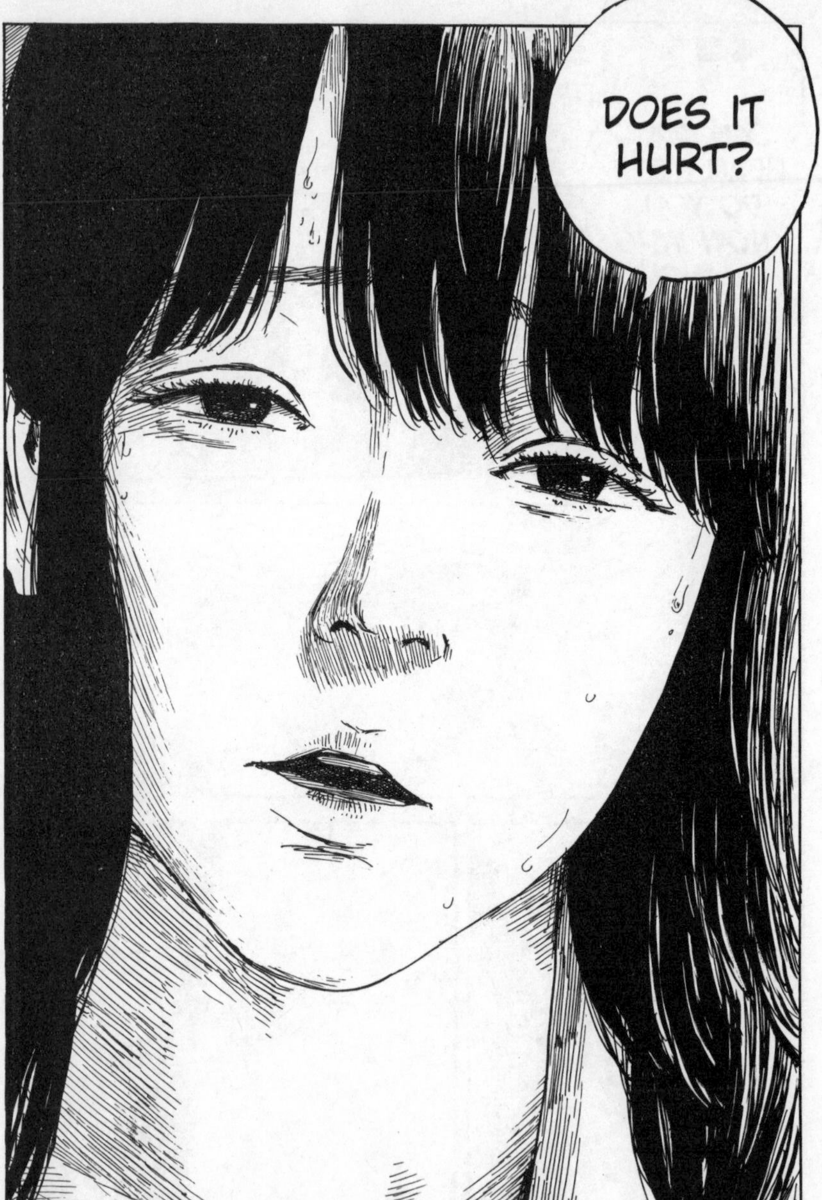
DOES IT HURT?

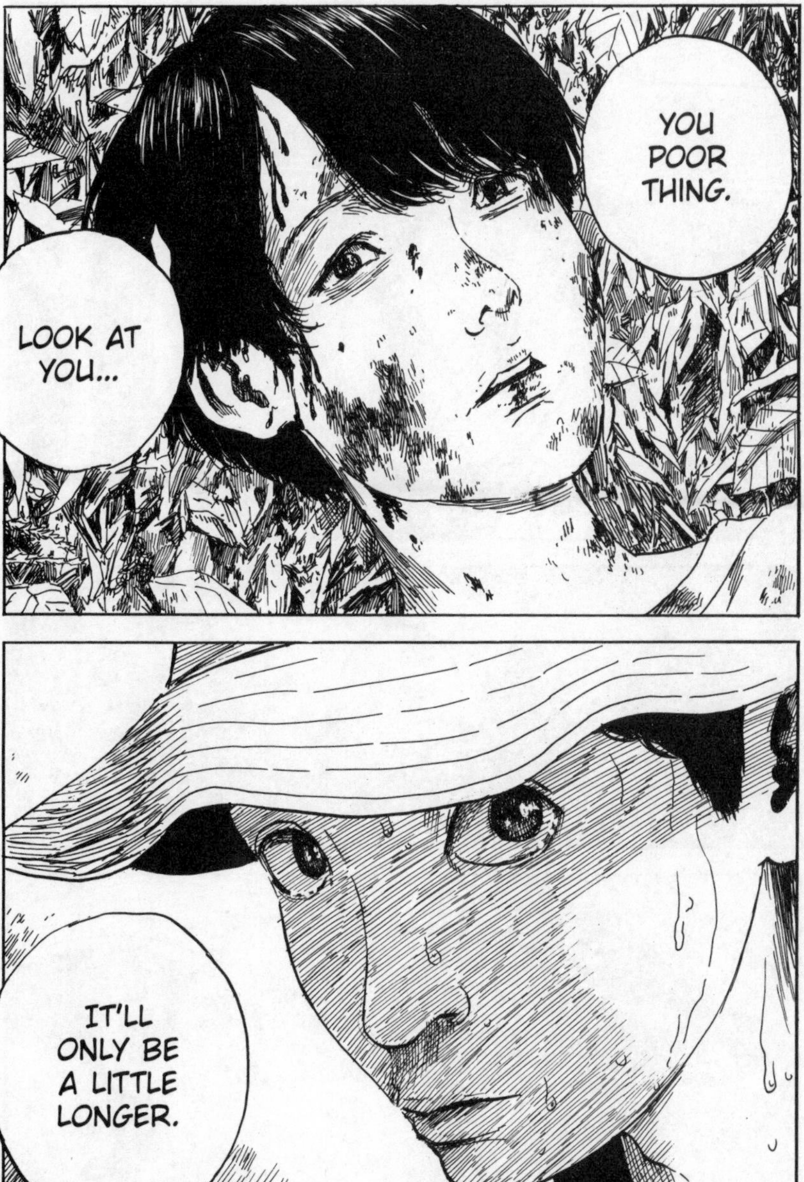
YOU POOR THING.
LOOK AT YOU...
IT'LL ONLY BE A LITTLE LONGER.

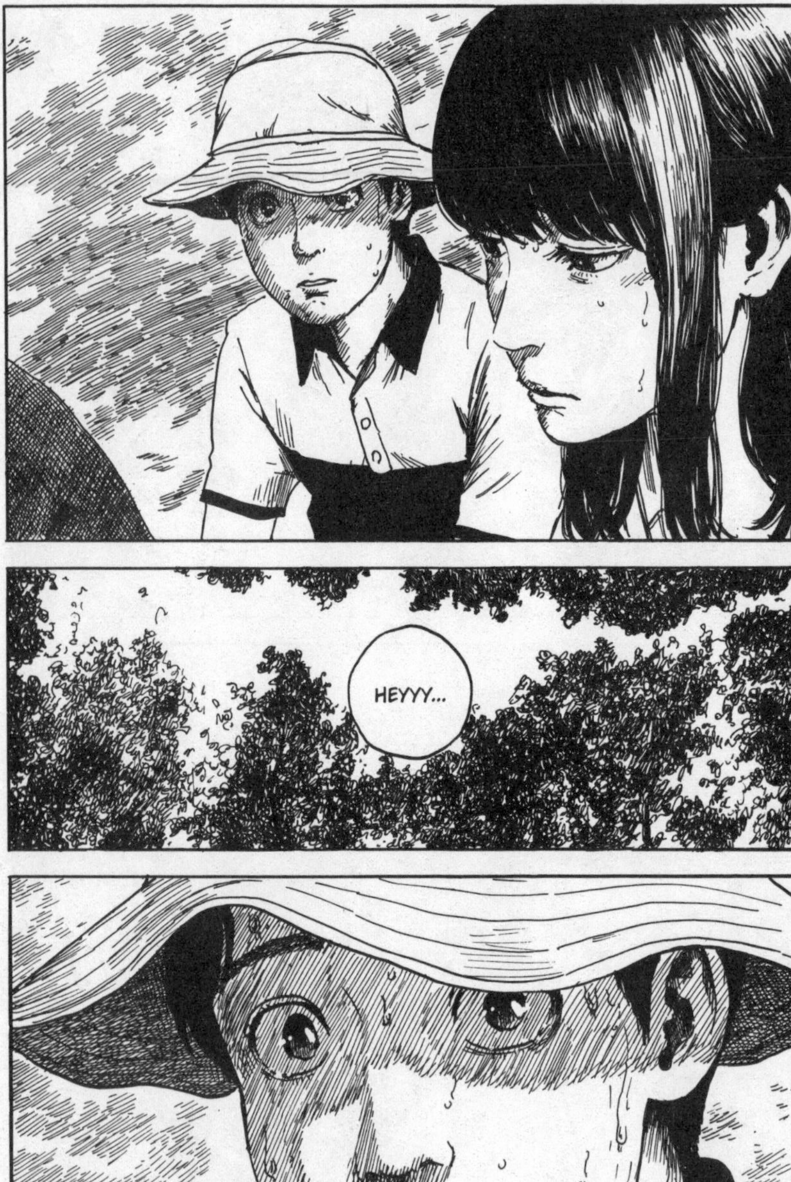
HEYYY...

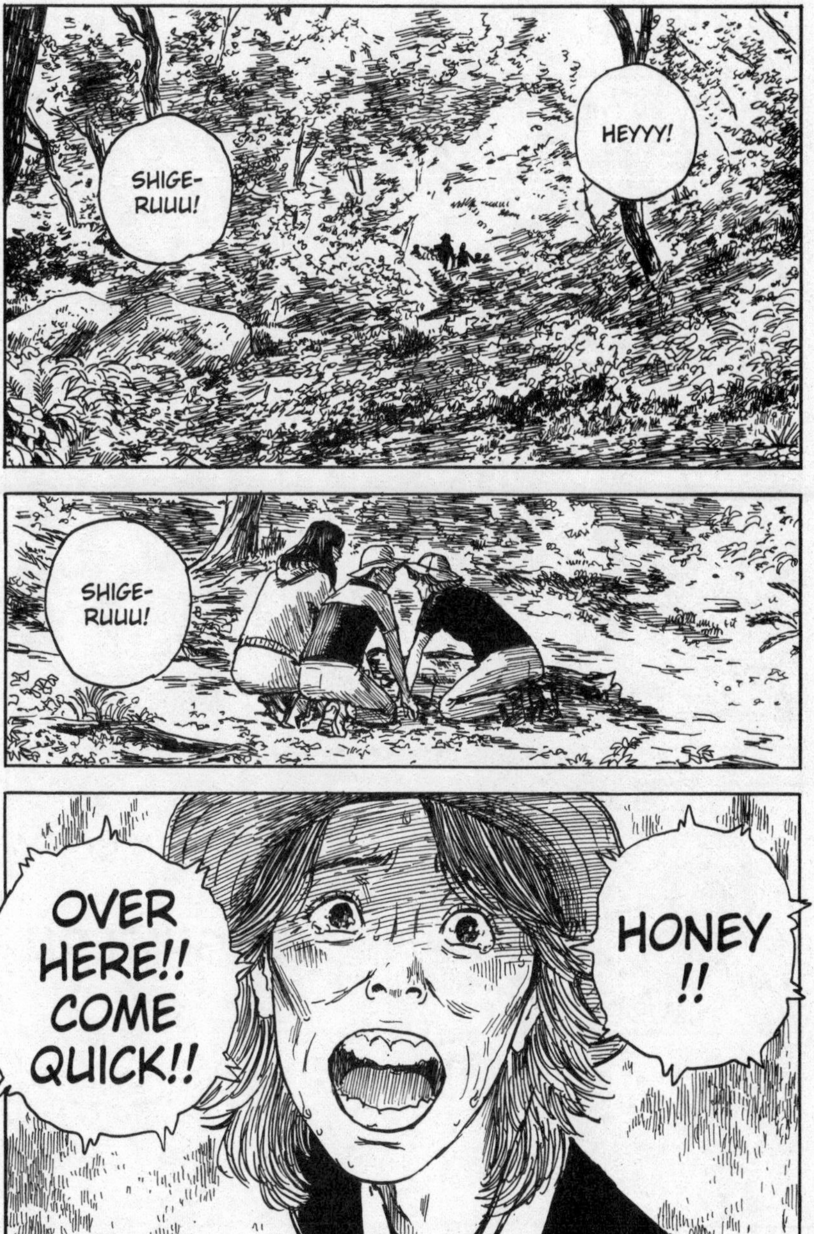
HEYYY!
SHIGE-RUUU!
SHIGE-RUUU!
HONEY !!
OVER HERE!! COME QUICK!!

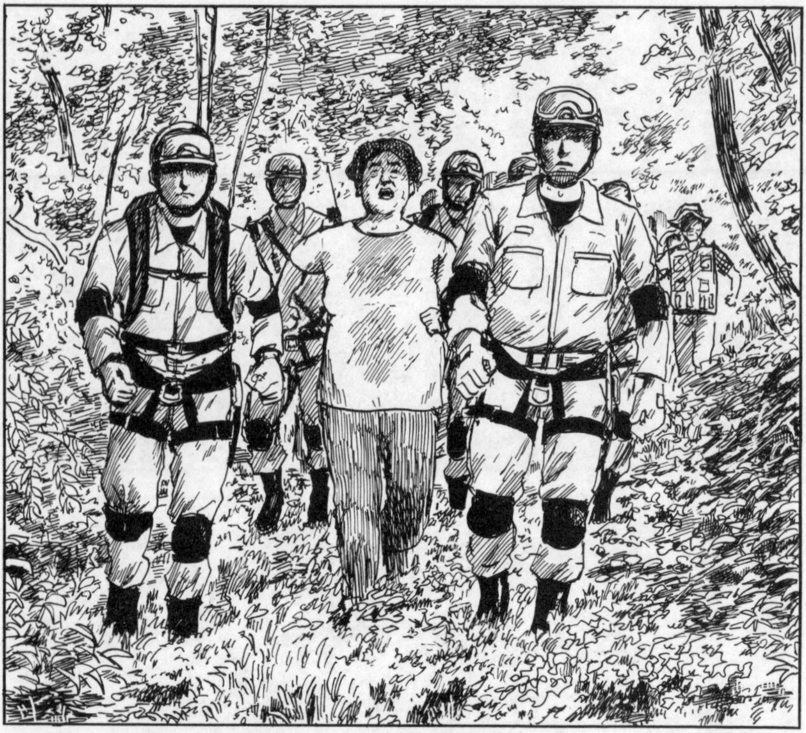

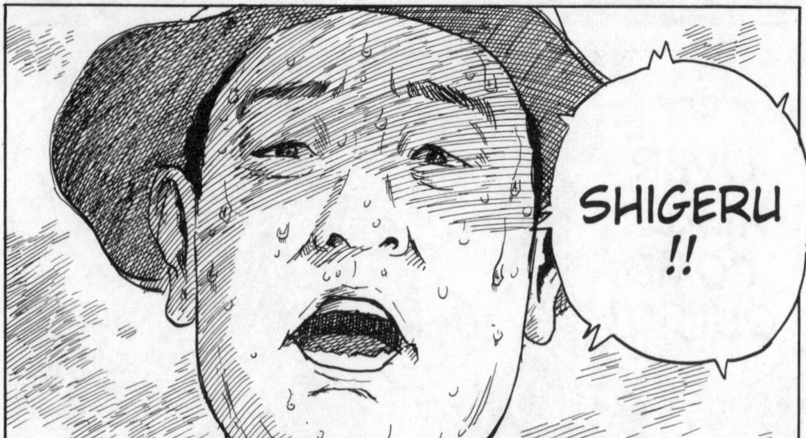
SHIGERU !!

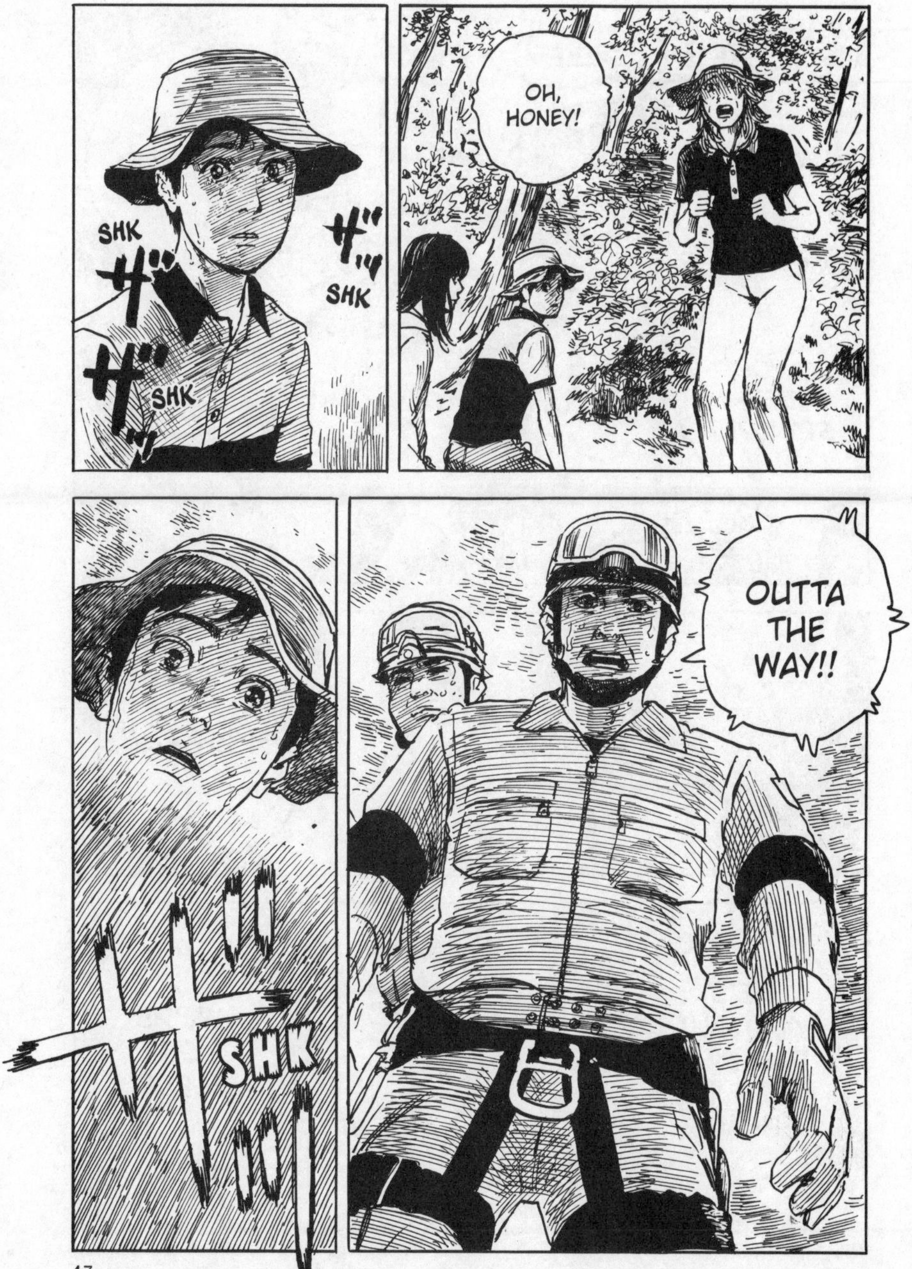
OH, HONEY!
SHK
SHK
SHK
OUTTA THE WAY!!
SHK

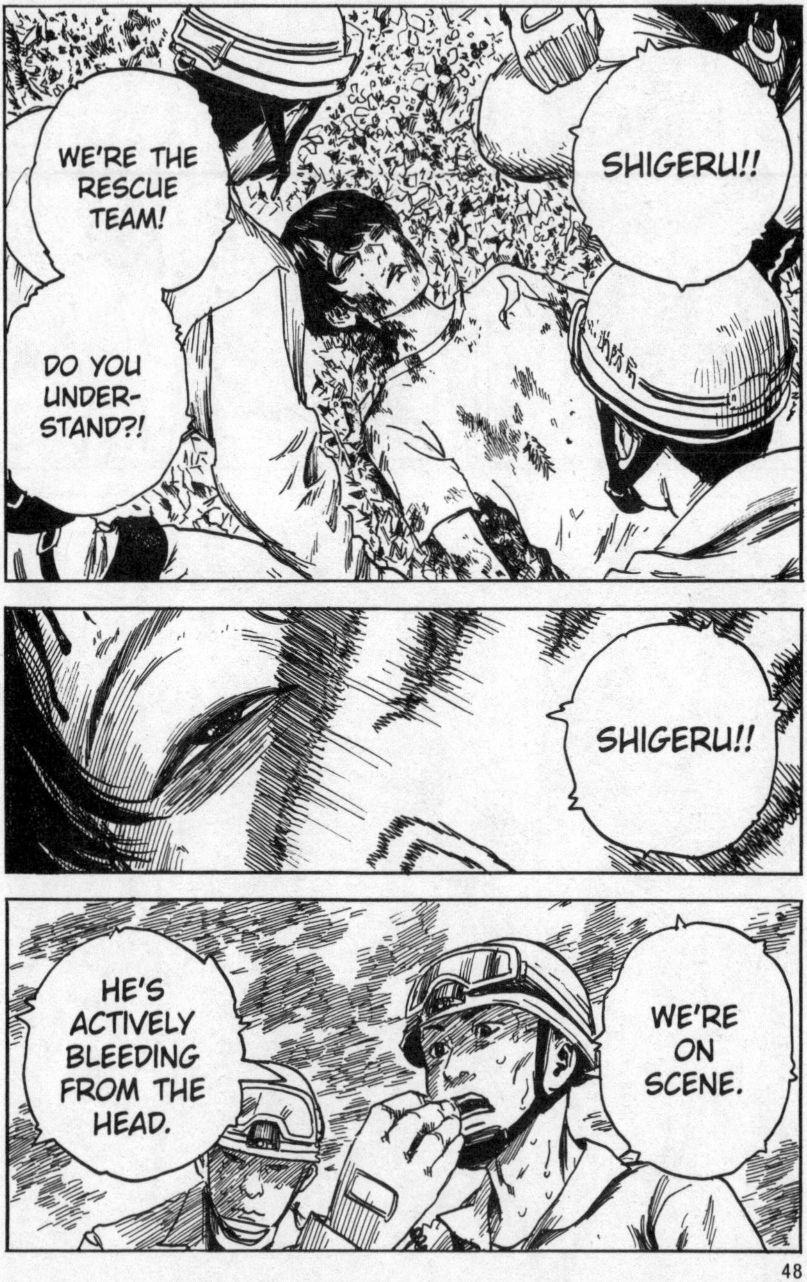
SHIGERU!!
WE'RE THE RESCUE TEAM!
DO YOU UNDER-STAND?!
SHIGERU!!
WE'RE ON SCENE.
HE'S ACTIVELY BLEEDING FROM THE HEAD.

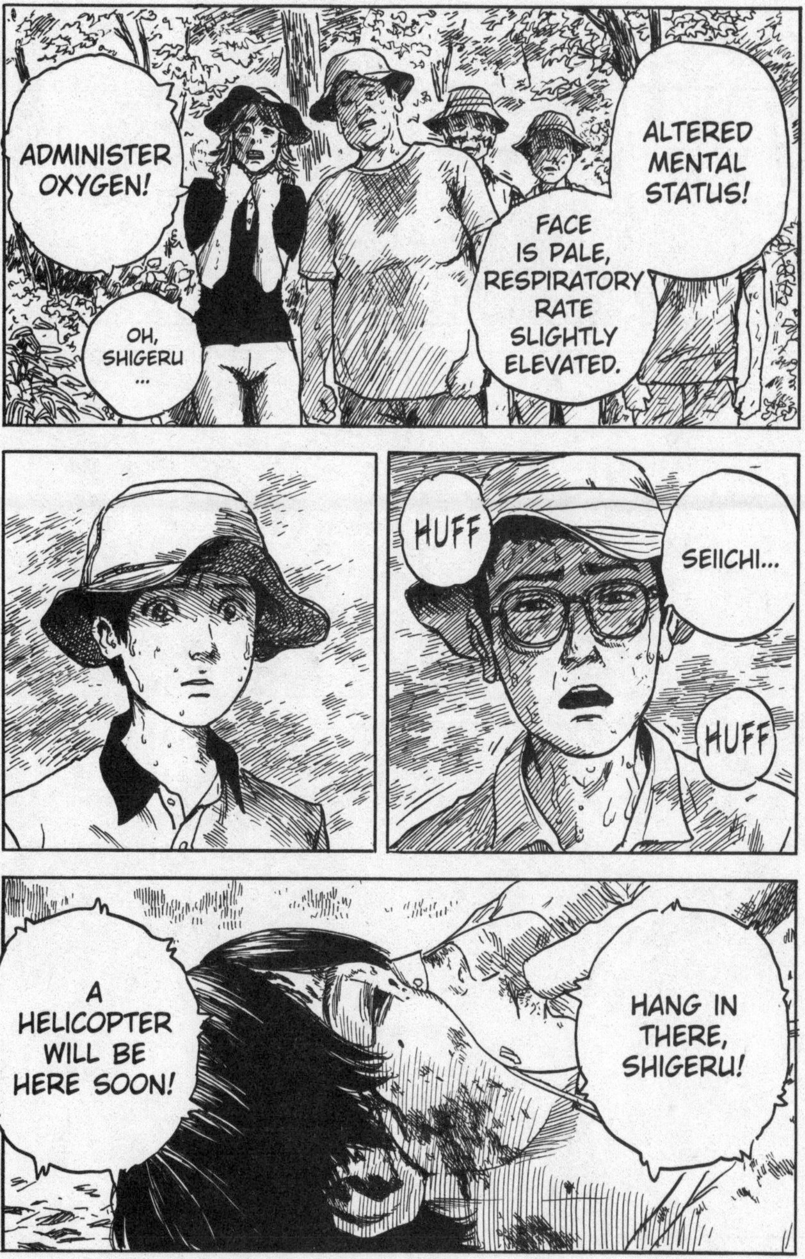
ALTERED MENTAL STATUS!
FACE IS PALE, RESPIRATORY RATE SLIGHTLY ELEVATED.
ADMINISTER OXYGEN!
OH, SHIGERU ...
SEIICHI...
HUFF
HUFF
HANG IN THERE, SHIGERU!
A HELICOPTER WILL BE HERE SOON!

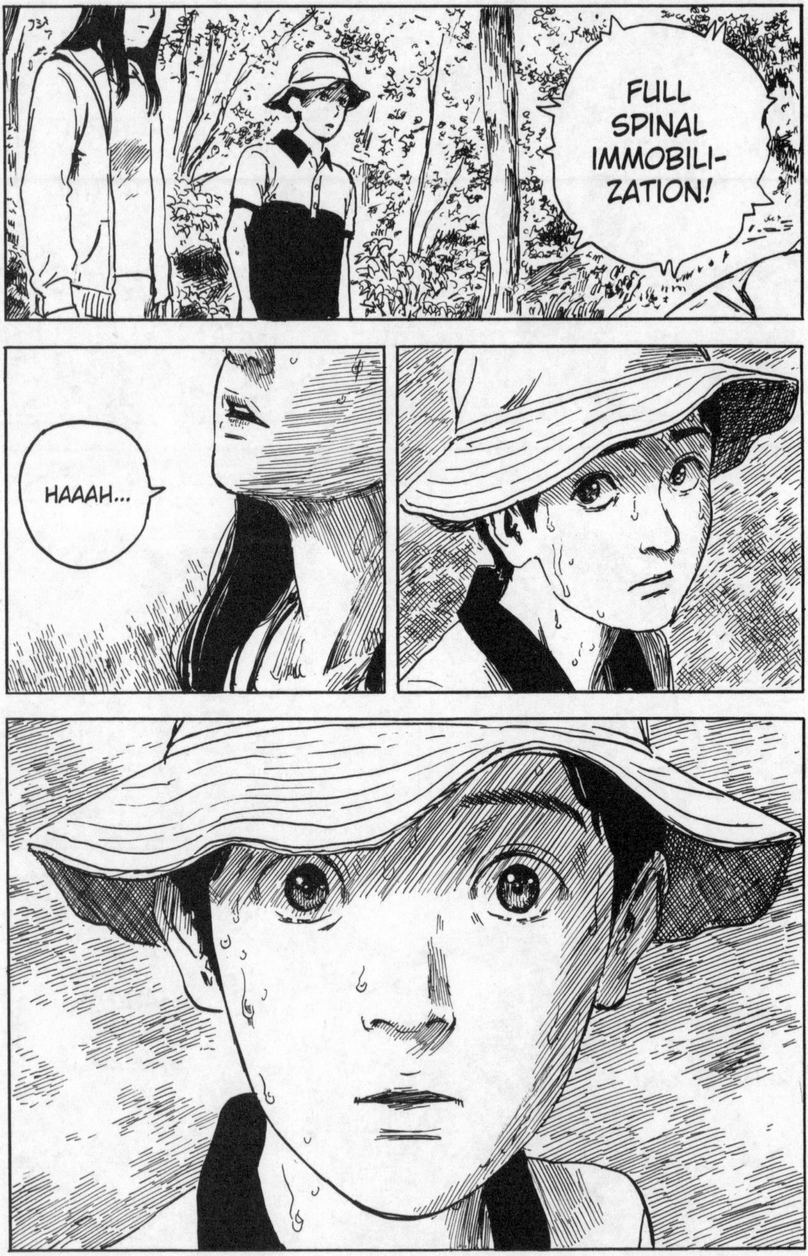
FULL SPINAL IMMOBILI- ZATION!
HAAAH...

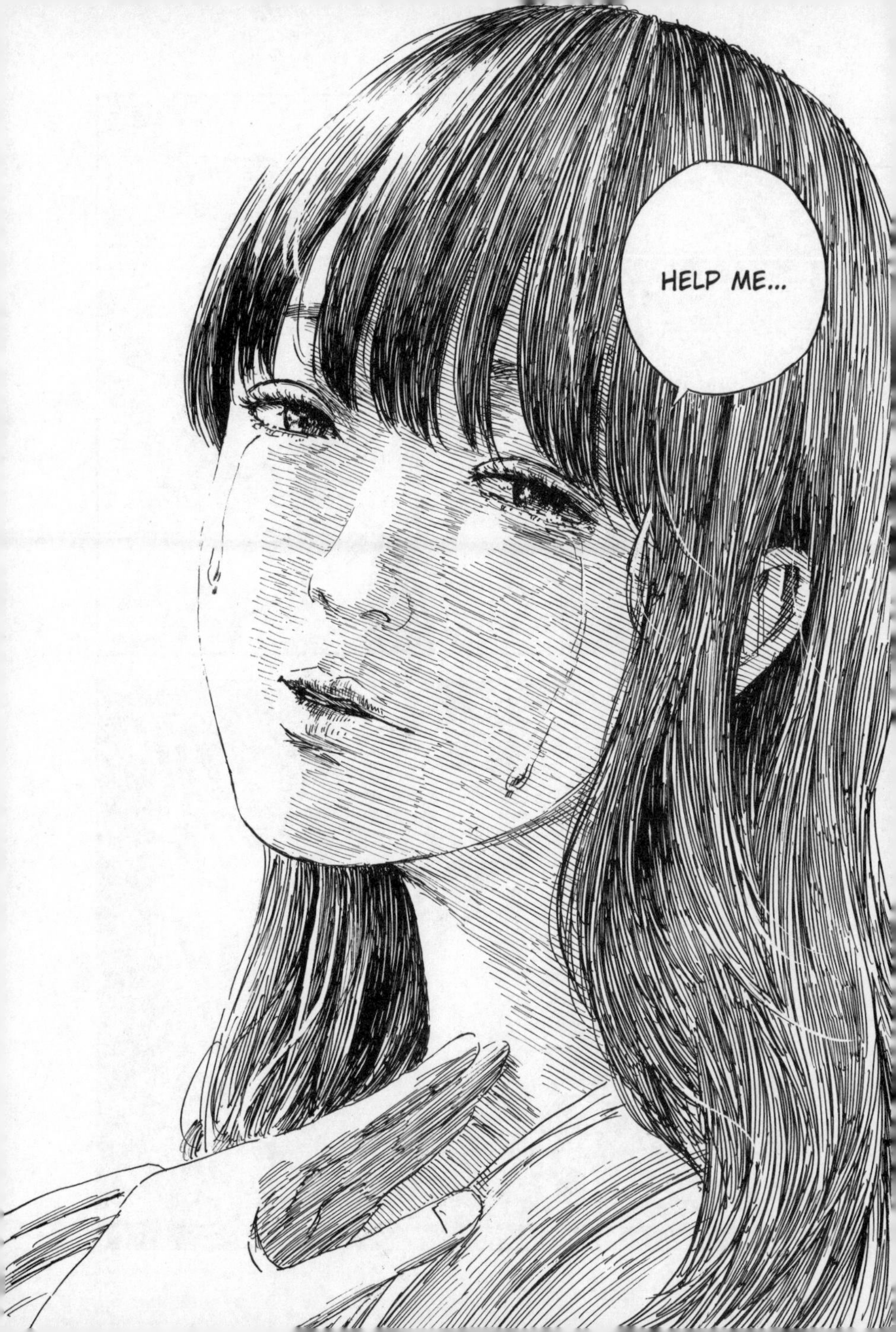
HELP ME...

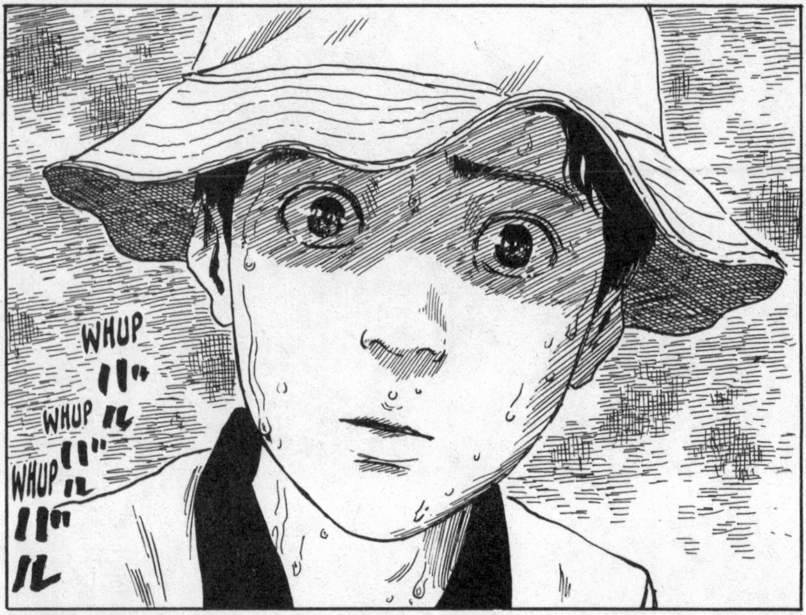
WHUP
バル
WHUP
バル
WHUP
バル

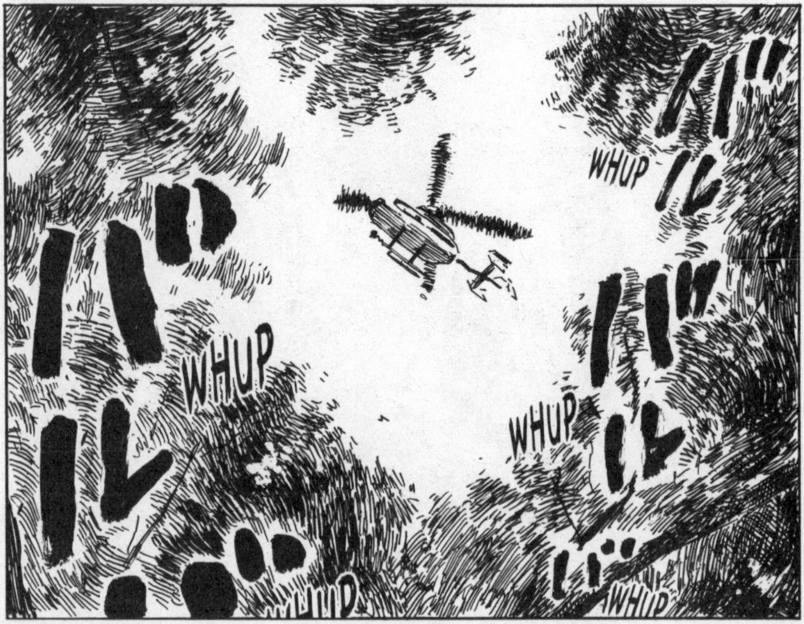
バル
WHUP
バル
WHUP
バル
WHUP

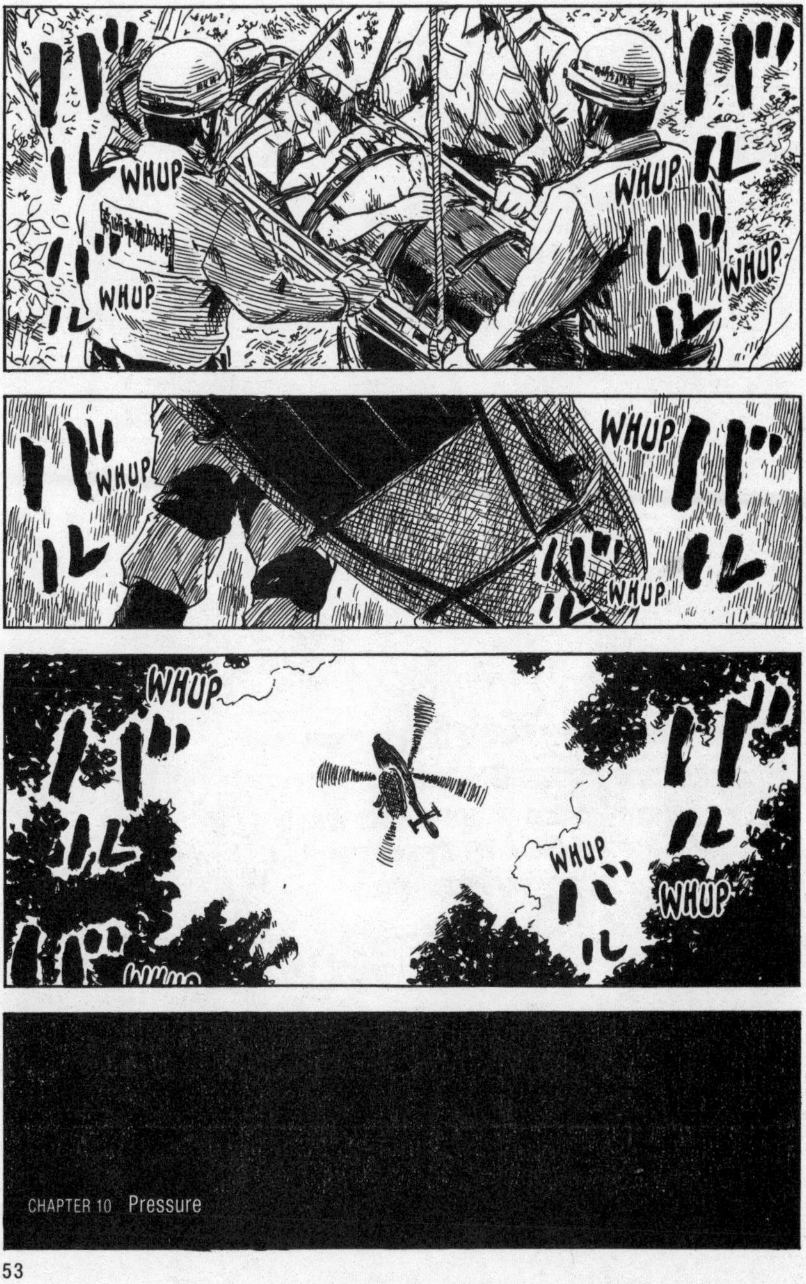
バル
WHUP
バル
WHUP
バル
WHUP
バル
WHUP
WHUP
バル
バル
WHUP
バル
WHUP
バル
WHUP
バル
WHUP
バル
WHUP
バル
WHUP

CHAPTER 10 Pressure

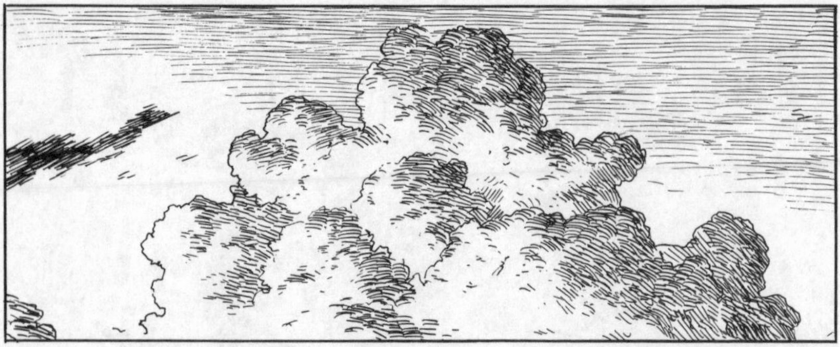

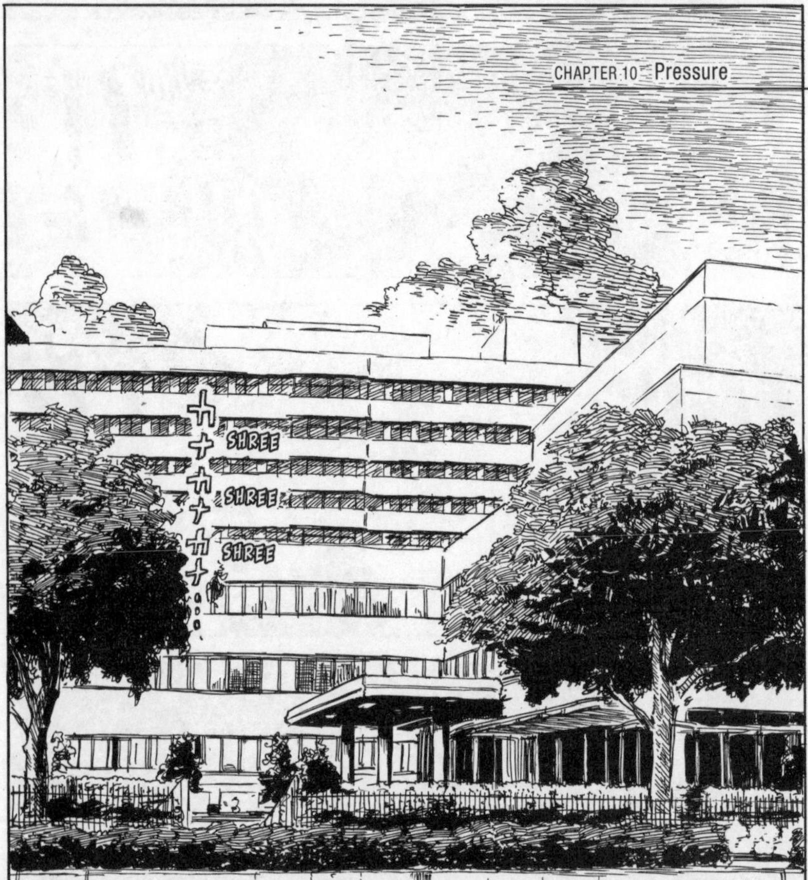
CHAPTER 10 Pressure
SHREE
SHREE
SHREE

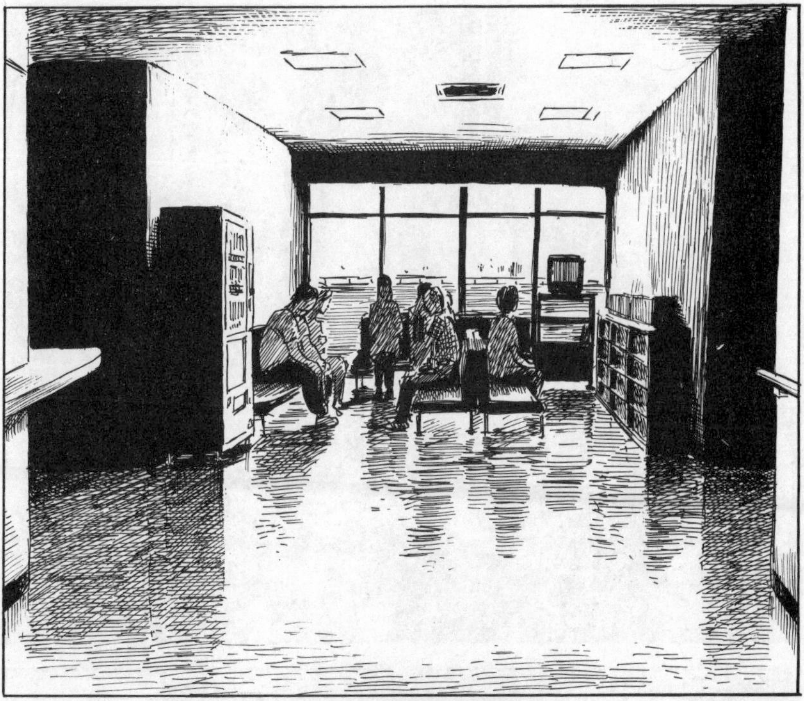

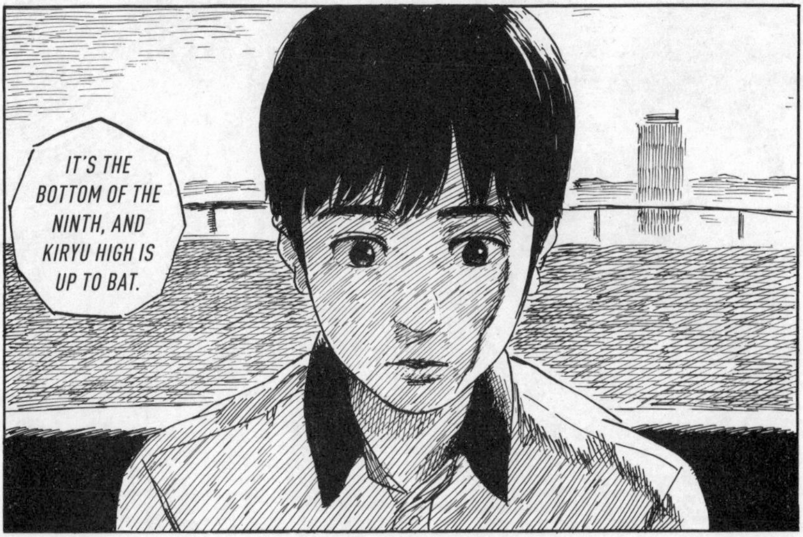
IT'S THE BOTTOM OF THE NINTH, AND KIRYU HIGH IS UP TO BAT.

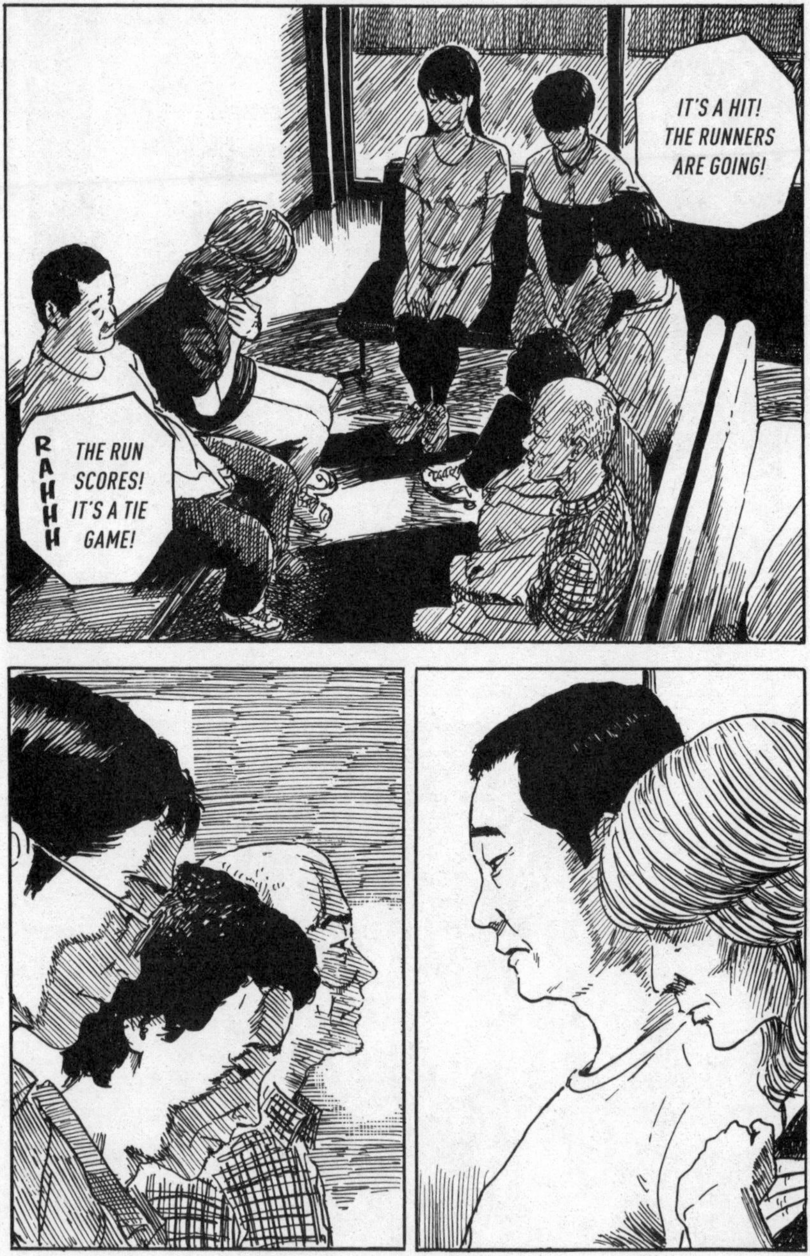
IT'S A HIT! THE RUNNERS ARE GOING!
RAHHH
THE RUN SCORES! IT'S A TIE GAME!

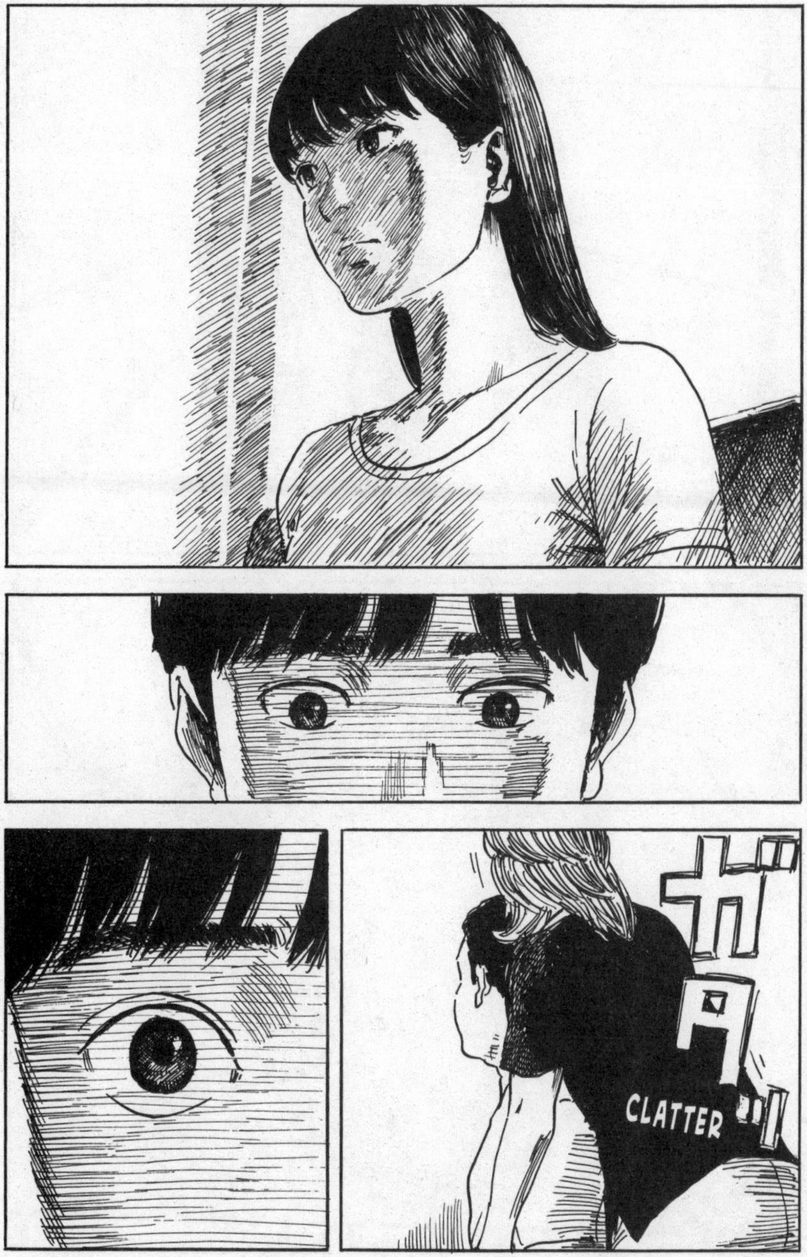
ガタ
CLATTER

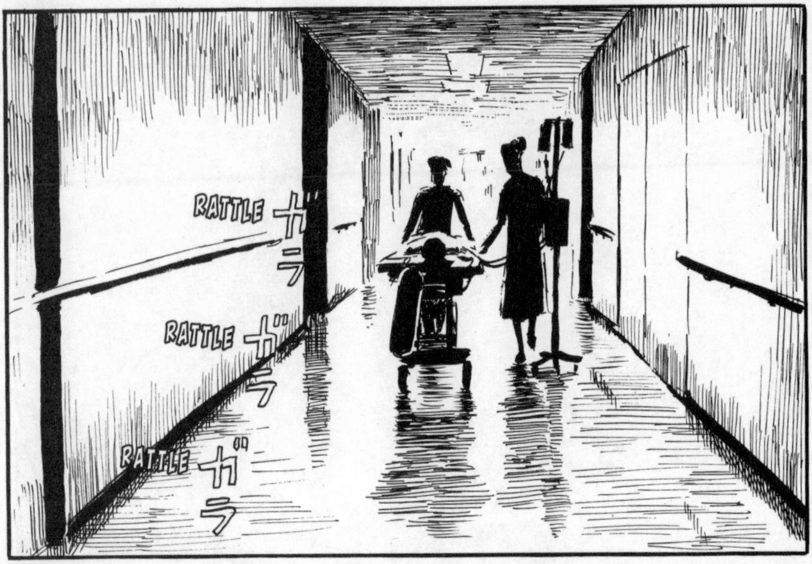
ガラ RATTLE
ガラ RATTLE
ガラ RATTLE

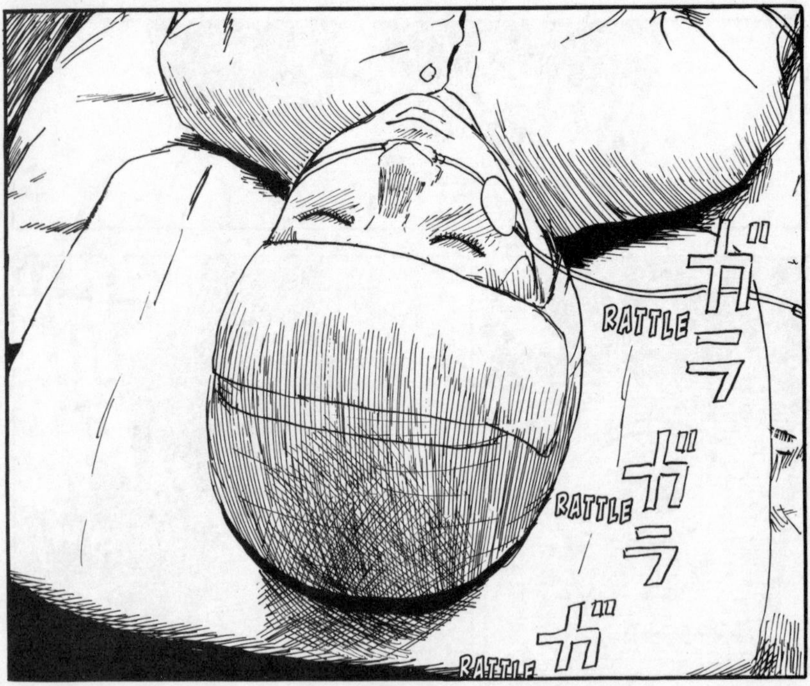
ガラ RATTLE
ガラ RATTLE
ガ RATTLE

SHIGERU !!
IS HE OKAY?!
DON'T WORRY.
THE SURGERY WAS SUCCESSFUL.

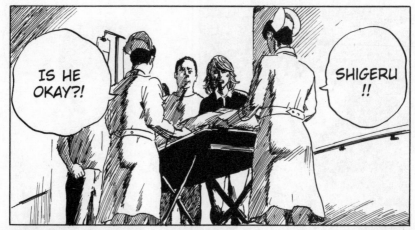

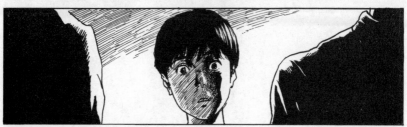

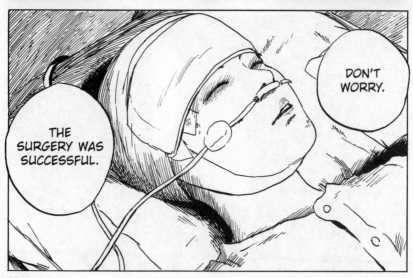

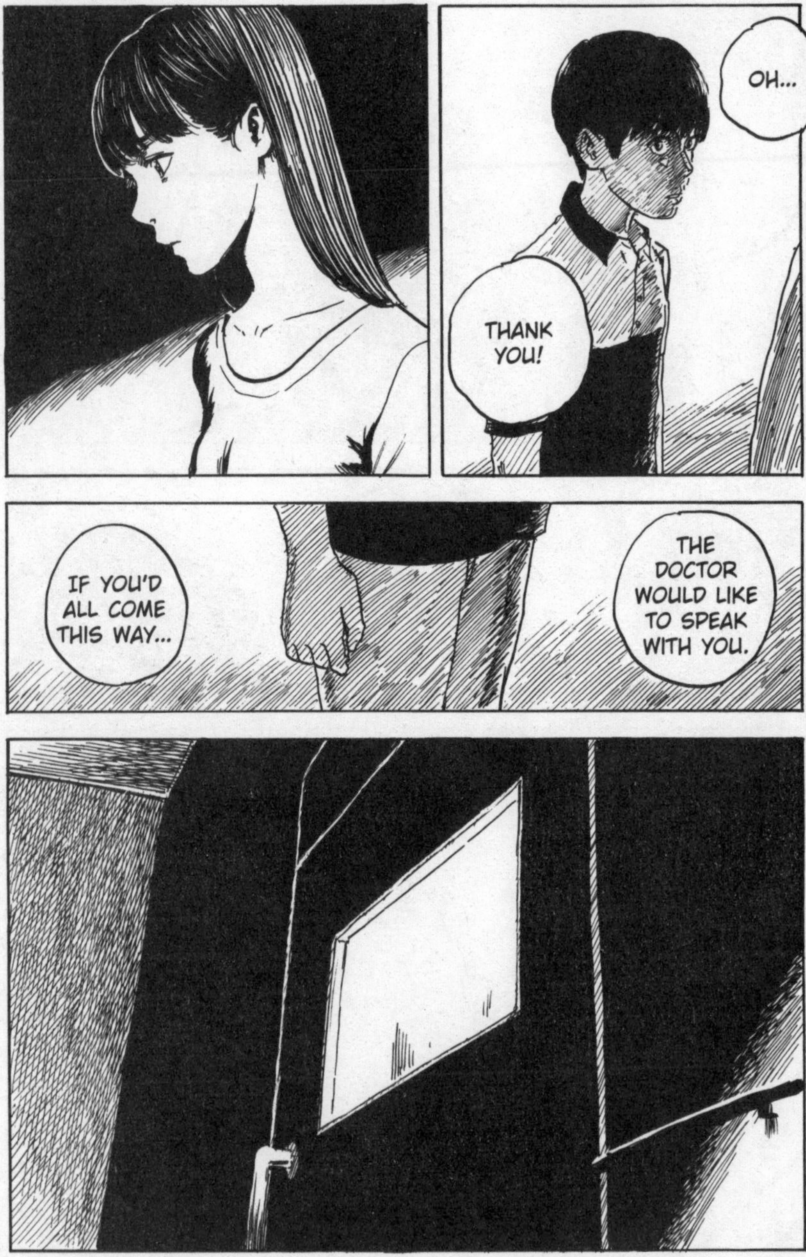
OH...
THANK YOU!
THE DOCTOR WOULD LIKE TO SPEAK WITH YOU.
IF YOU'D ALL COME THIS WAY...

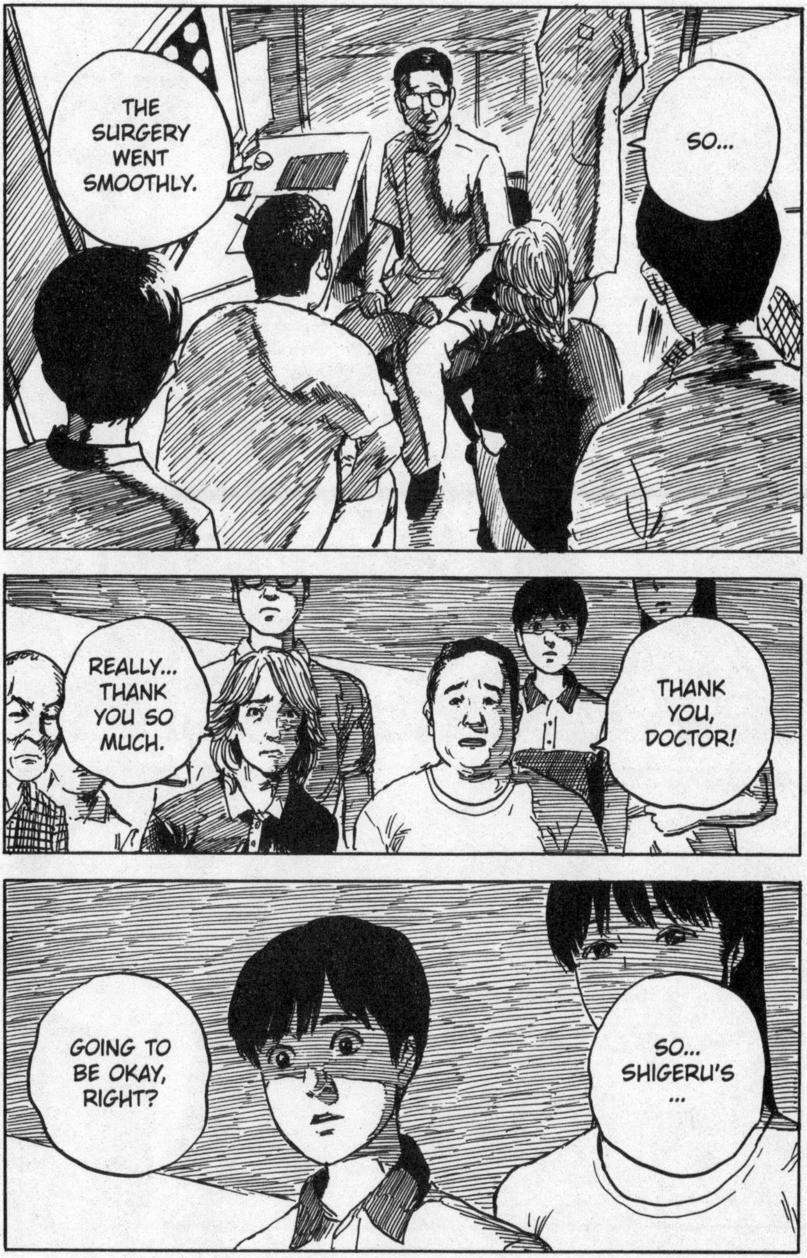
SO...
THE SURGERY WENT SMOOTHLY.
THANK YOU, DOCTOR!
REALLY... THANK YOU SO MUCH.
SO... SHIGERU'S ...
GOING TO BE OKAY, RIGHT?

PLEASE TAKE A LOOK AT THIS.

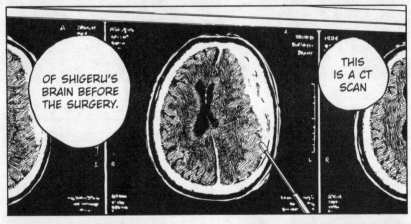

THIS IS A CT SCAN

OF SHIGERU'S BRAIN BEFORE THE SURGERY.

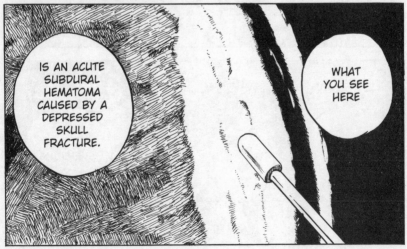

WHAT YOU SEE HERE

IS AN ACUTE SUBDURAL HEMATOMA CAUSED BY A DEPRESSED SKULL FRACTURE.

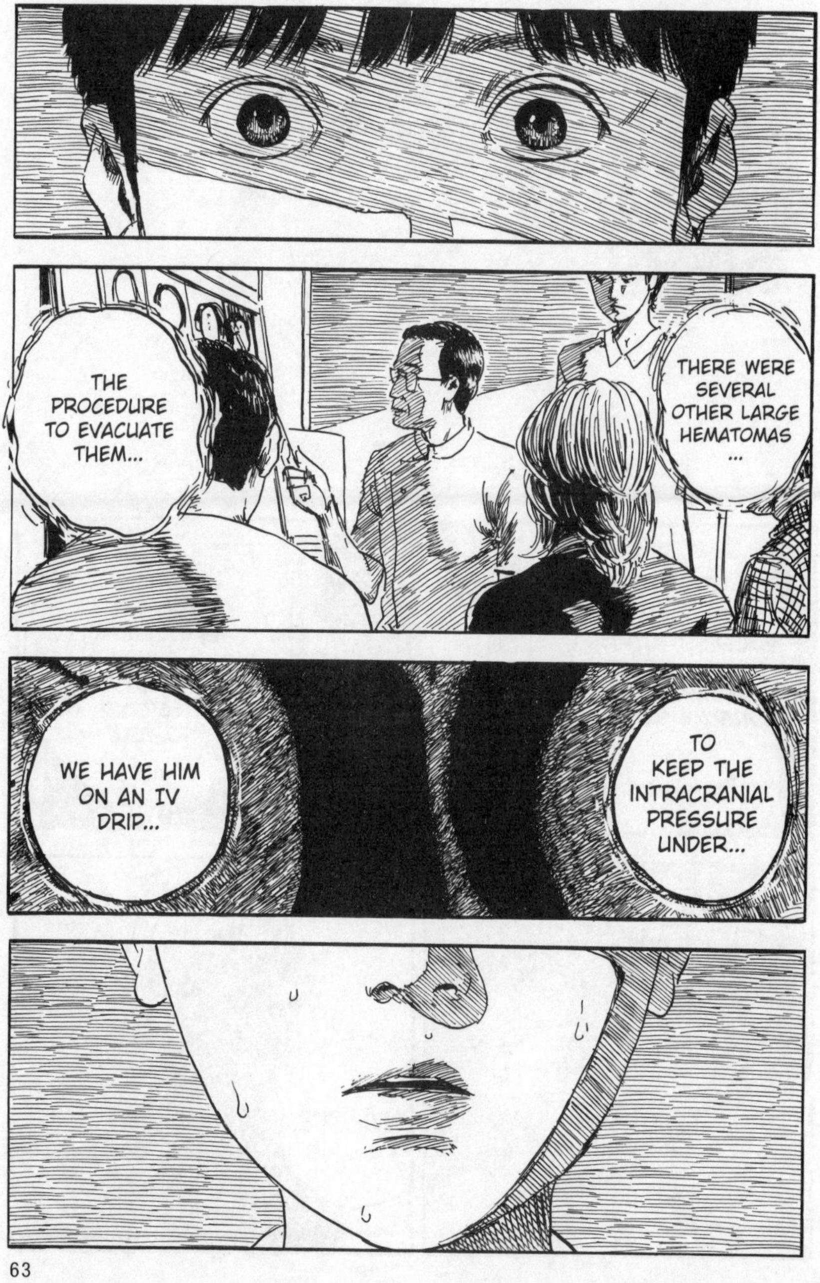
THERE WERE SEVERAL OTHER LARGE HEMATOMAS ...
THE PROCEDURE TO EVACUATE THEM...
TO KEEP THE INTRACRANIAL PRESSURE UNDER...
WE HAVE HIM ON AN IV DRIP...

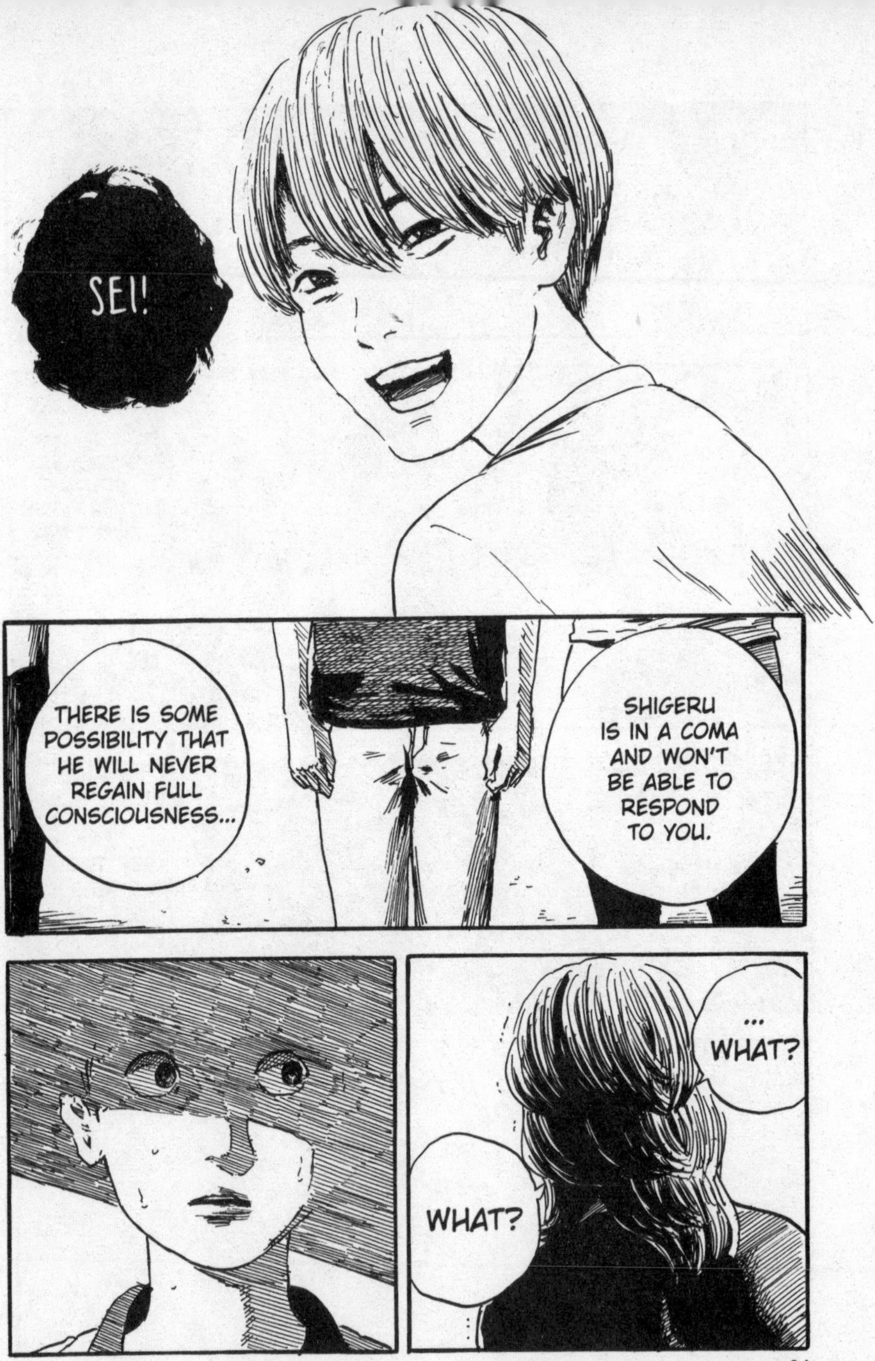
SEI!
SHIGERU IS IN A COMA AND WON'T BE ABLE TO RESPOND TO YOU.
THERE IS SOME POSSIBILITY THAT HE WILL NEVER REGAIN FULL CONSCIOUSNESS...
... WHAT?
WHAT?

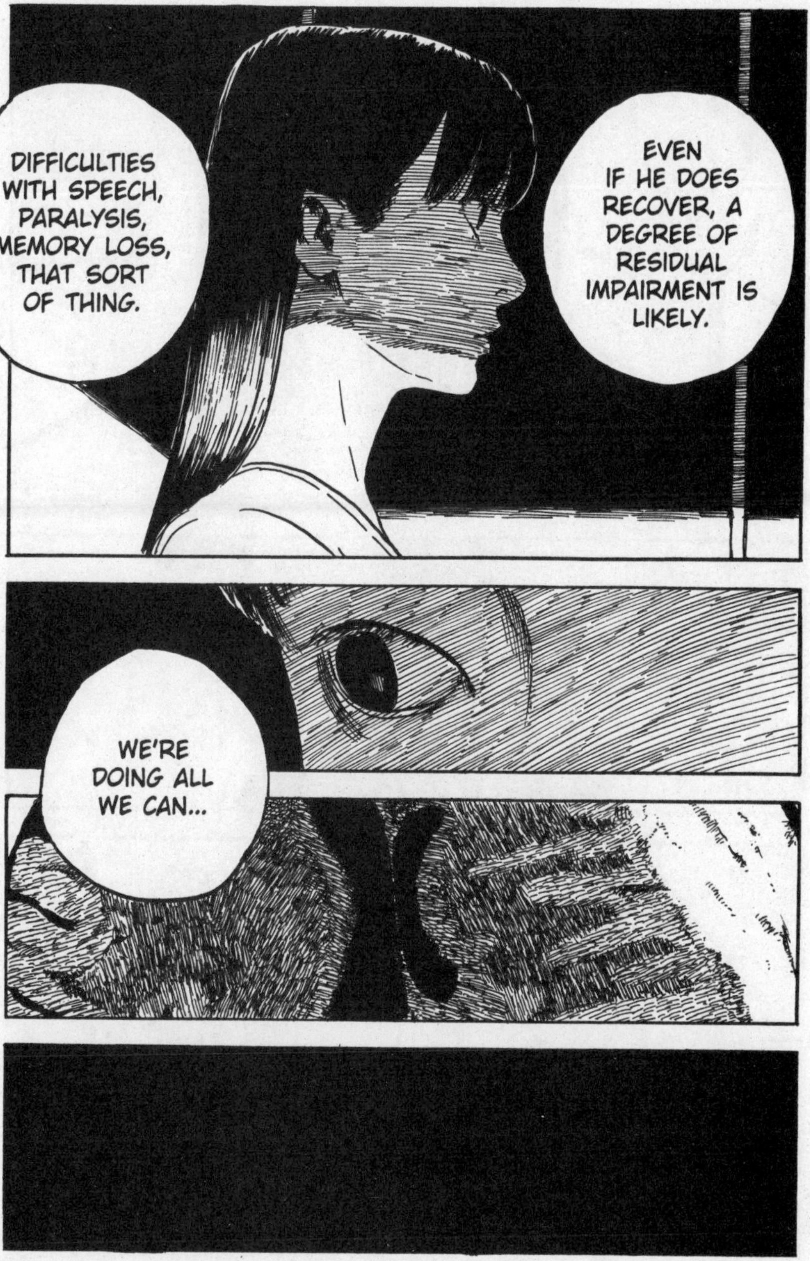
EVEN IF HE DOES RECOVER, A DEGREE OF RESIDUAL IMPAIRMENT IS LIKELY.
DIFFICULTIES WITH SPEECH, PARALYSIS, MEMORY LOSS, THAT SORT OF THING.
WE'RE DOING ALL WE CAN...

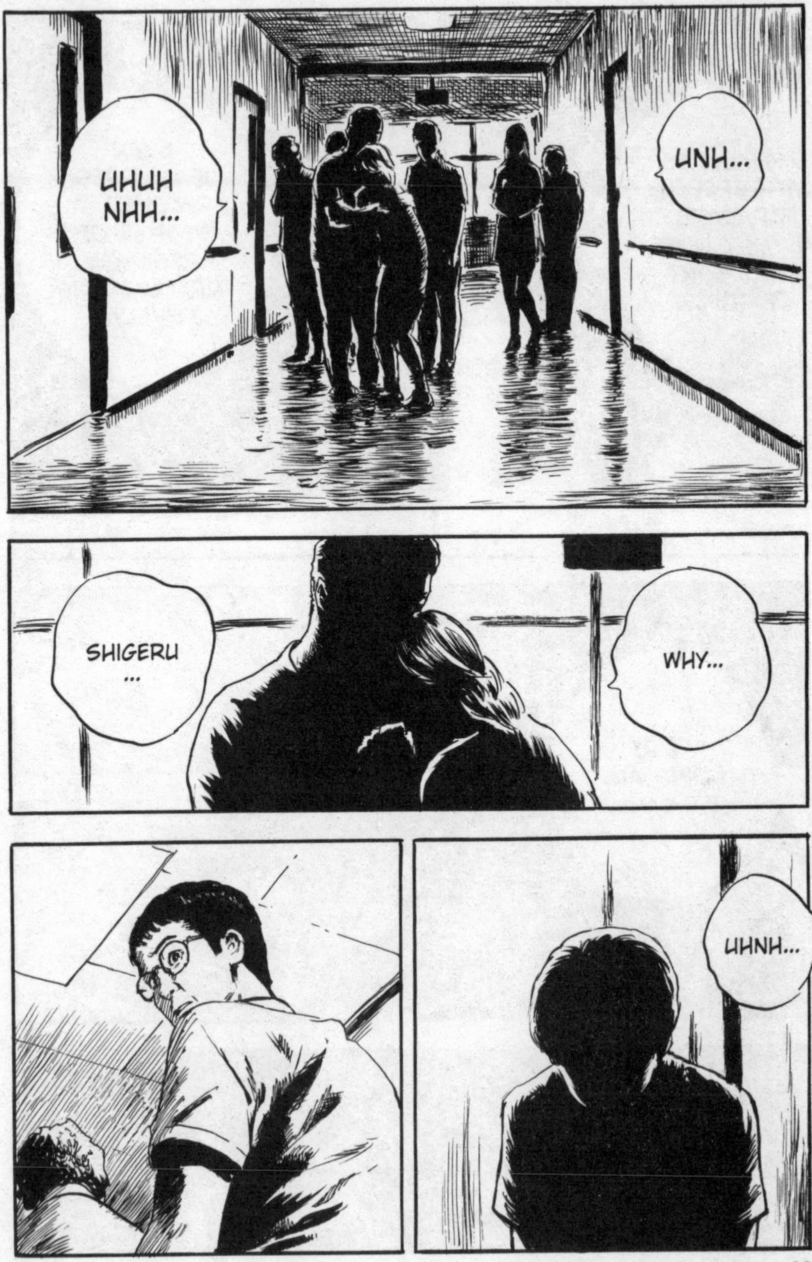
UNH...
UHUH NHH...
WHY...
SHIGERU ...
UHNH...

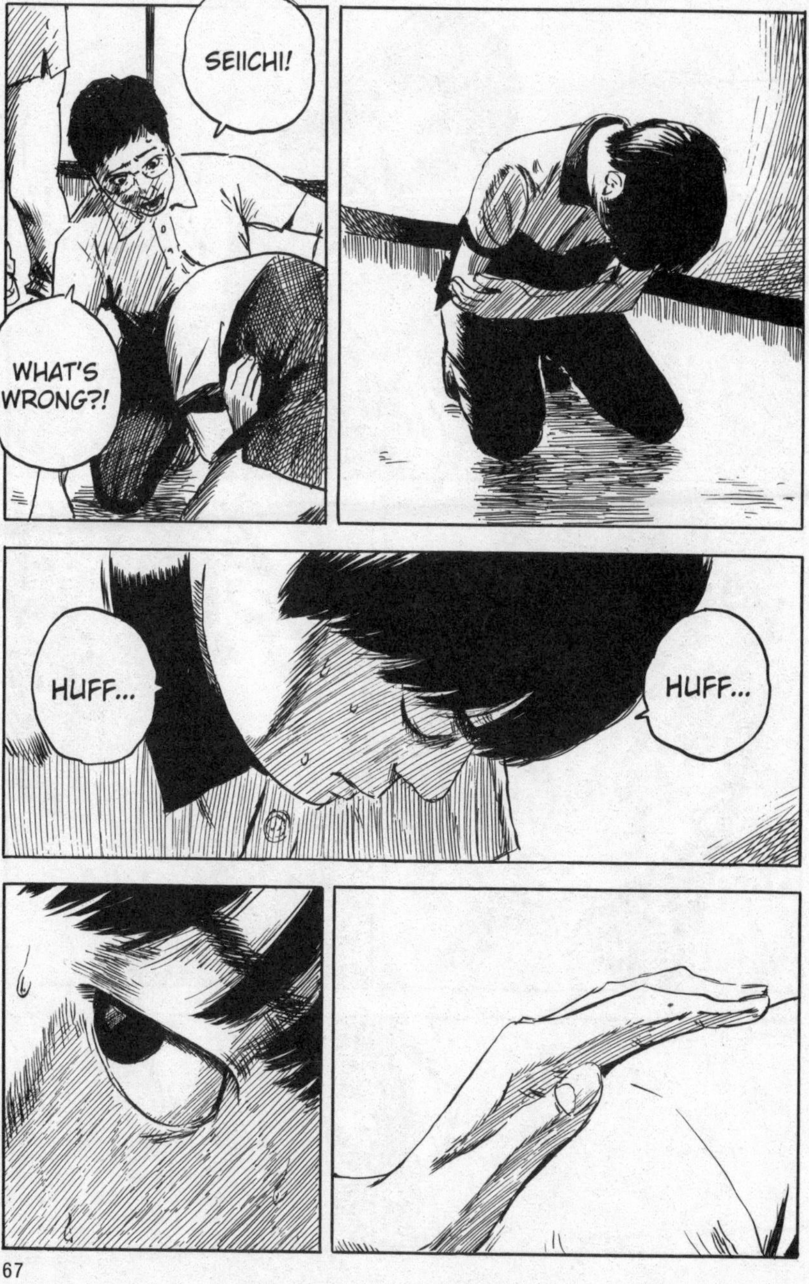
SEIICHI!
WHAT'S WRONG?!
HUFF...
HUFF...

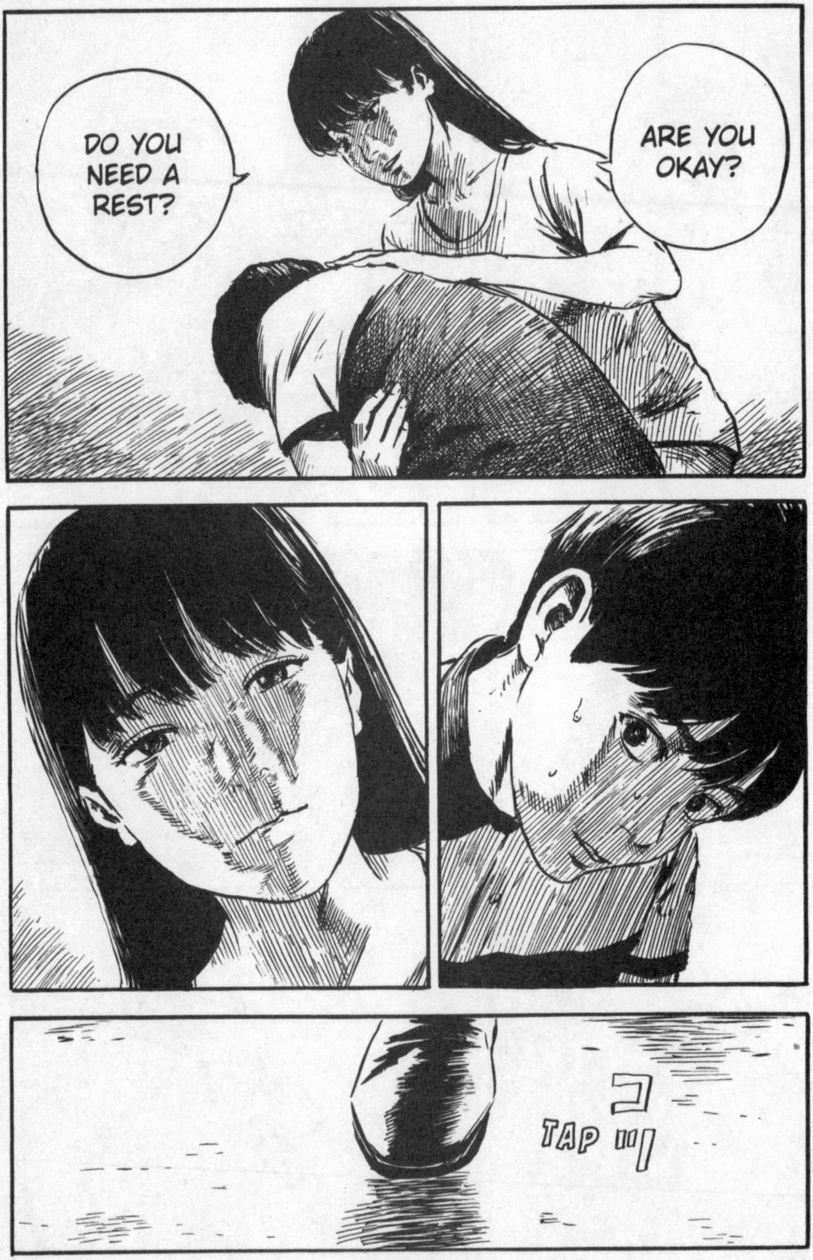
ARE YOU OKAY?
DO YOU NEED A REST?
TAP

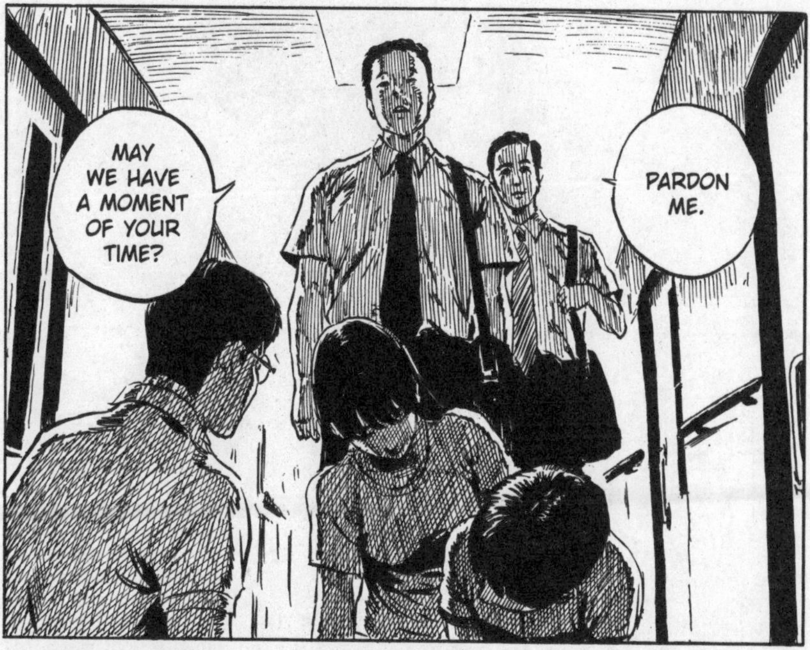
PARDON ME.
MAY WE HAVE A MOMENT OF YOUR TIME?

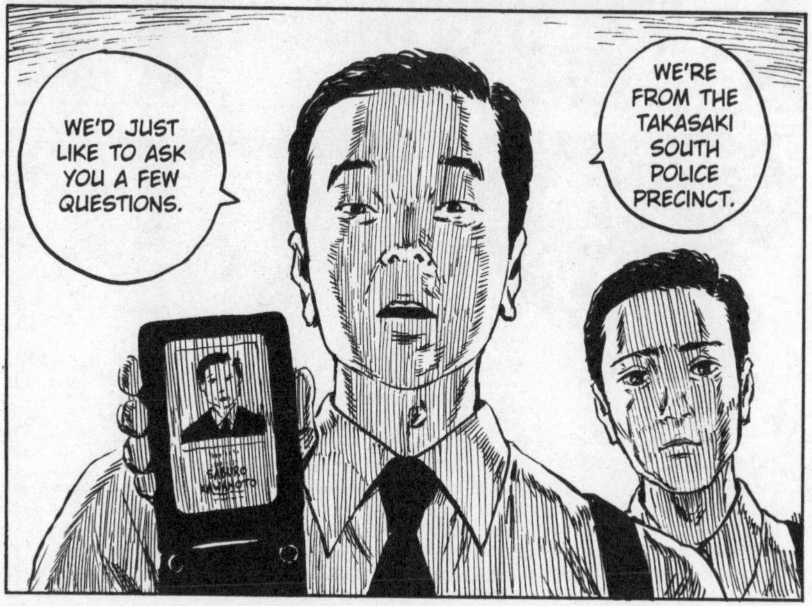
WE'RE FROM THE TAKASAKI SOUTH POLICE PRECINCT.
WE'D JUST LIKE TO ASK YOU A FEW QUESTIONS.

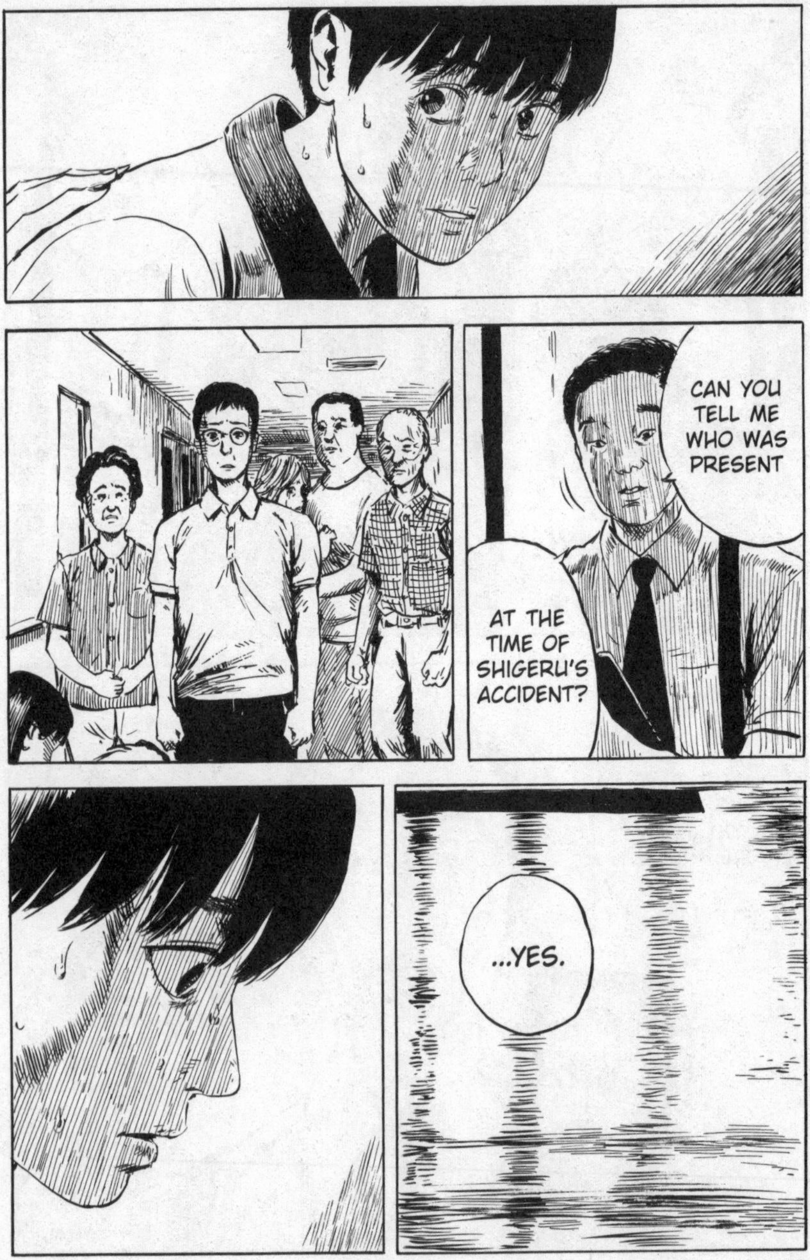
CAN YOU TELL ME WHO WAS PRESENT
AT THE TIME OF SHIGERU'S ACCIDENT?
...YES.

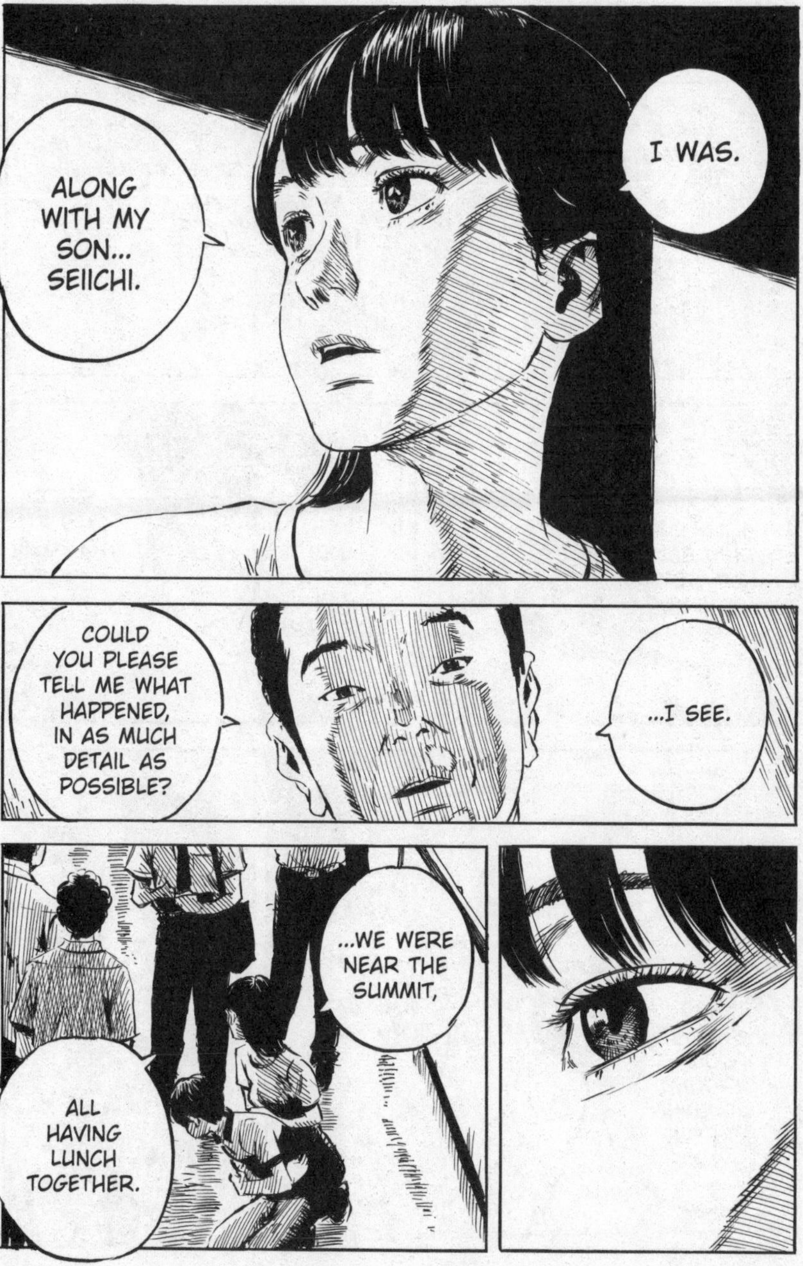
I WAS.
ALONG WITH MY SON... SEIICHI.
...I SEE.
COULD YOU PLEASE TELL ME WHAT HAPPENED, IN AS MUCH DETAIL AS POSSIBLE?
...WE WERE NEAR THE SUMMIT,
ALL HAVING LUNCH TOGETHER.

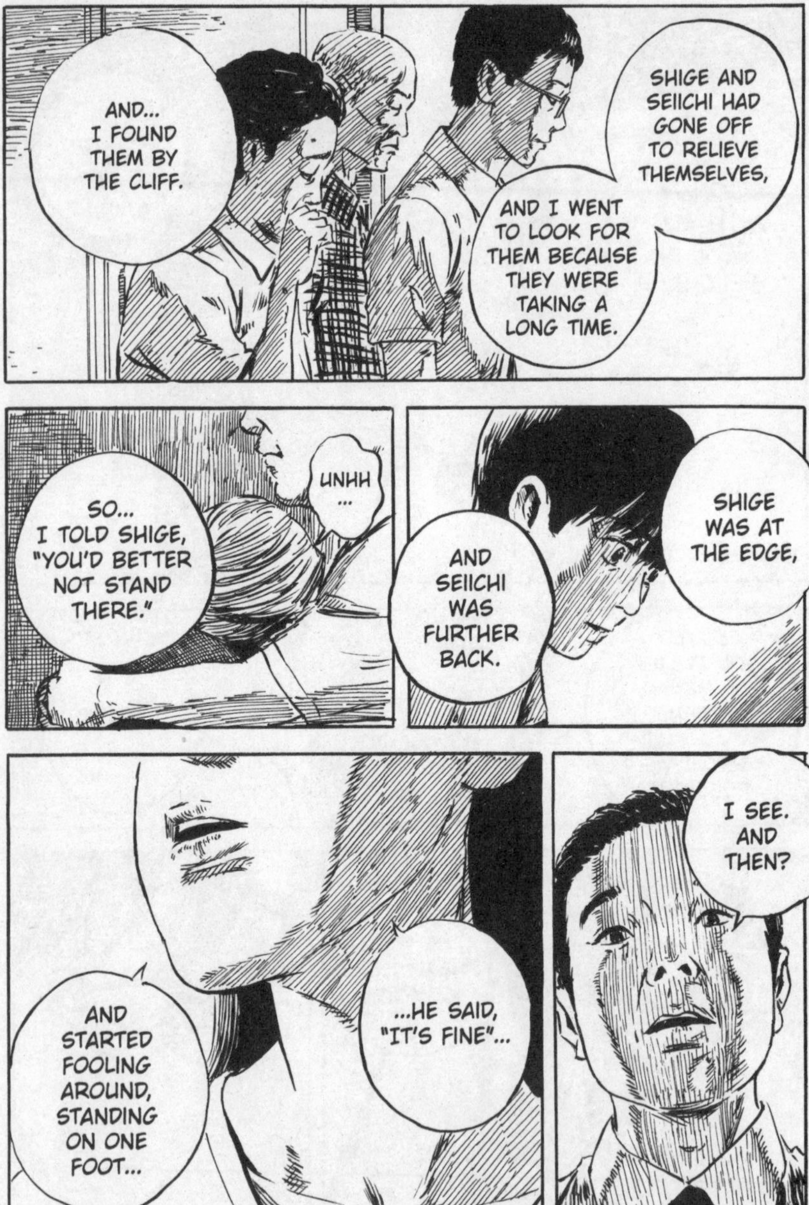
SHIGE AND SEIICHI HAD GONE OFF TO RELIEVE THEMSELVES,
AND I WENT TO LOOK FOR THEM BECAUSE THEY WERE TAKING A LONG TIME.
AND... I FOUND THEM BY THE CLIFF.
SHIGE WAS AT THE EDGE,
AND SEIICHI WAS FURTHER BACK.
UNHH ...
SO... I TOLD SHIGE, "YOU'D BETTER NOT STAND THERE."
I SEE. AND THEN?
...HE SAID, "IT'S FINE"...
AND STARTED FOOLING AROUND, STANDING ON ONE FOOT...

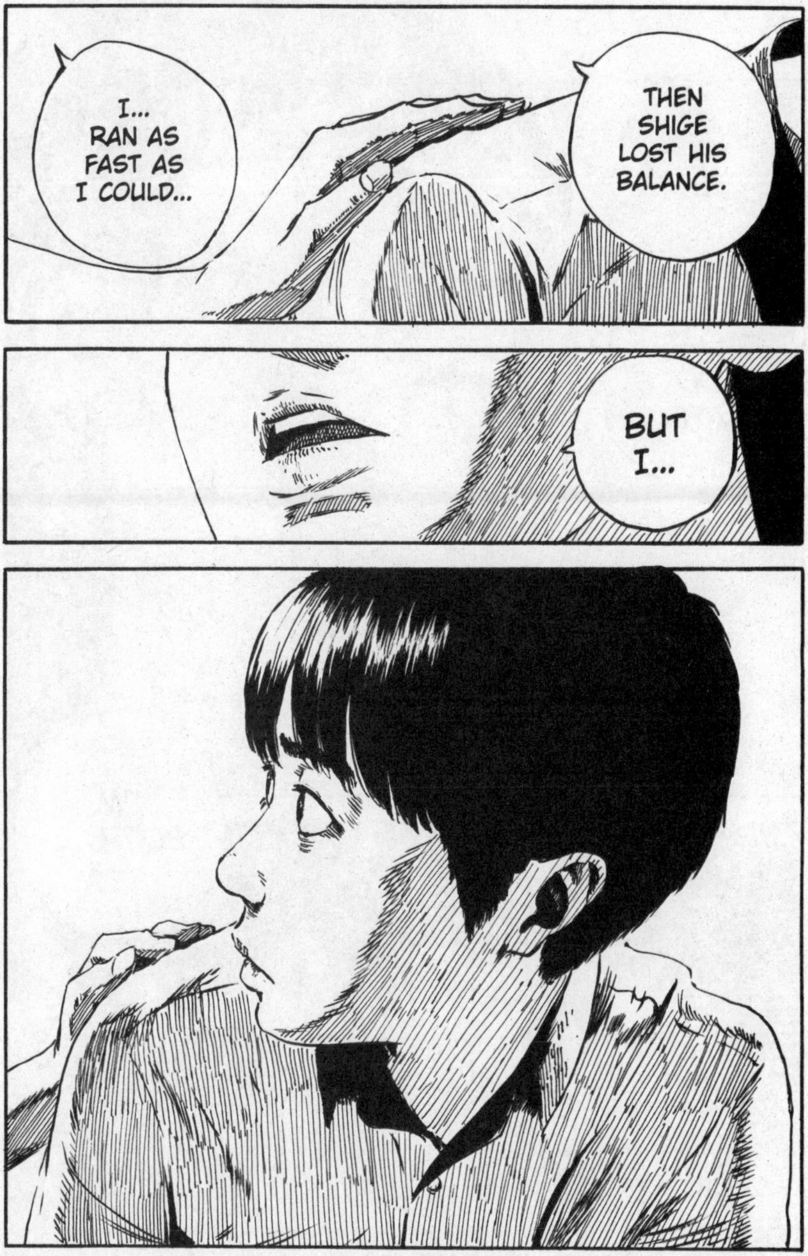
THEN SHIGE LOST HIS BALANCE.
I... RAN AS FAST AS I COULD...
BUT I...

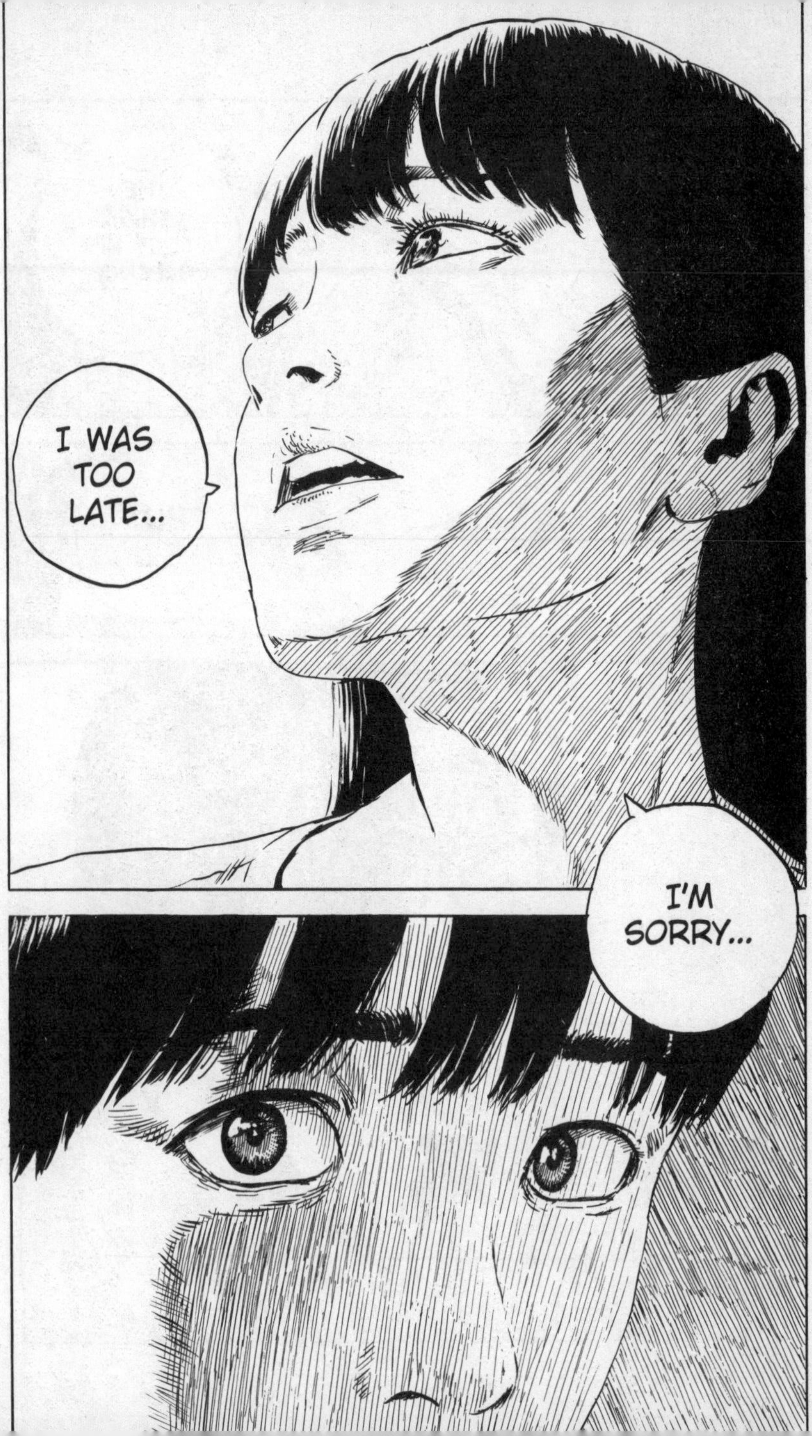
I WAS TOO LATE...
I'M SORRY...

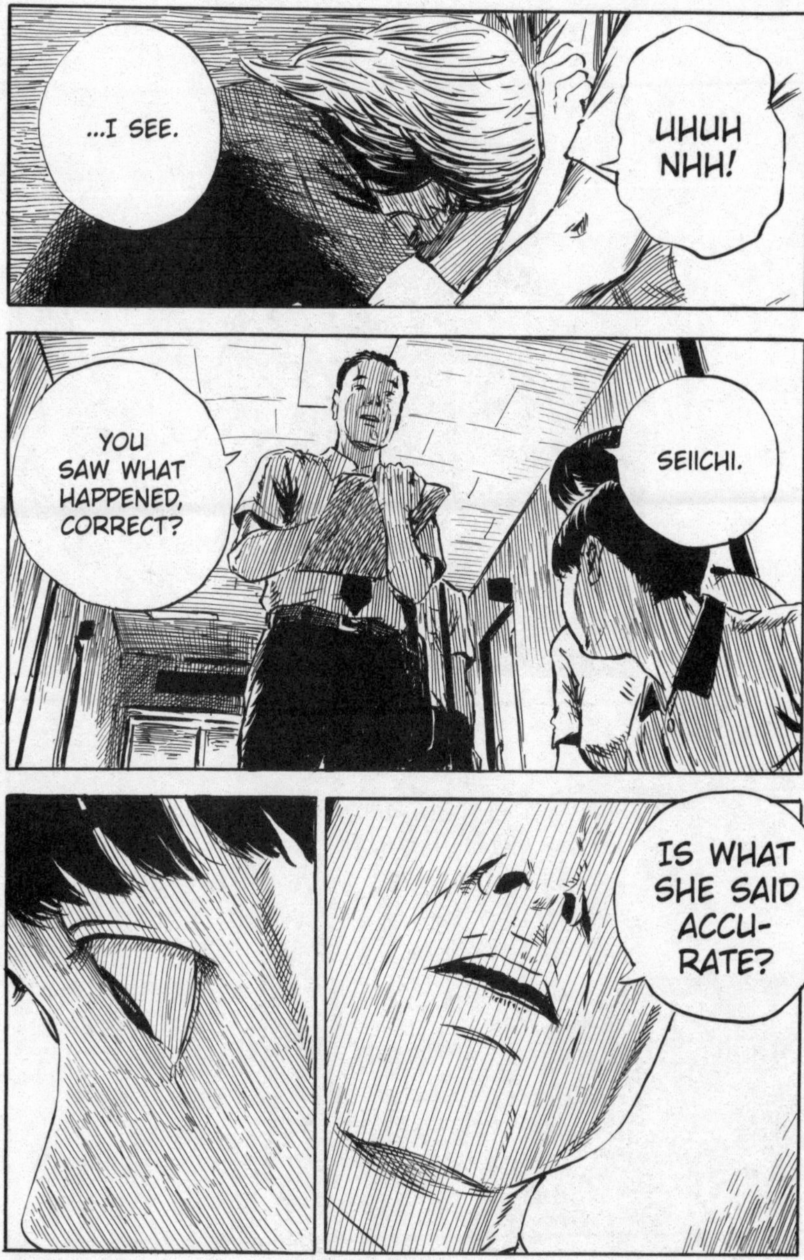
UHUH NHH!
...I SEE.
SEIICHI.
YOU SAW WHAT HAPPENED, CORRECT?
IS WHAT SHE SAID ACCURATE?

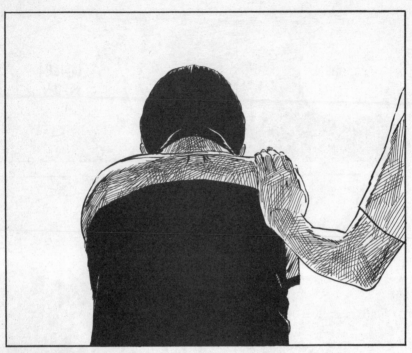

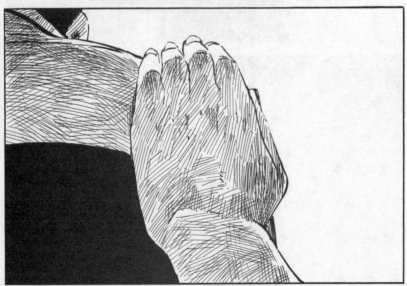

CHAPTER 11　Cross to Bear

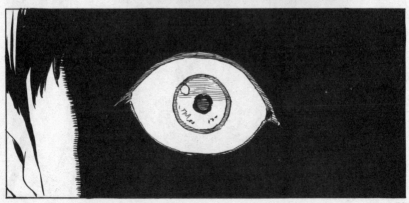

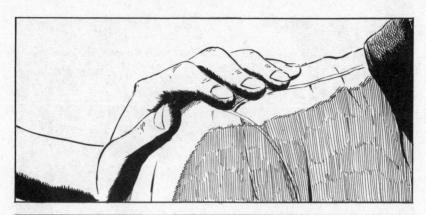

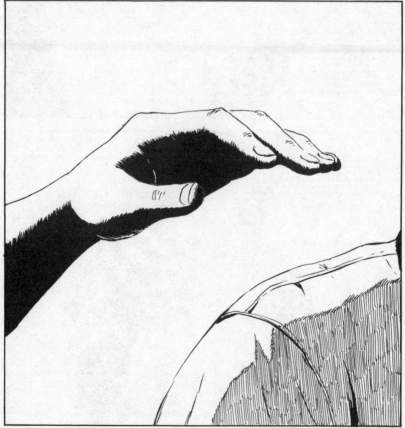

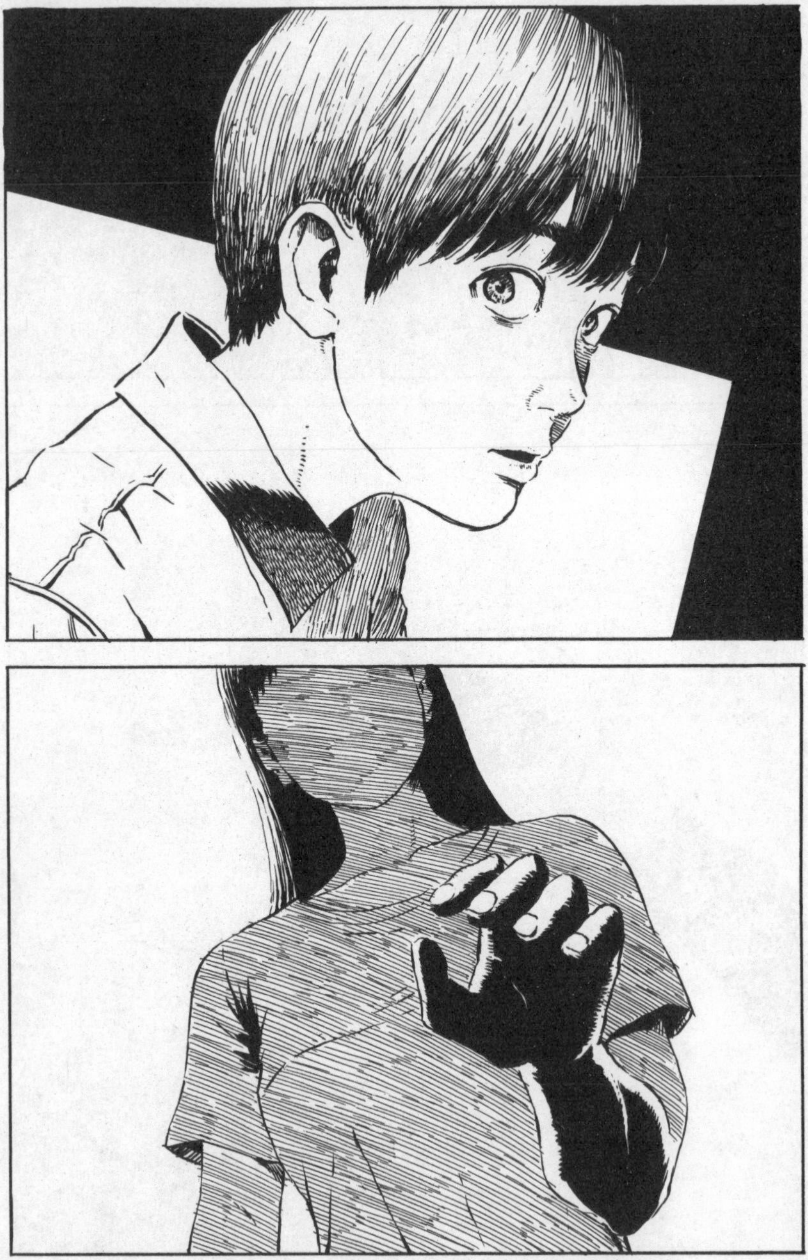

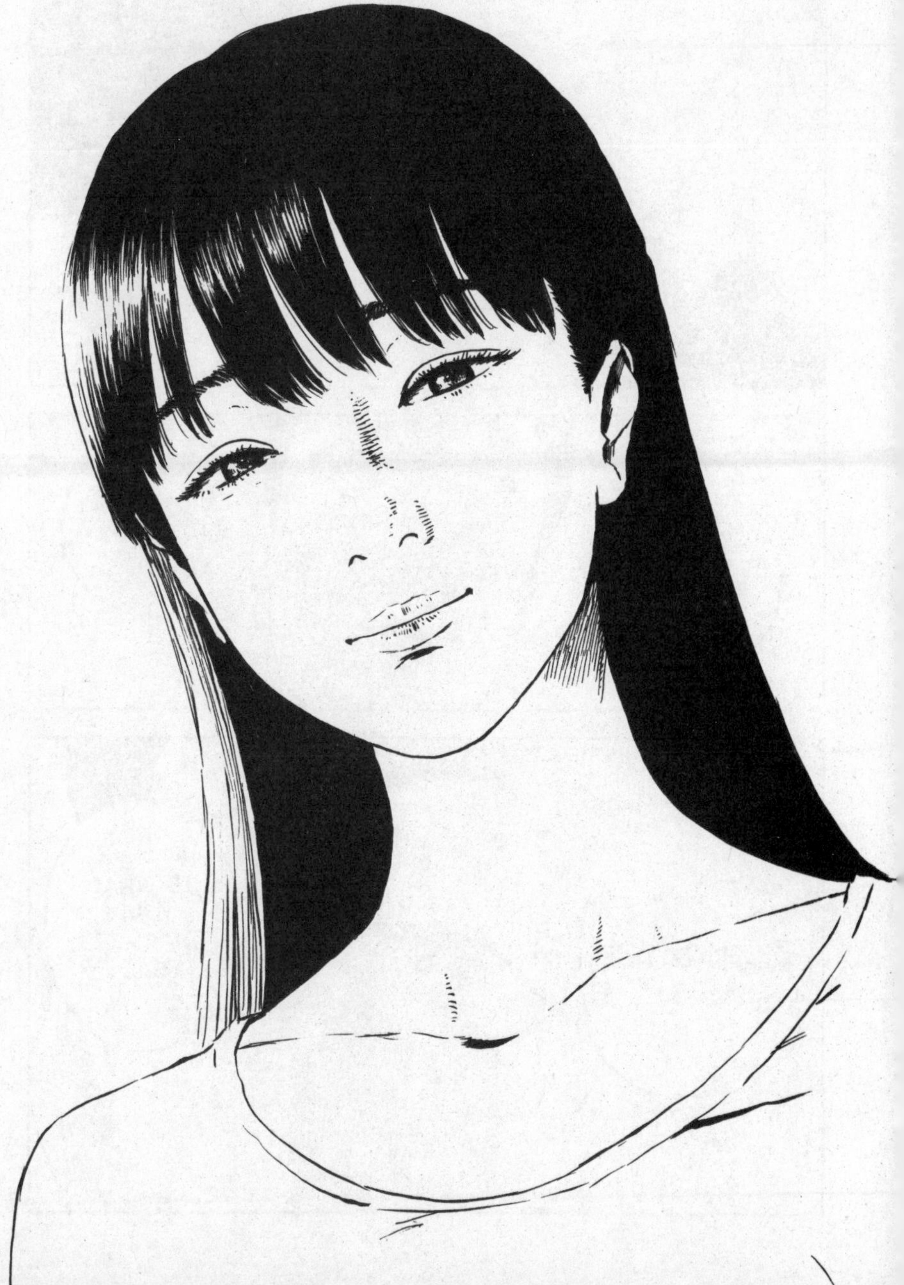

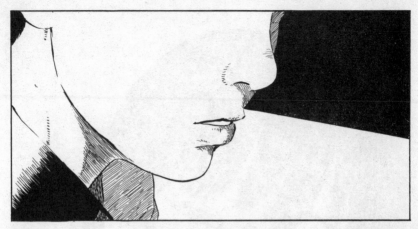

WHAT'S WRONG, SEIICHI?

HM?

ACCURATE?

IS WHAT YOUR MOTHER SAID

...YES.

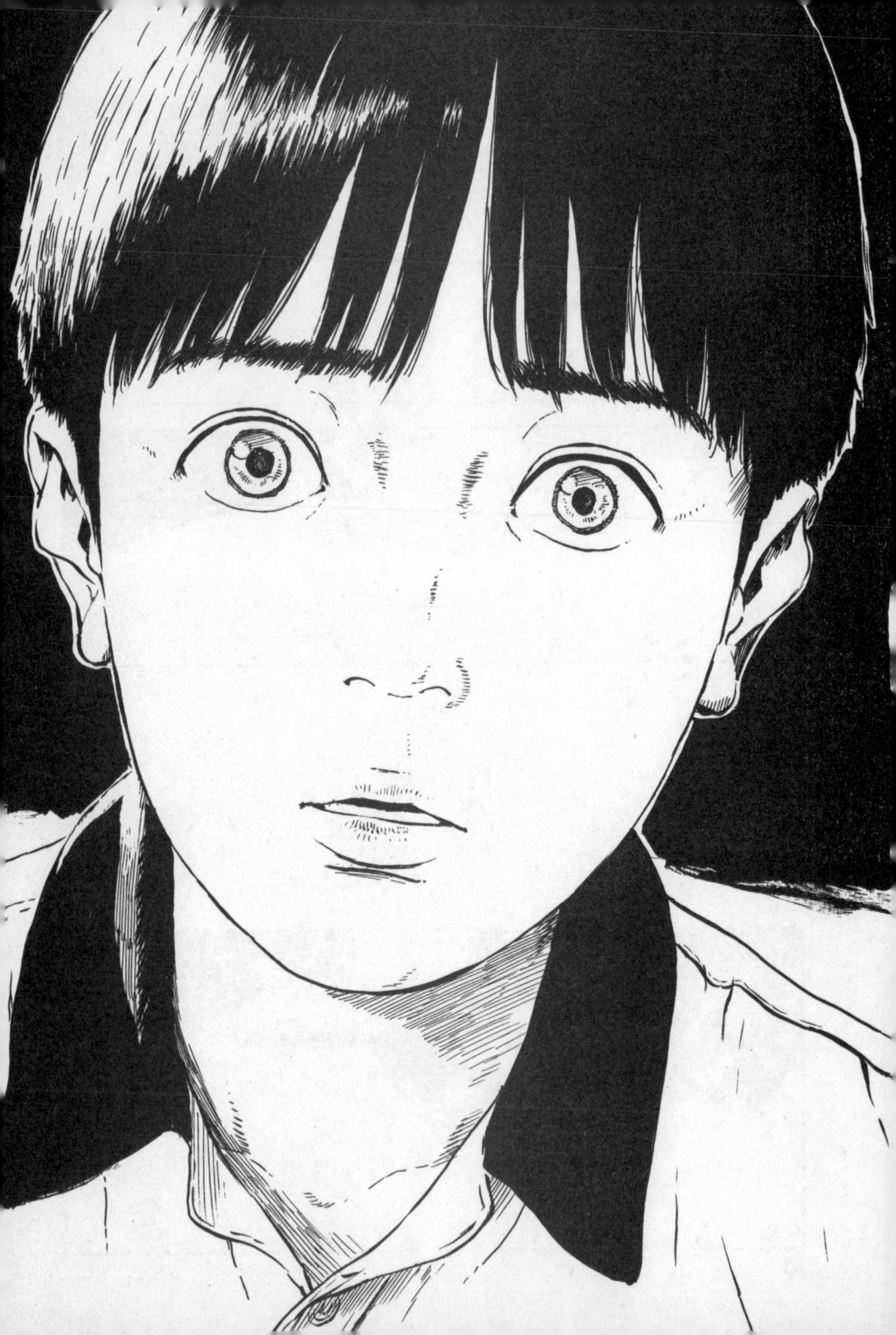

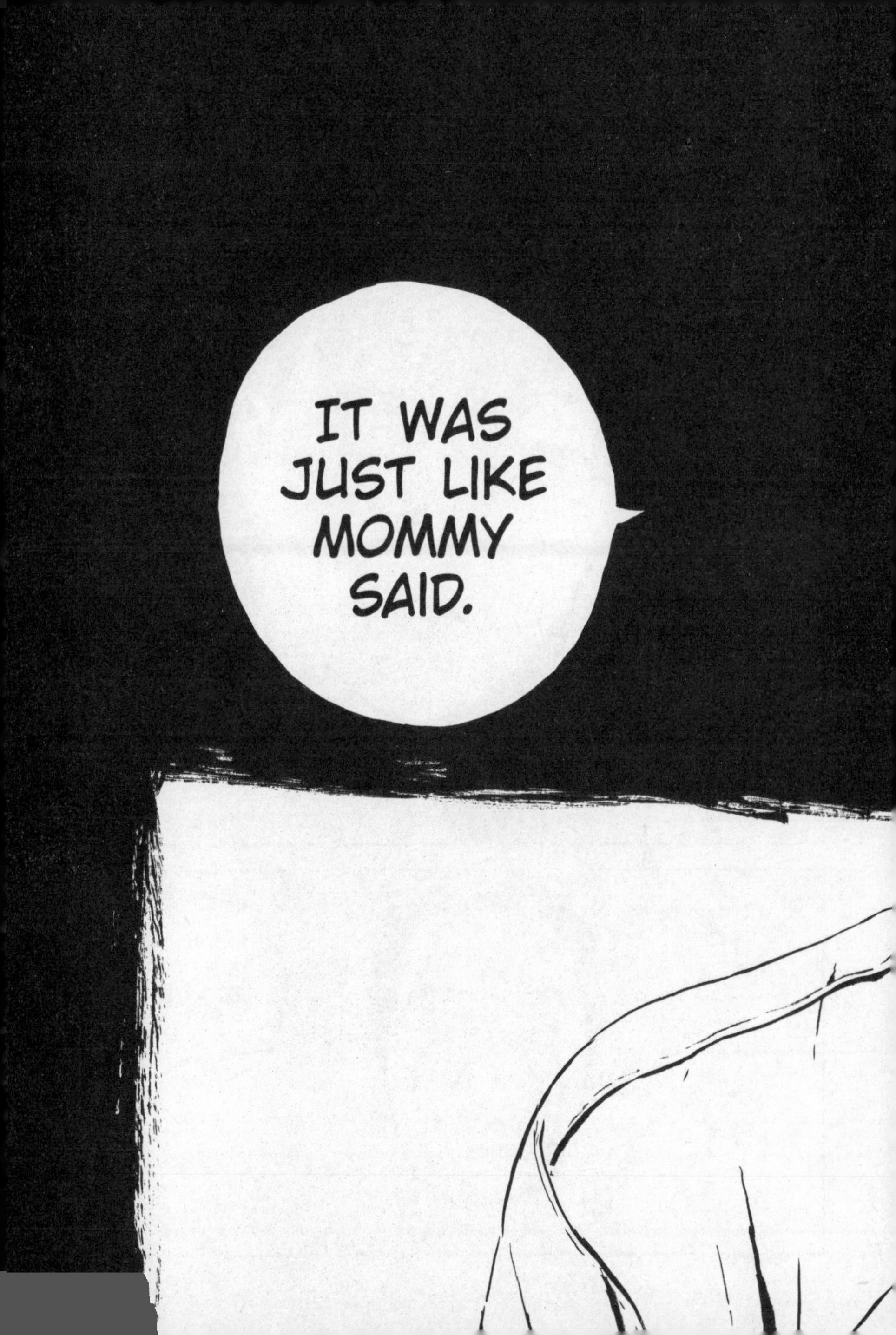
IT WAS JUST LIKE MOMMY SAID.

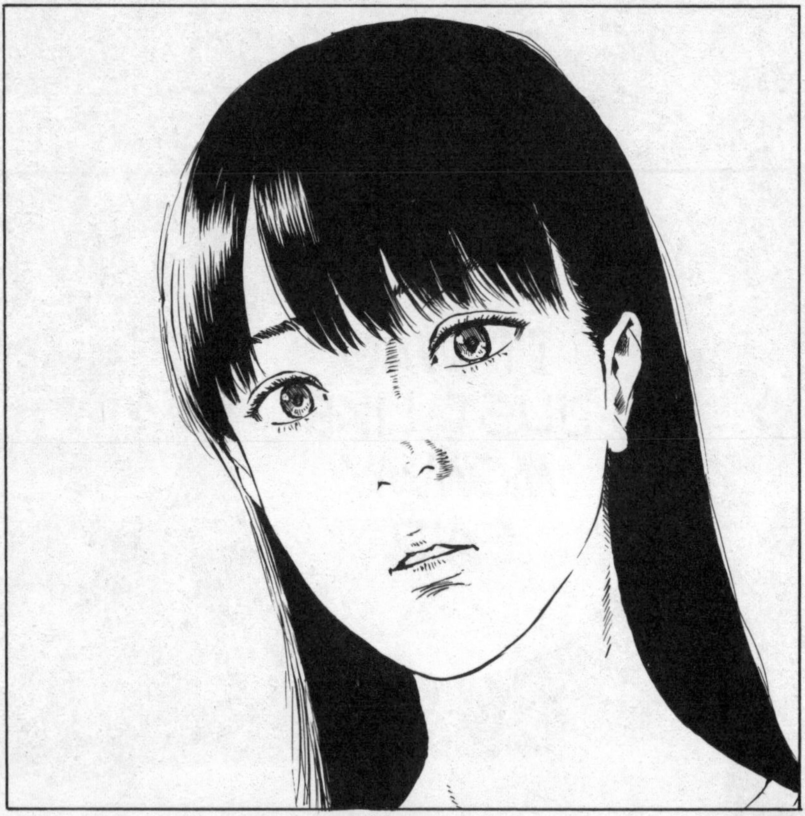

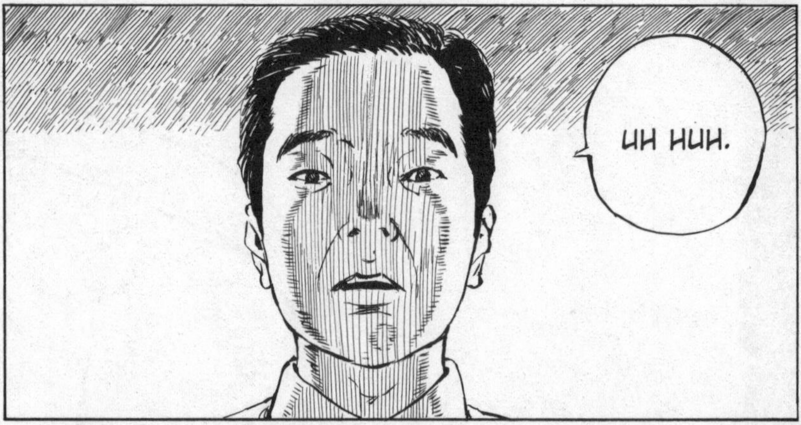
UH HUH.

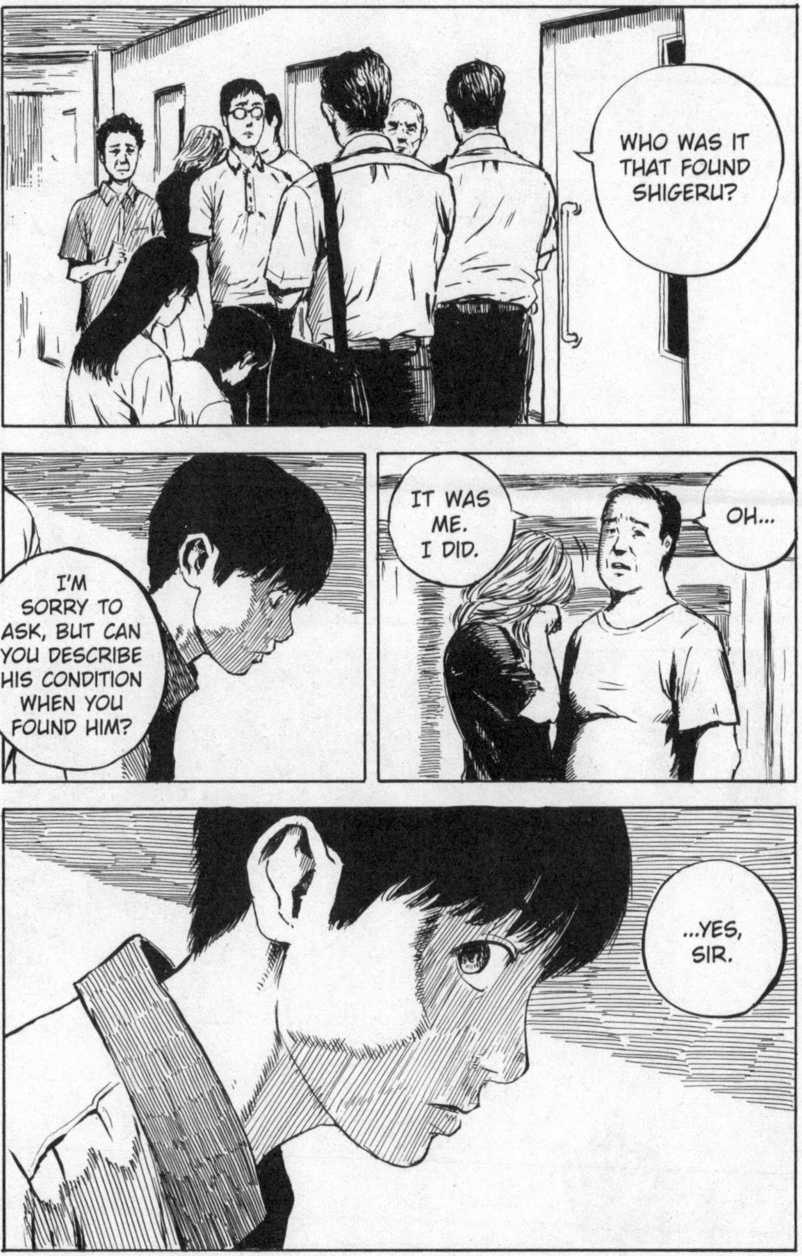
WHO WAS IT THAT FOUND SHIGERU?
OH...
IT WAS ME. I DID.
I'M SORRY TO ASK, BUT CAN YOU DESCRIBE HIS CONDITION WHEN YOU FOUND HIM?
...YES, SIR.

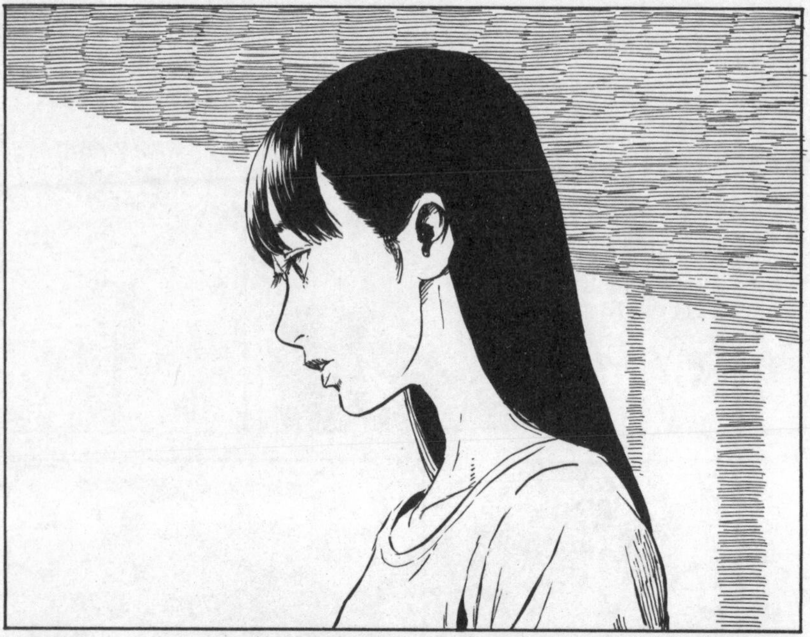

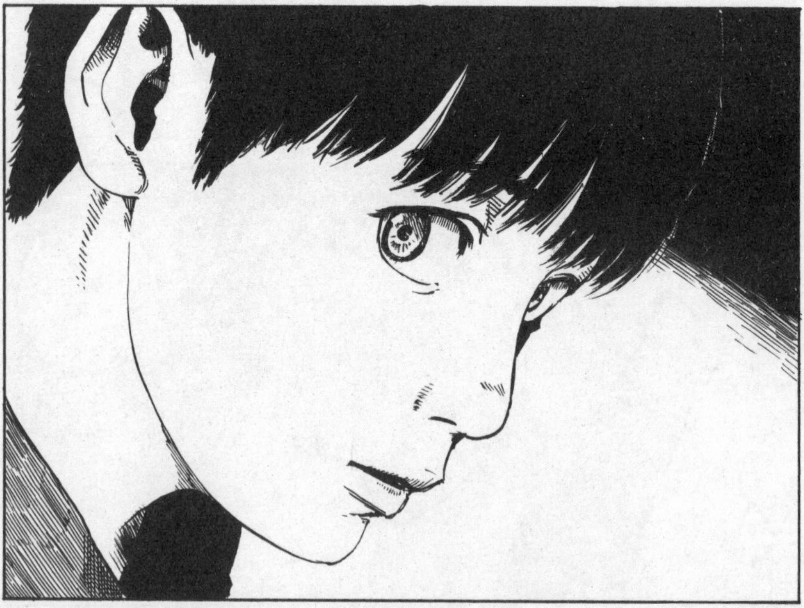

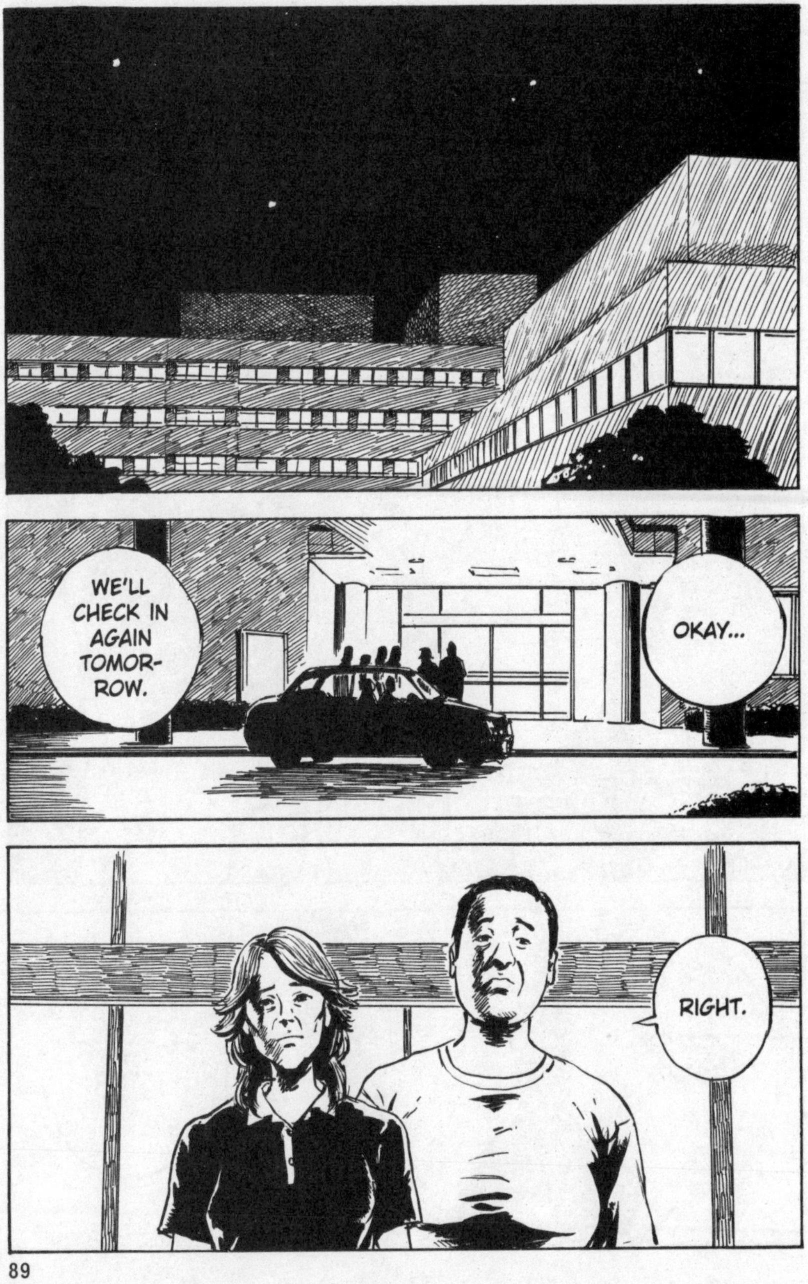
WE'LL CHECK IN AGAIN TOMORROW.
OKAY...
RIGHT.

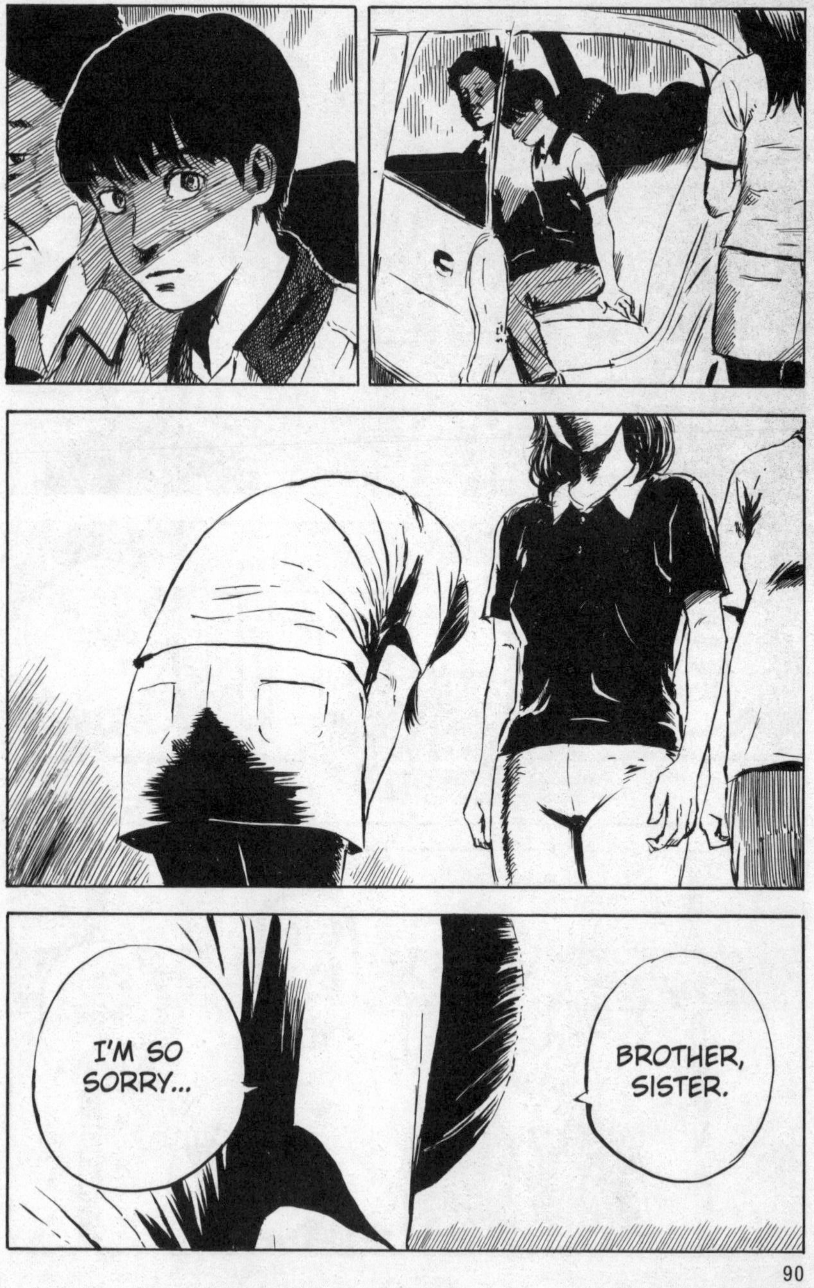
BROTHER, SISTER.
I'M SO SORRY...

...SEIKO.

IT'S MINE...

IT'S NOT YOUR FAULT.

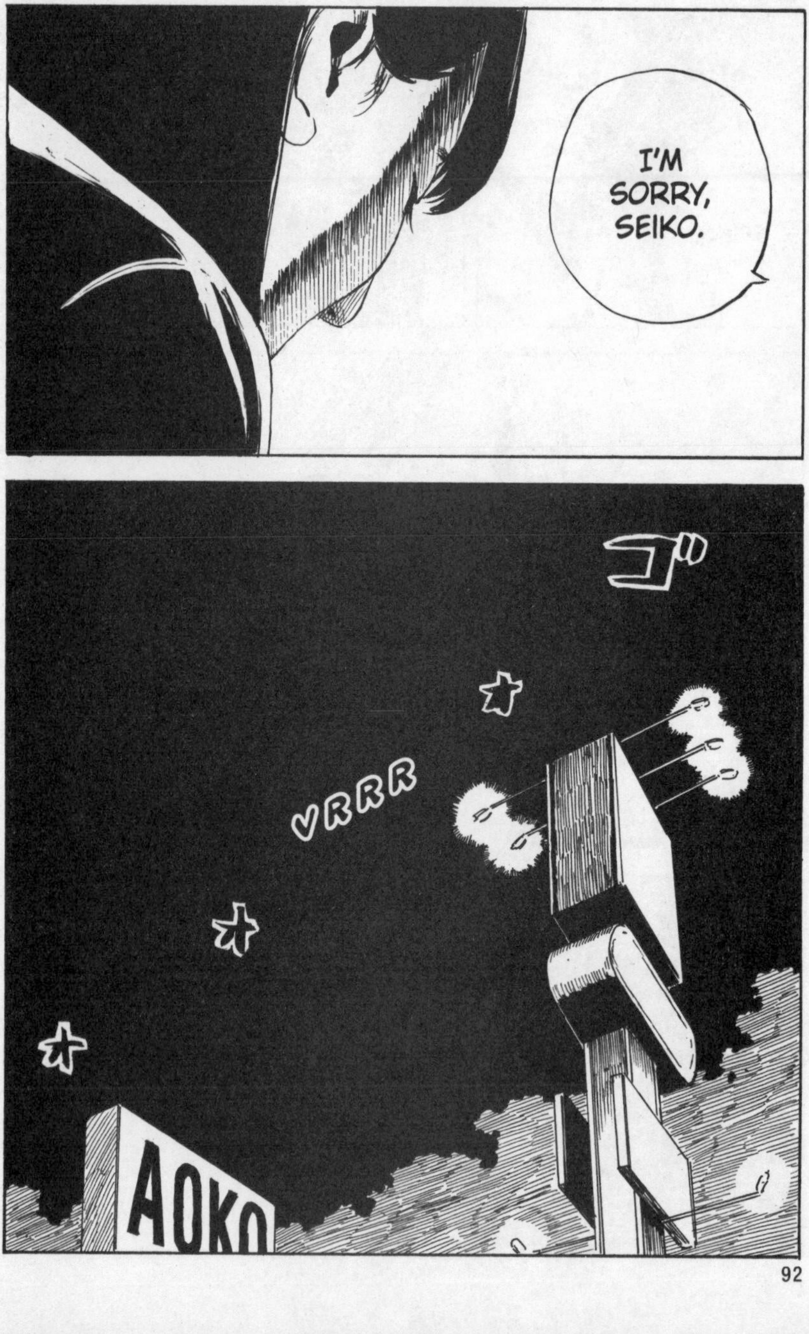
I'M SORRY, SEIKO.
ゴ
オ
VRRR
オ
オ
AOKO

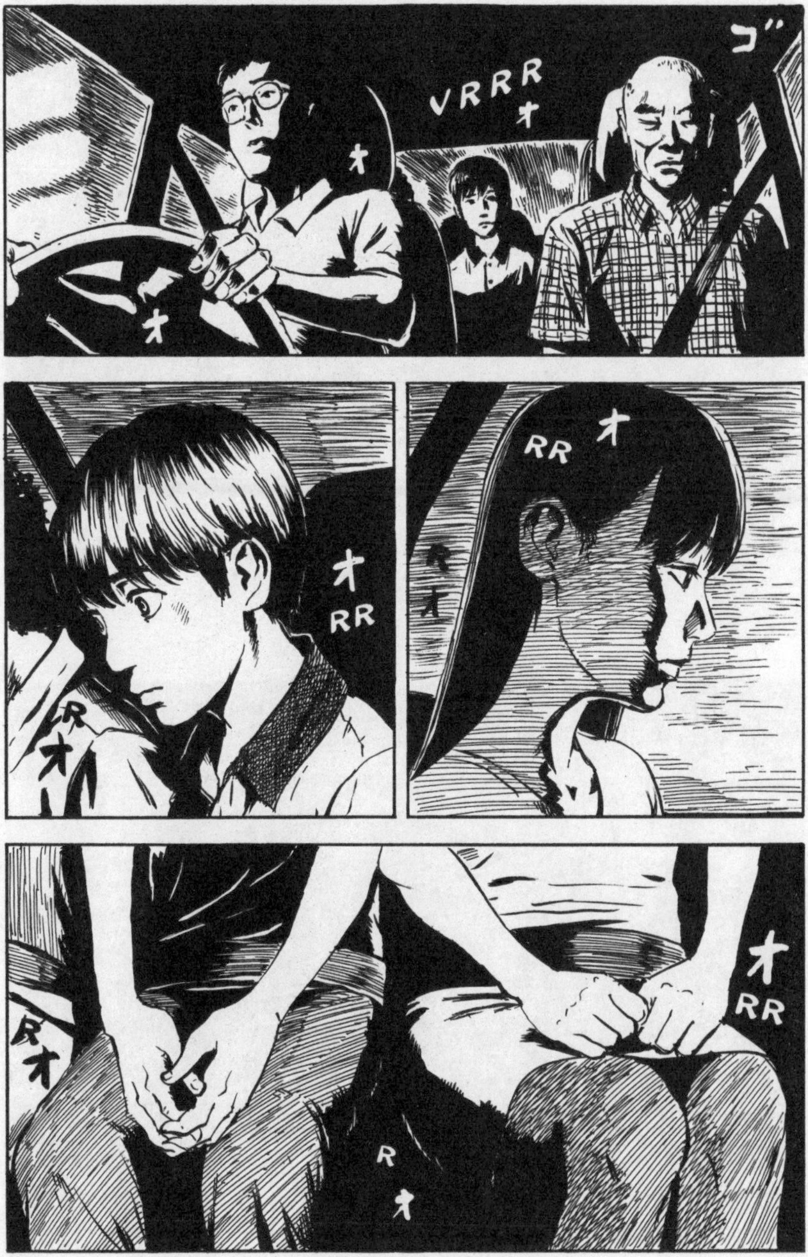
ゴ
VRRR
オ
オ
オ
オ
RR
R
オ
オ
RR
R
オ
オ
RR
R
オ
R
オ

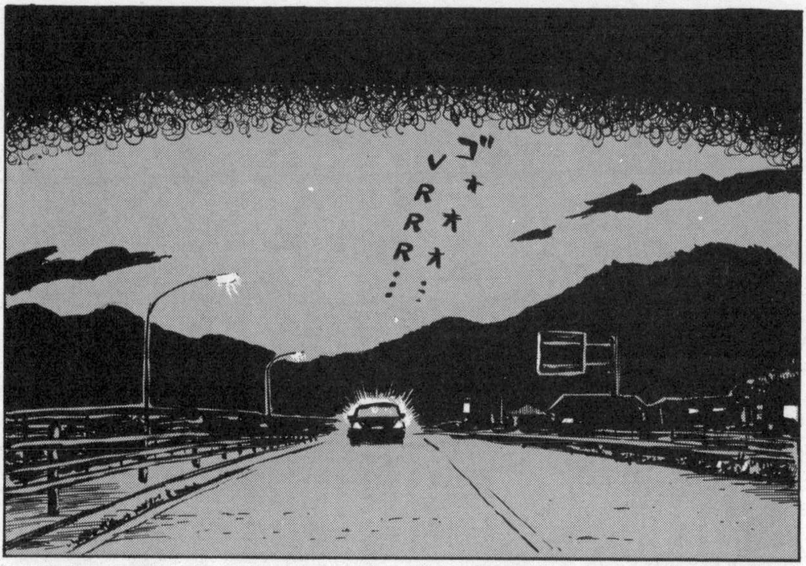
ゴォォォ
VRRR...

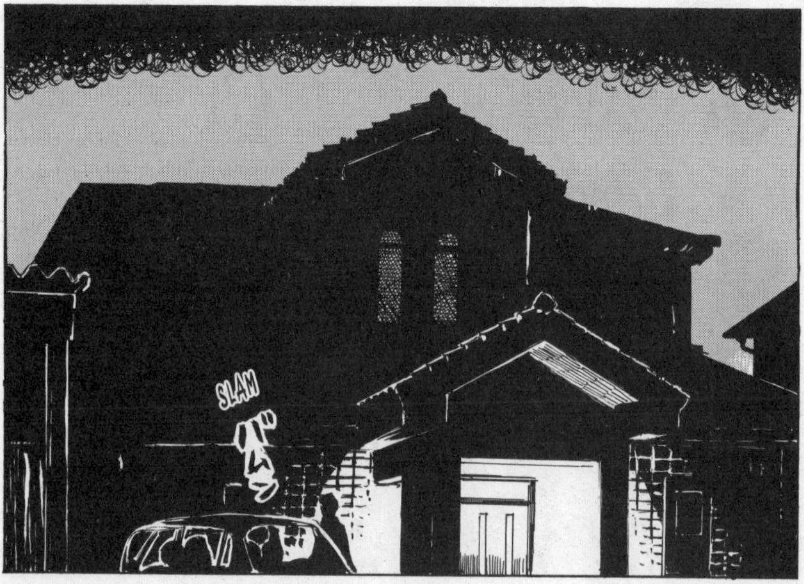
SLAM
バム

KACHIK
ガチャ
KACHIK
ガチャ
ガチャ
KACHIK
KREE
ギィ…

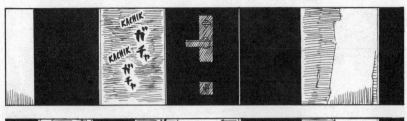

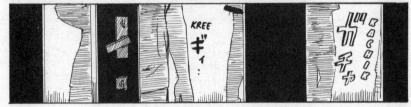

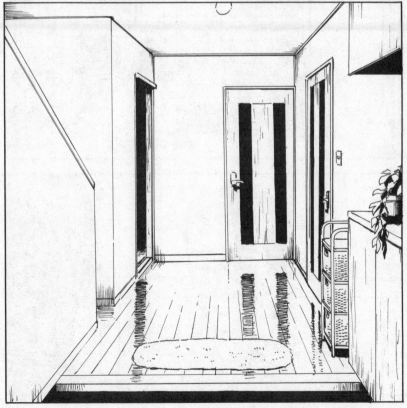

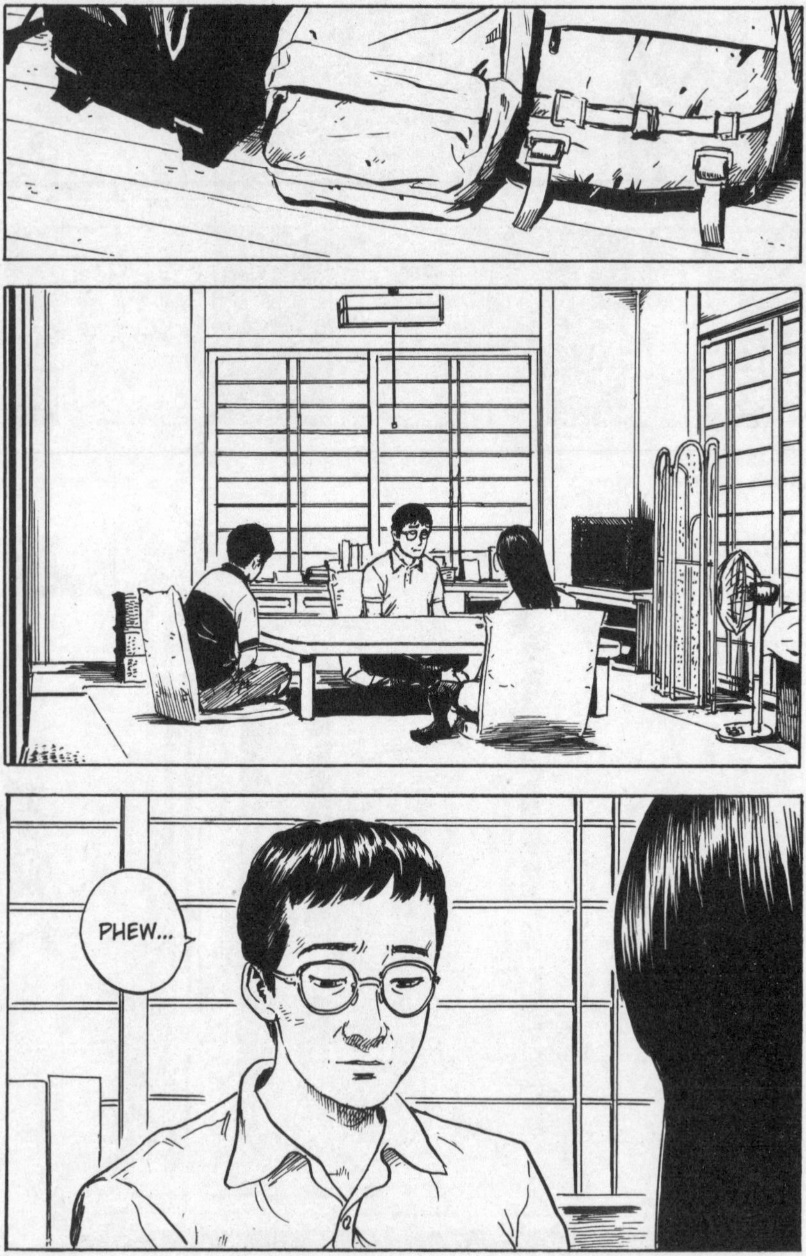
PHEW...

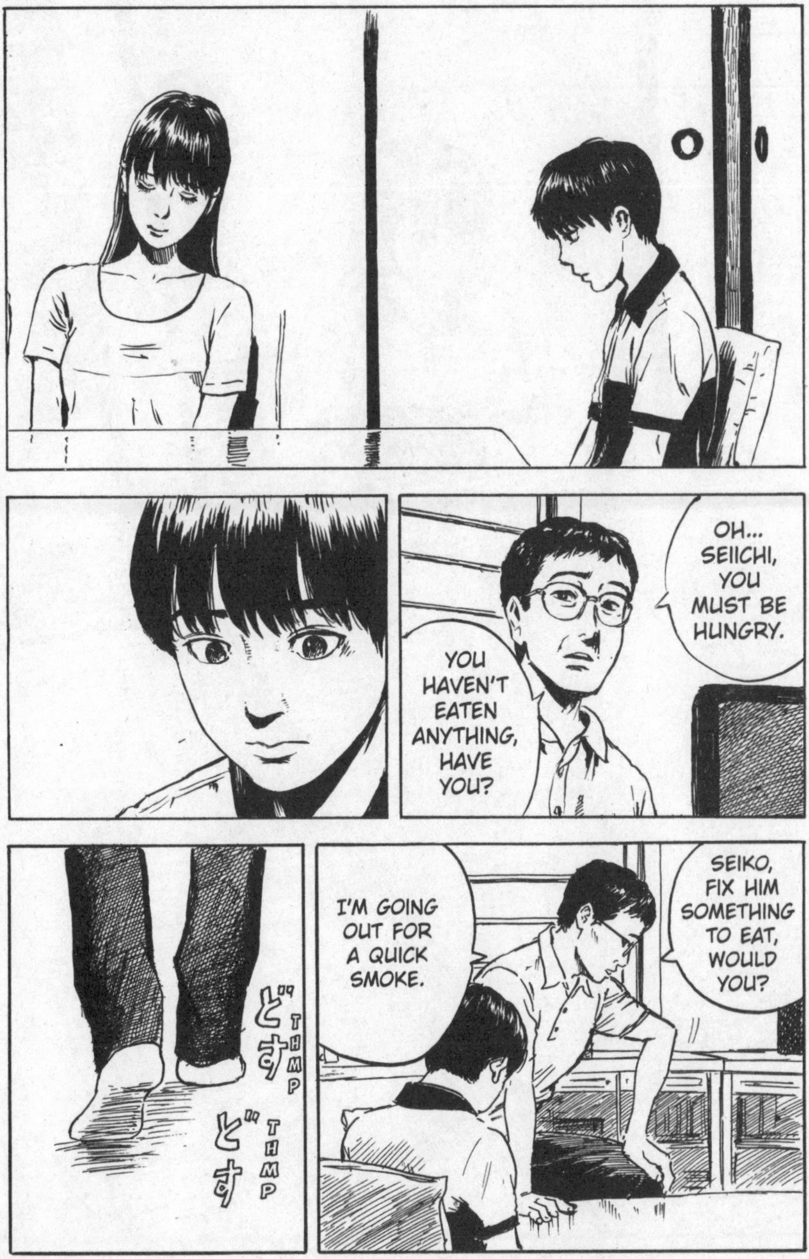
OH... SEIICHI, YOU MUST BE HUNGRY.
YOU HAVEN'T EATEN ANYTHING, HAVE YOU?
SEIKO, FIX HIM SOMETHING TO EAT, WOULD YOU?
I'M GOING OUT FOR A QUICK SMOKE.
どす
THMP
どす
THMP

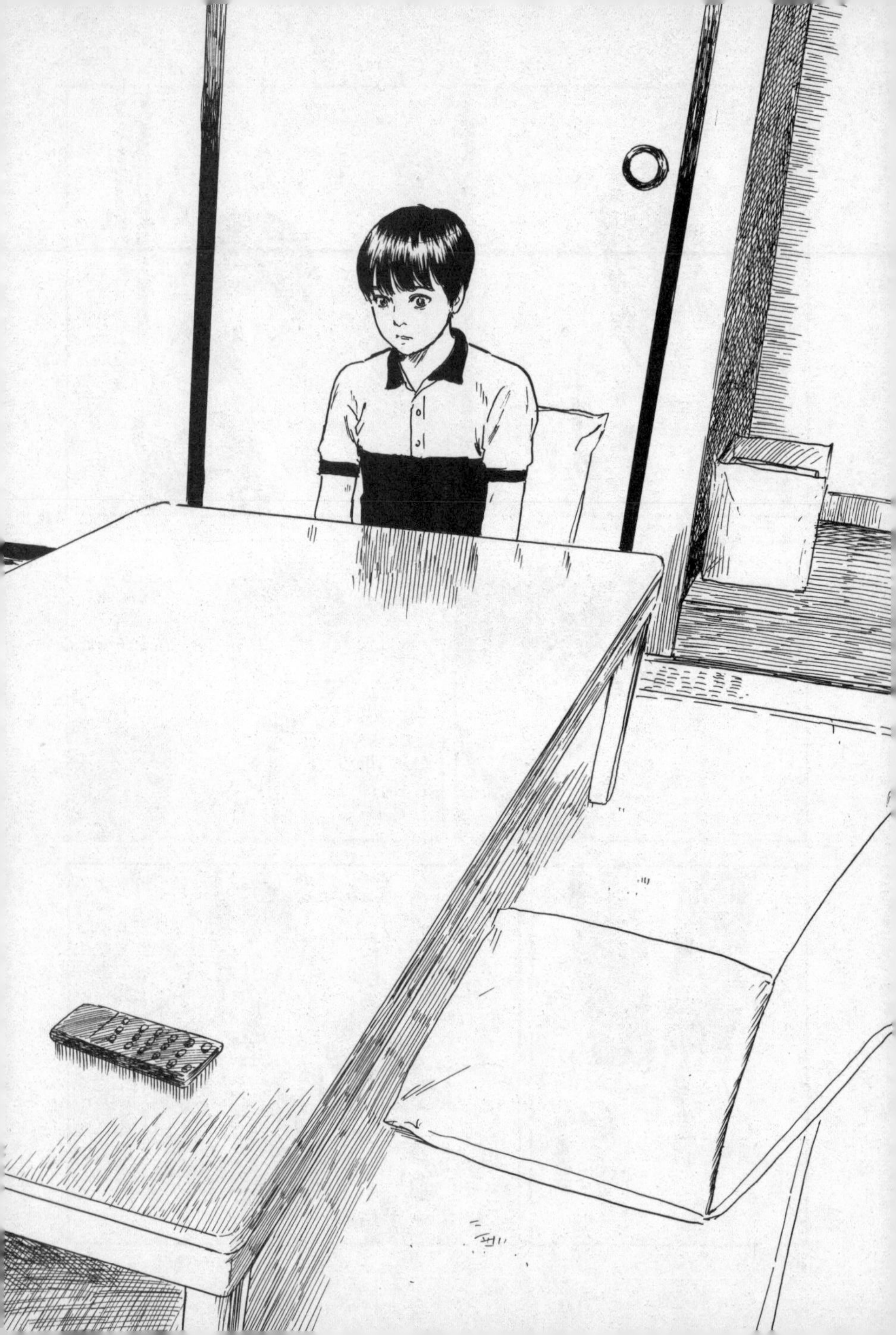

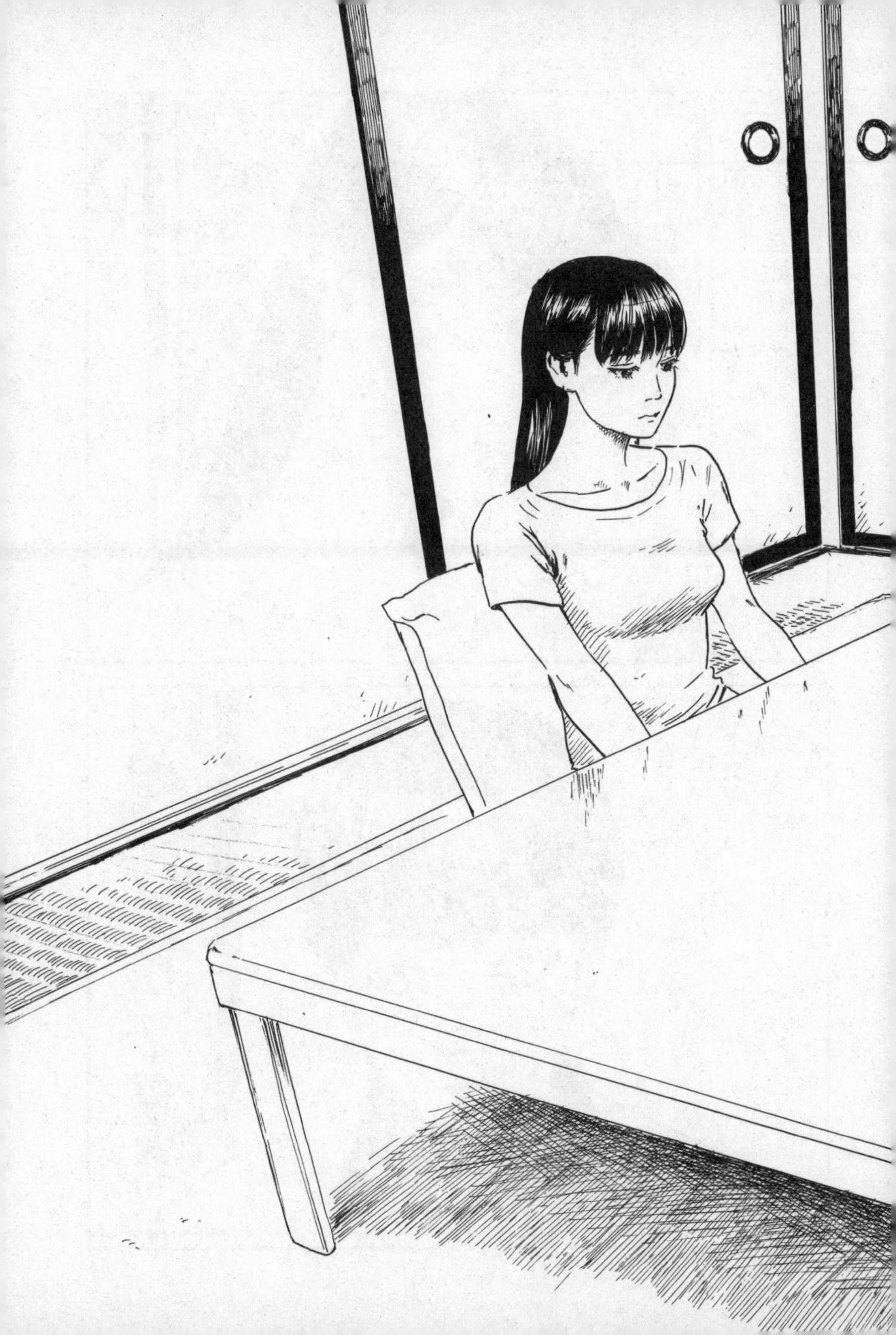

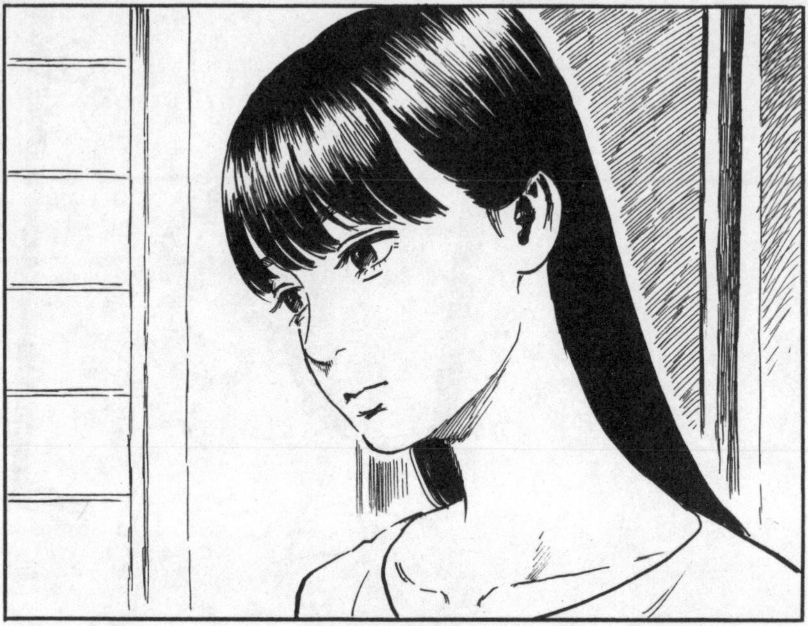
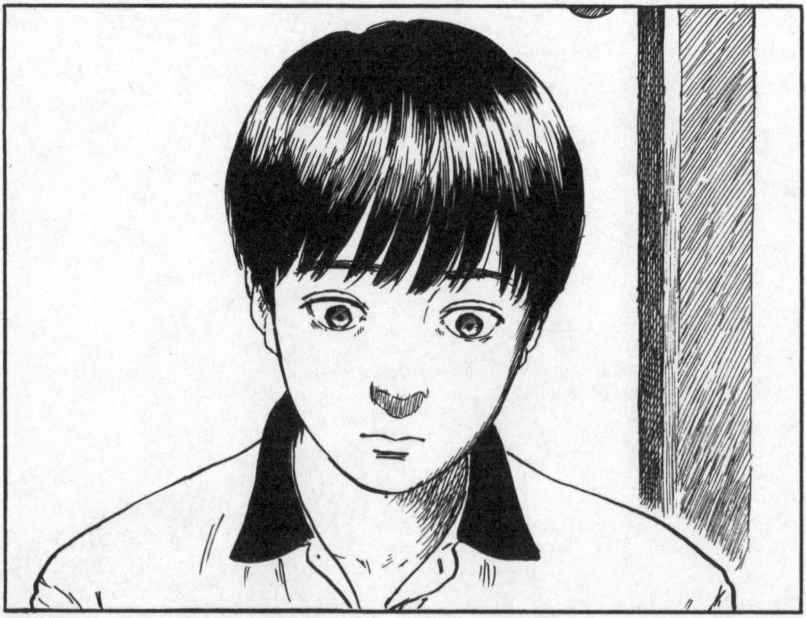

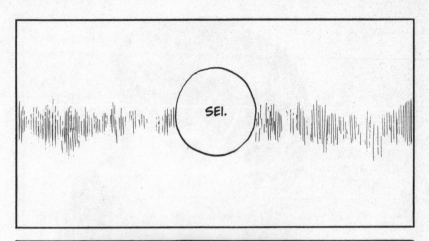

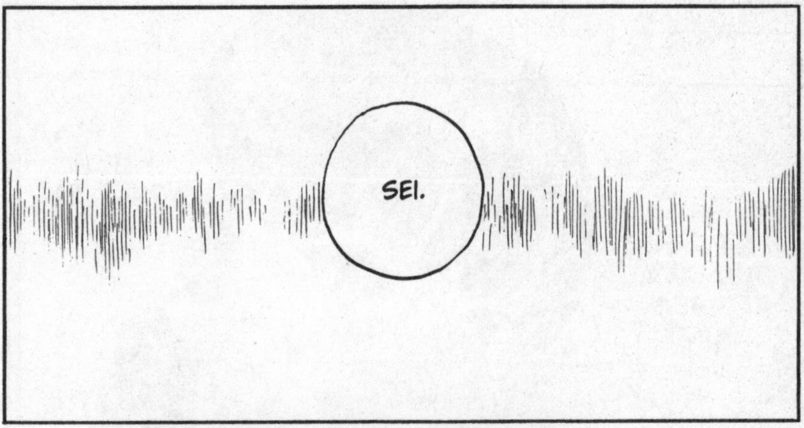
SEI.
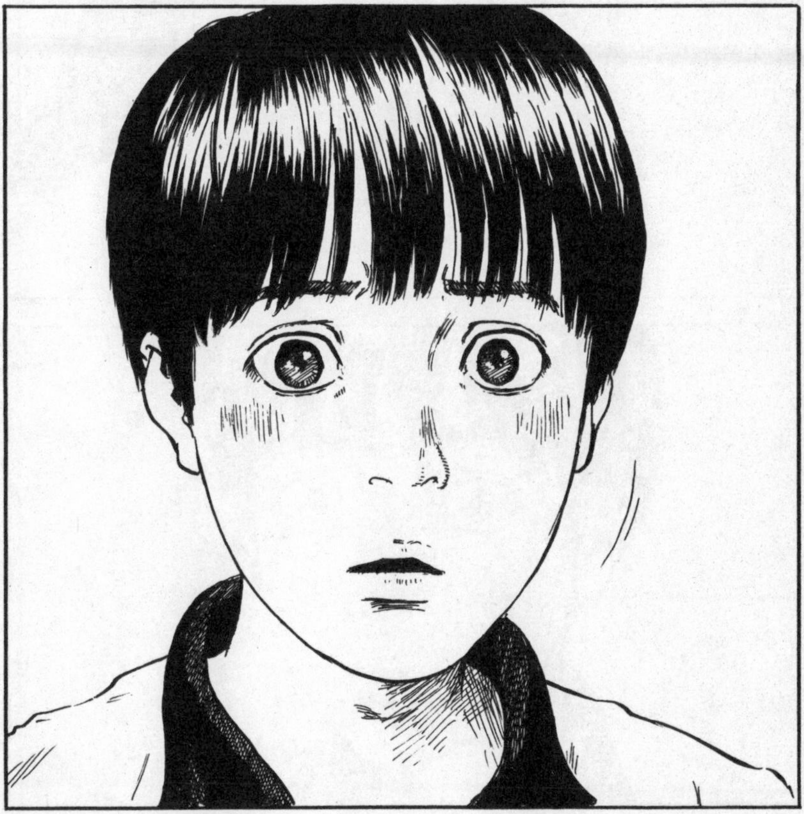

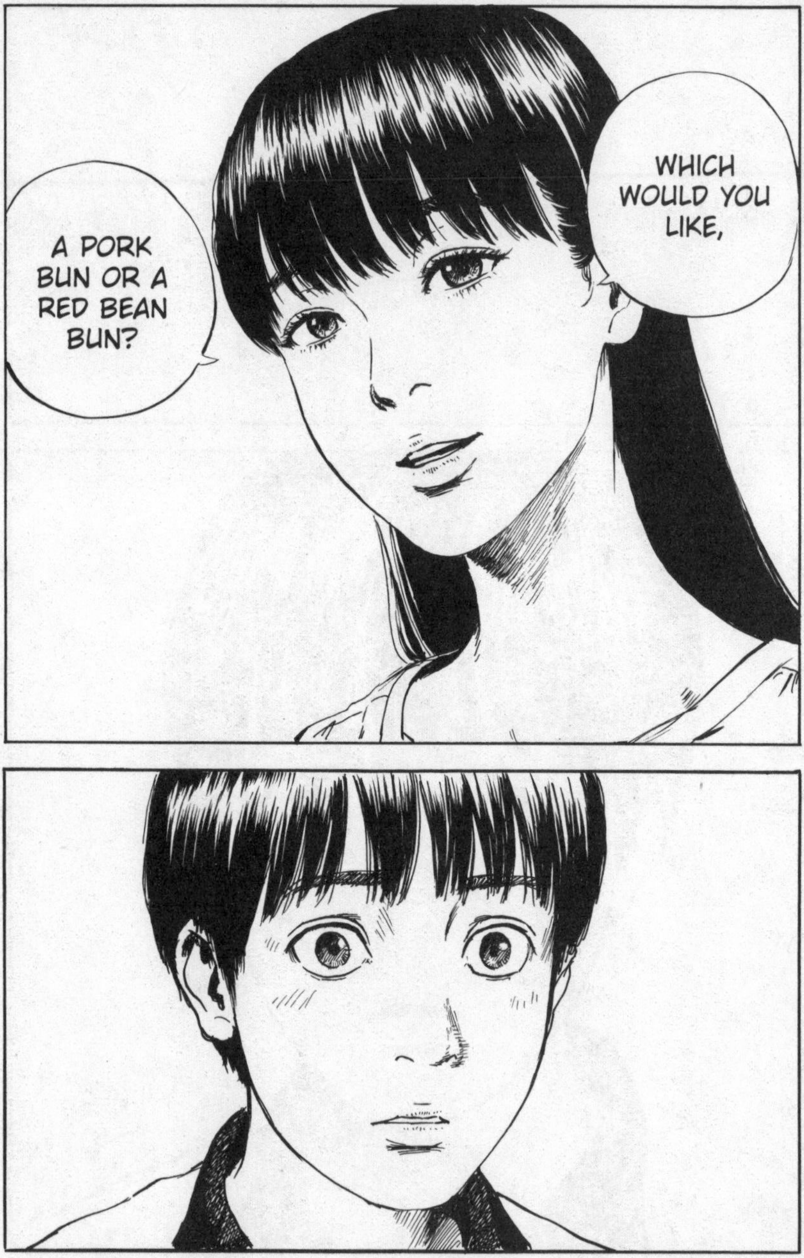
WHICH WOULD YOU LIKE,
A PORK BUN OR A RED BEAN BUN?

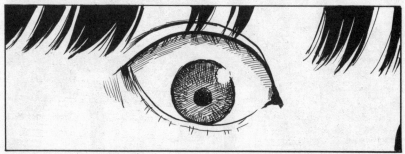

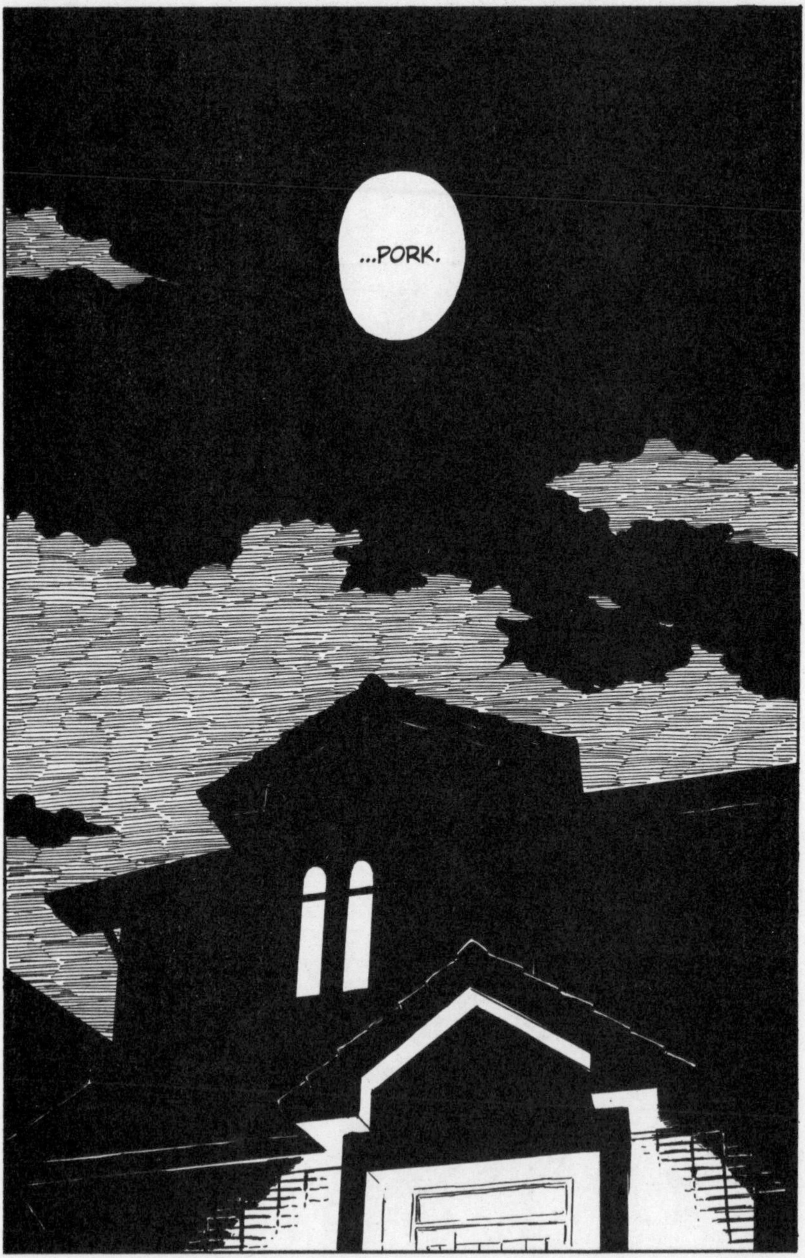
...PORK.

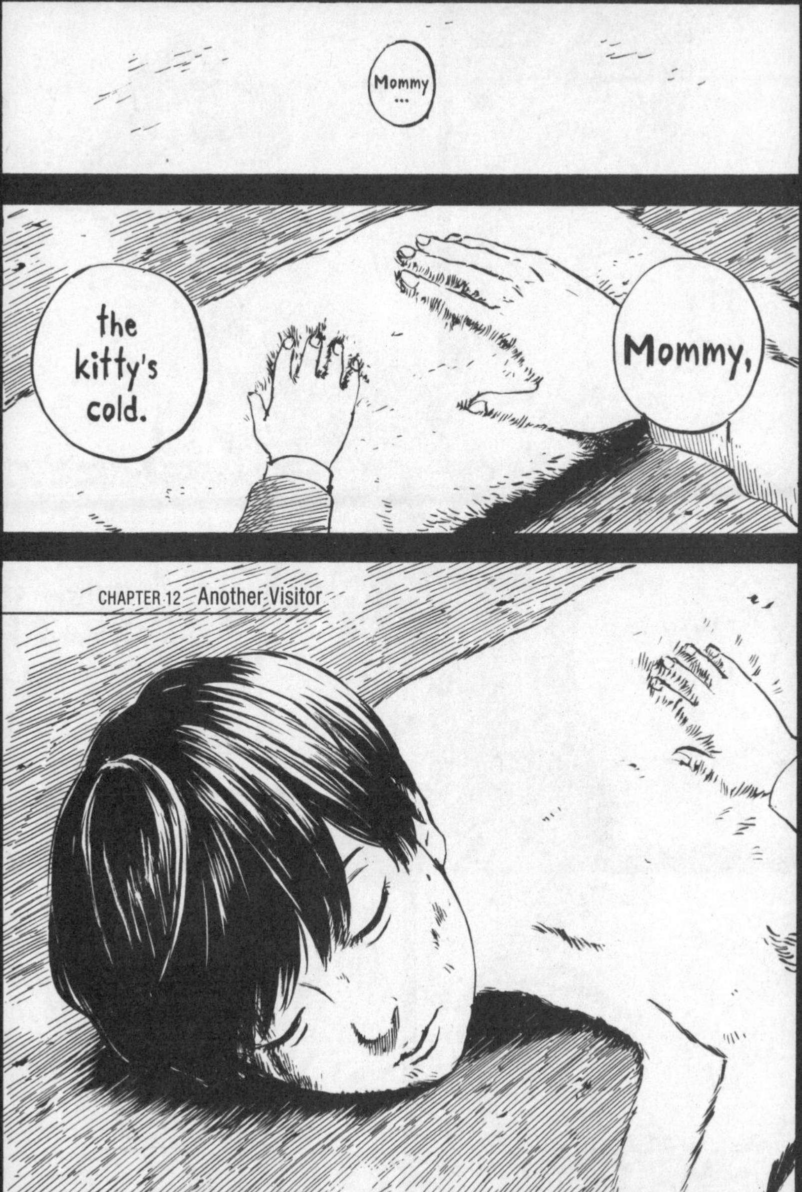
Mommy ...
Mommy,
the kitty's cold.
CHAPTER 12 Another Visitor

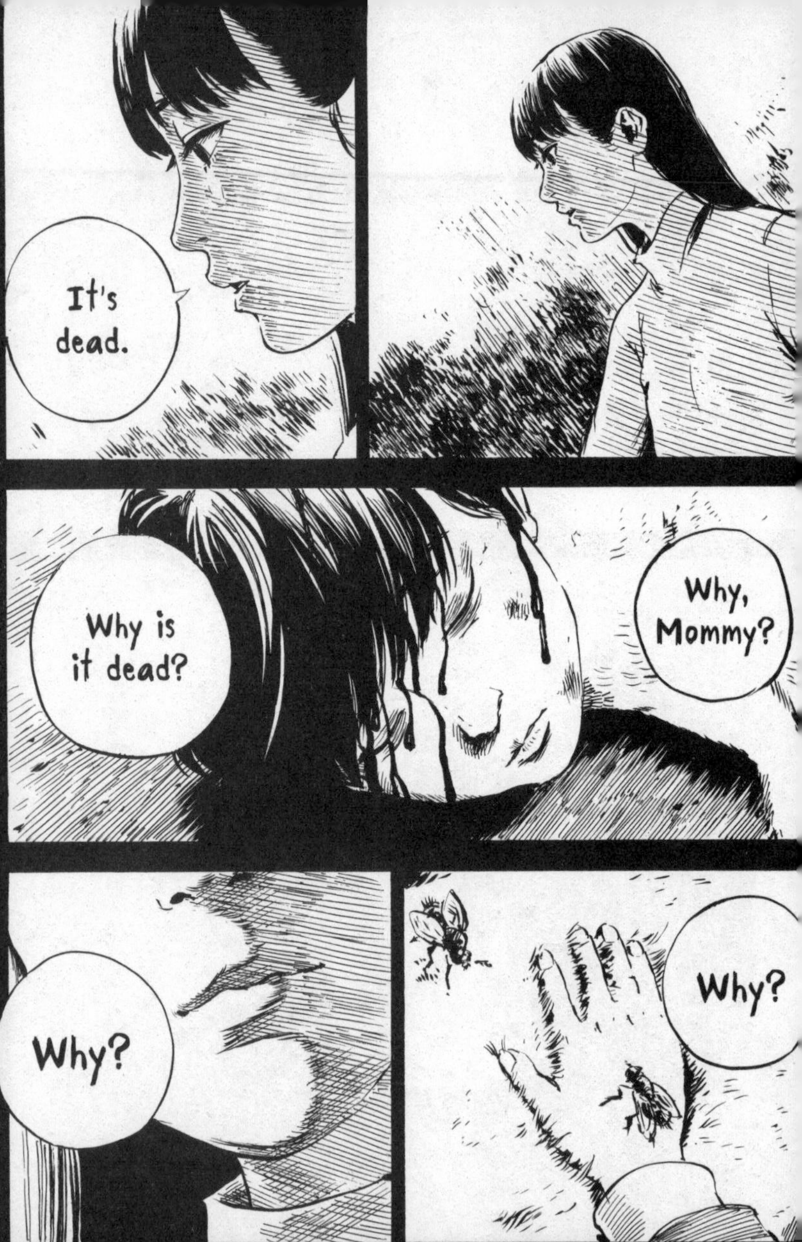
It's dead.
Why, Mommy?
Why is it dead?
Why?
Why?

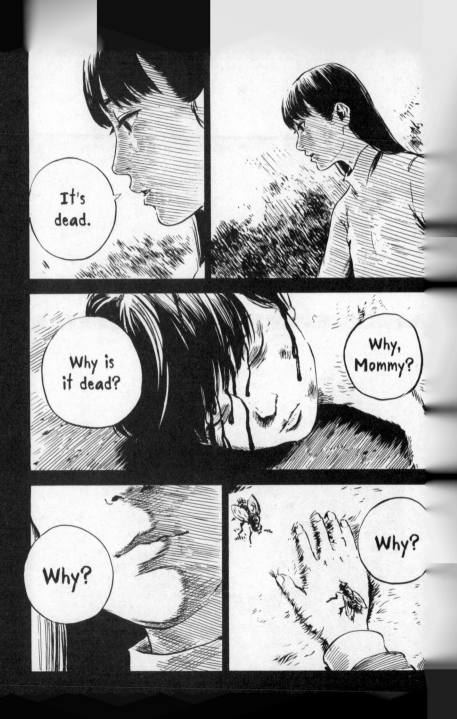

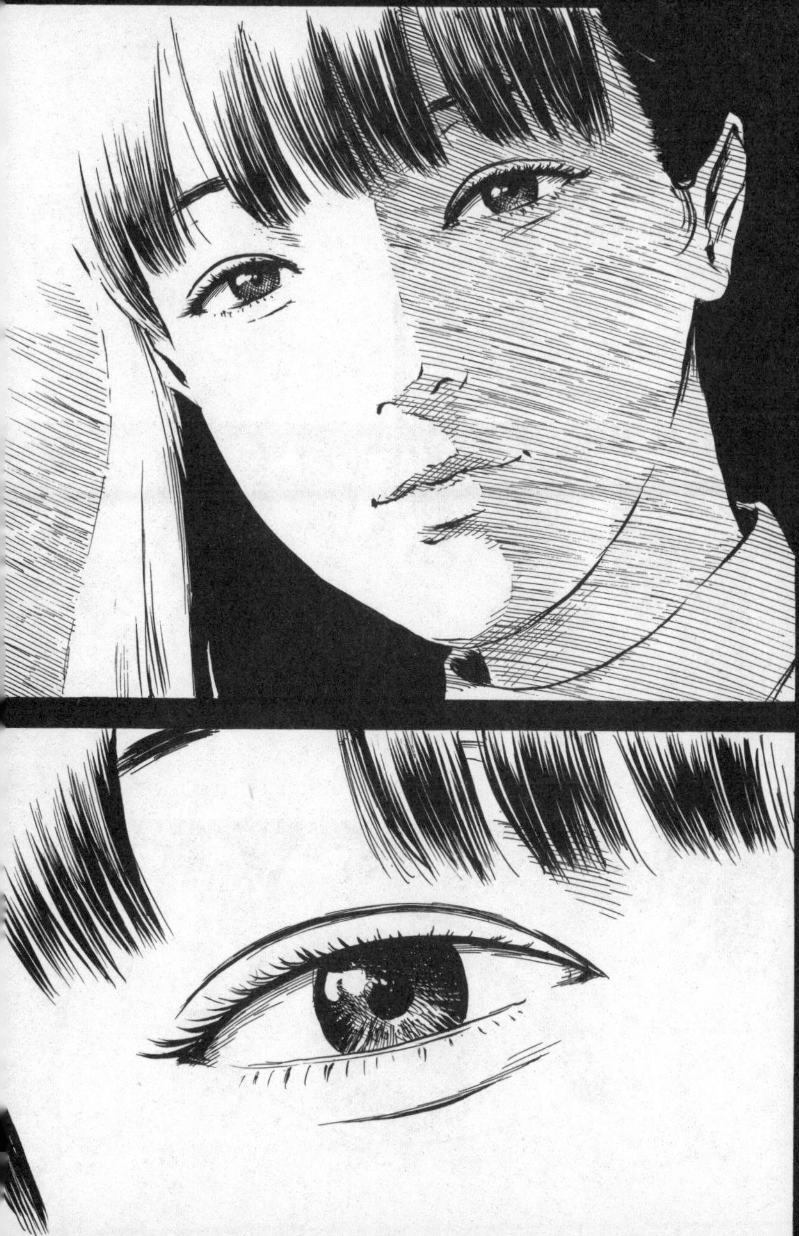

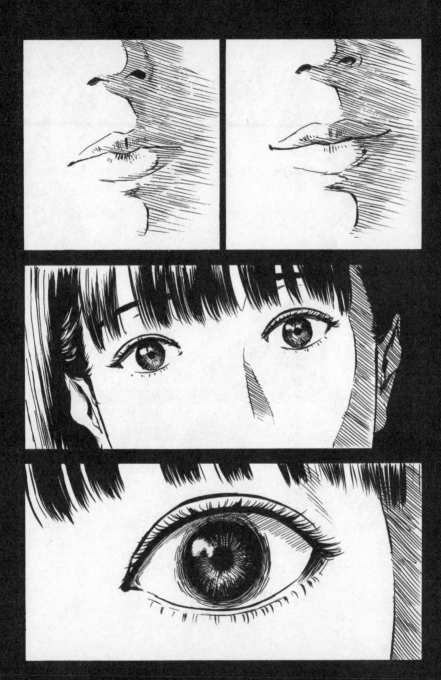

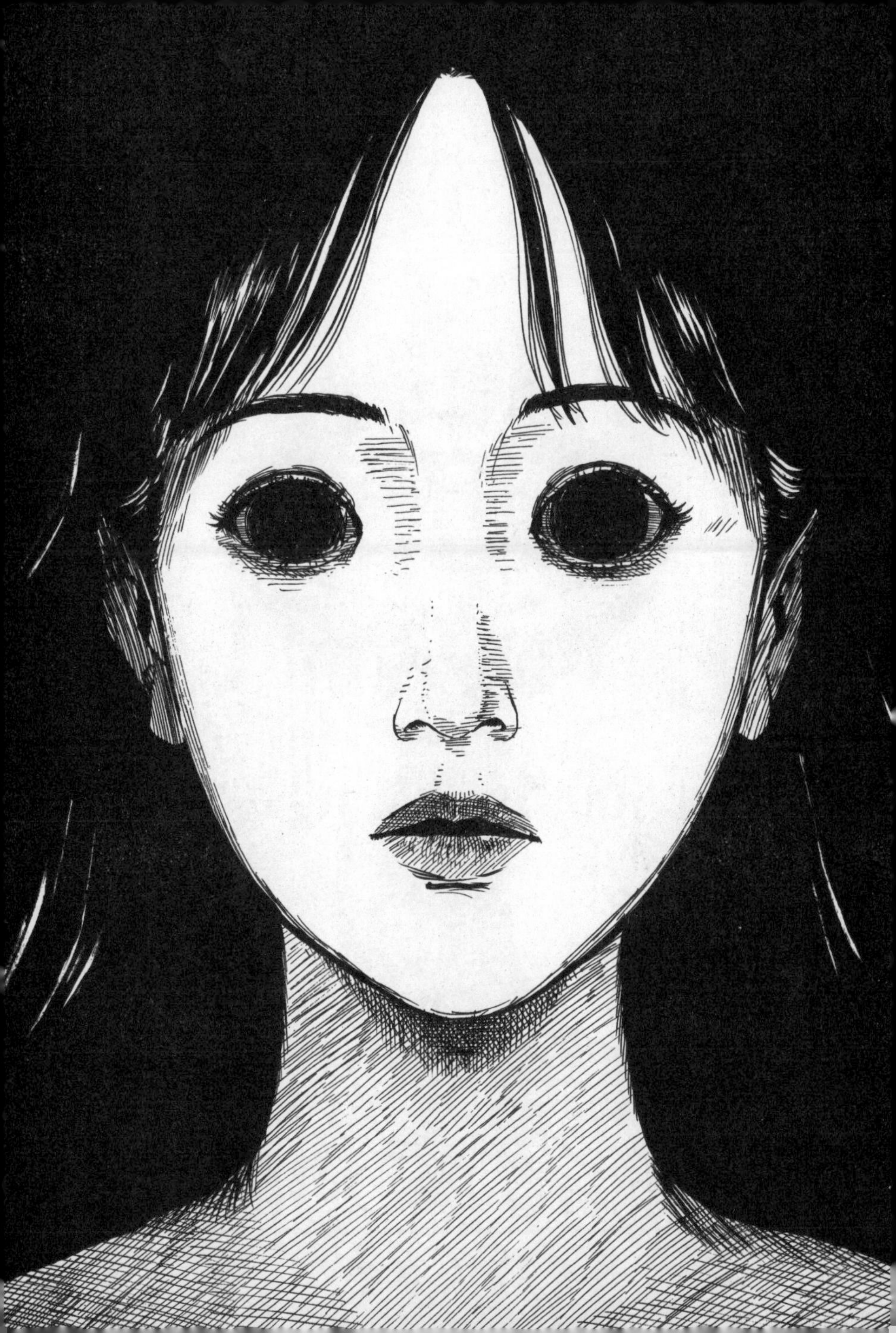

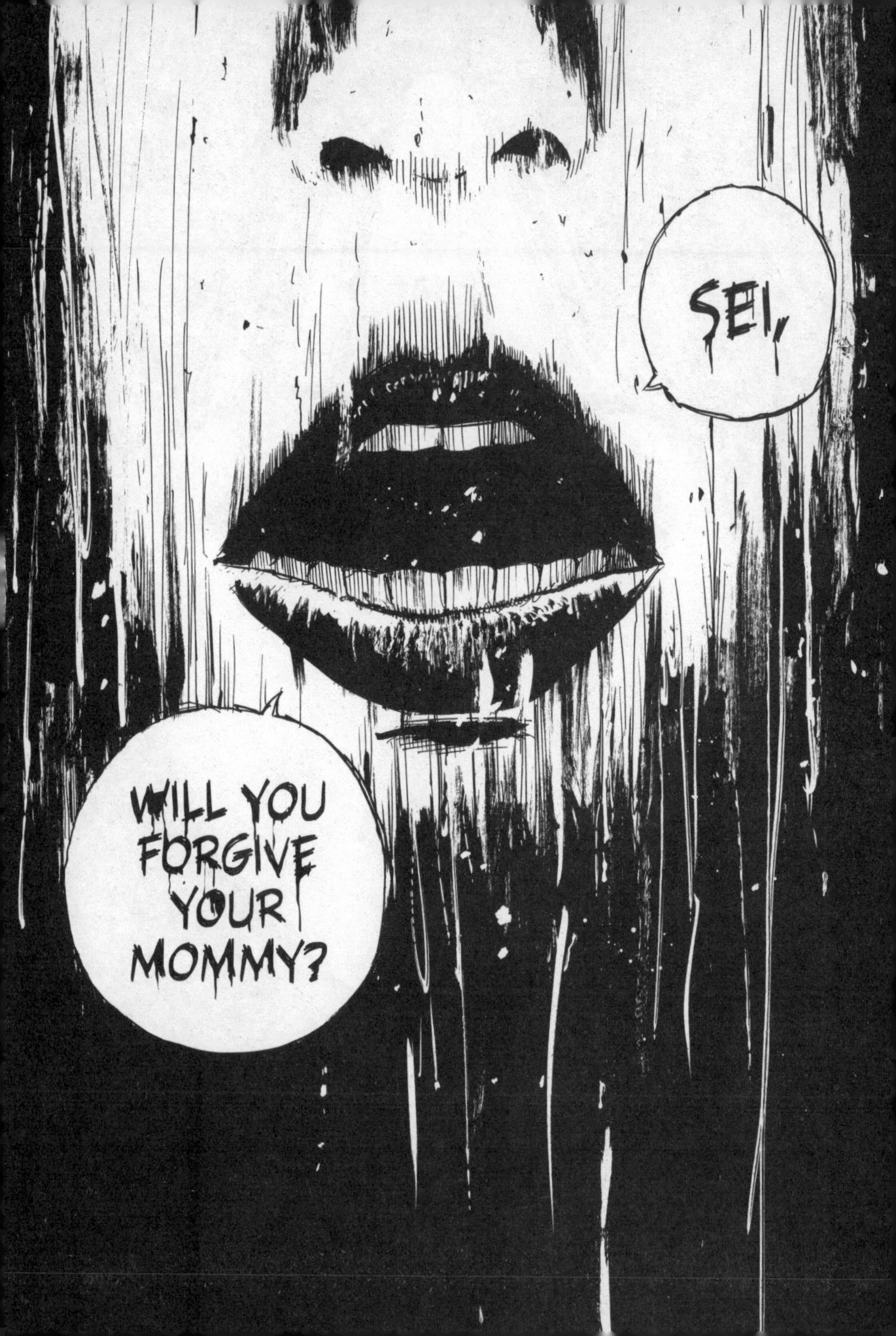
SEI,
WILL YOU FORGIVE YOUR MOMMY?

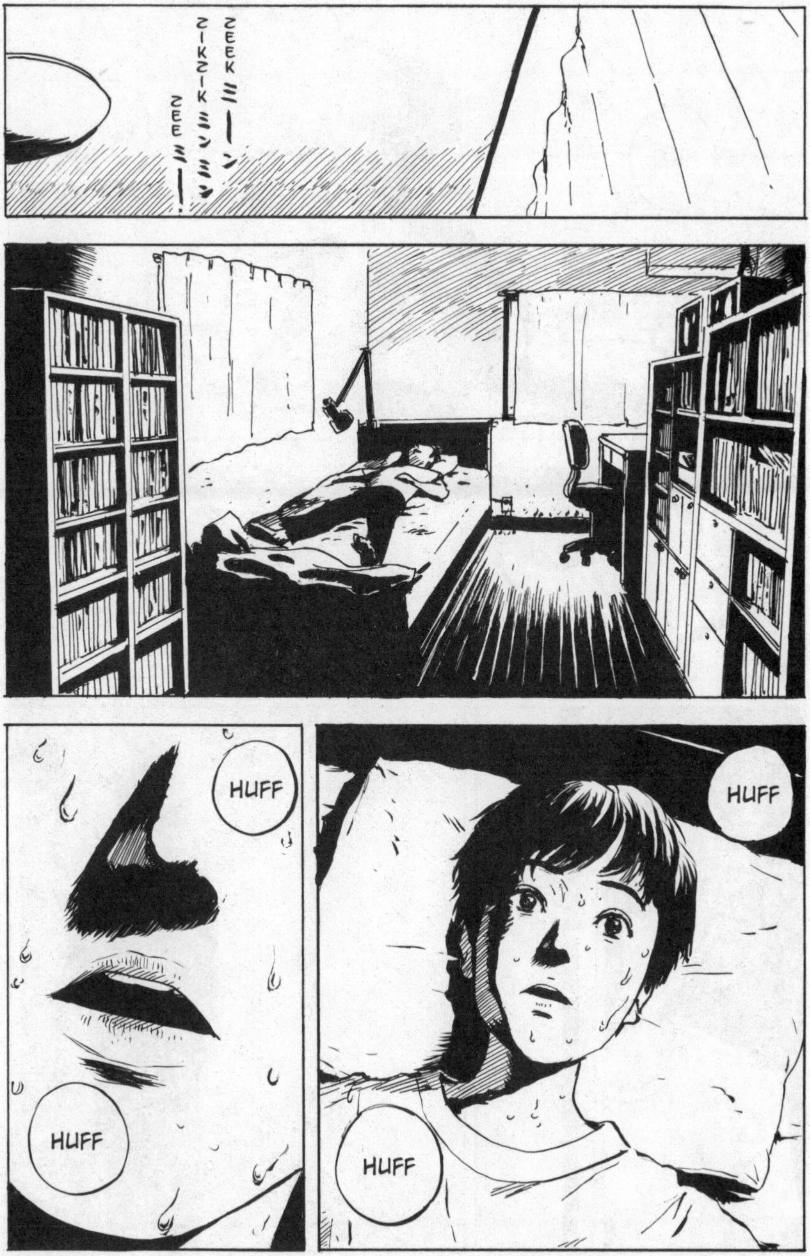
ZEEK ミーン
ZIKZIK ミンミン
ZEE ミー…
HUFF
HUFF
HUFF
HUFF

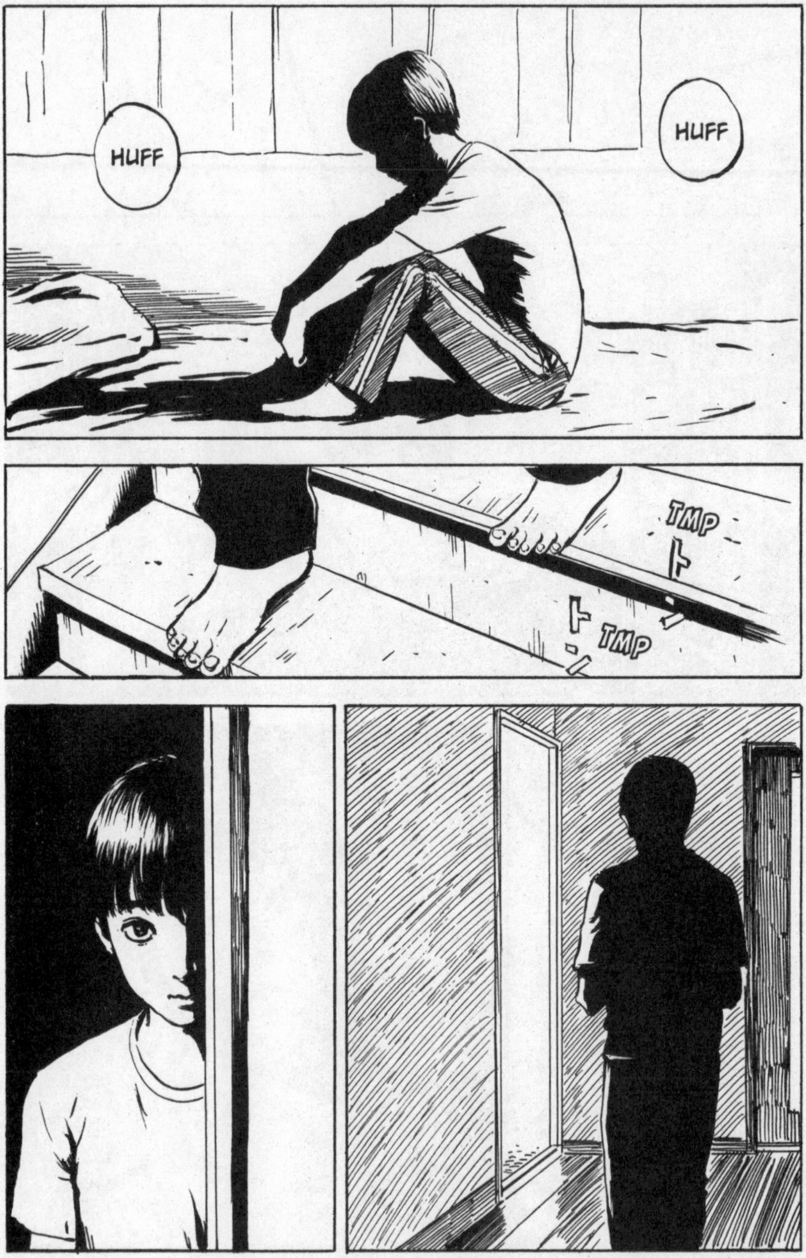
HUFF
HUFF
TMP
ト
ト
TMP

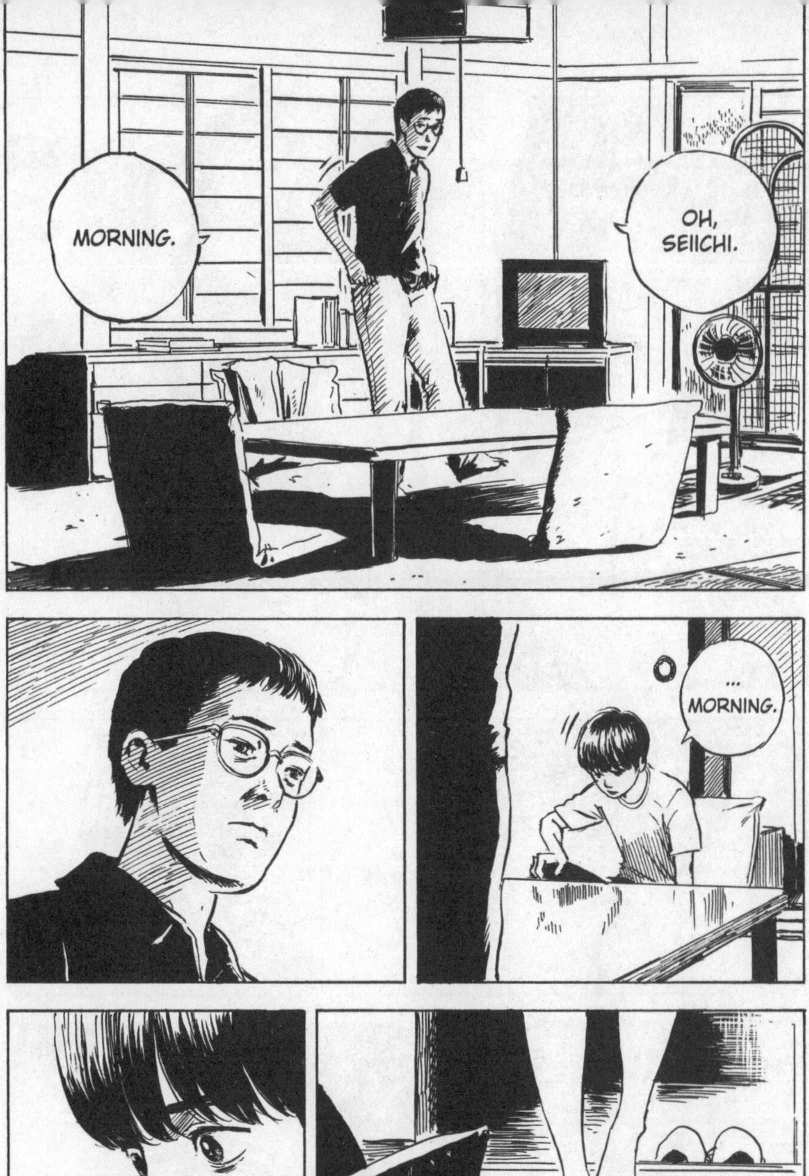
OH, SEIICHI.
MORNING.
... MORNING.
ぎし
CREAK

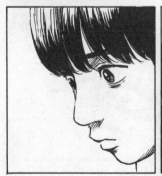

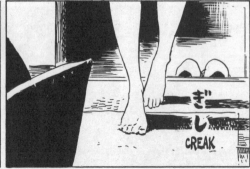

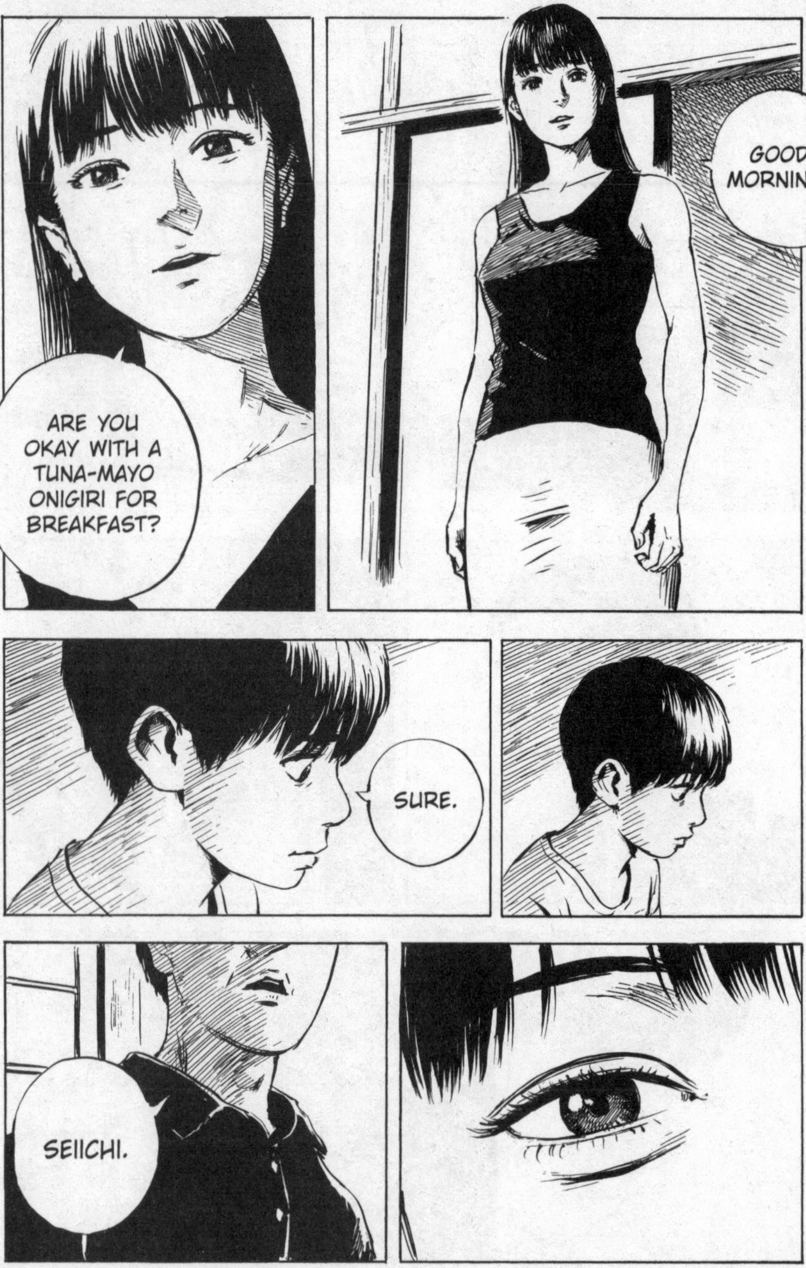
GOOD MORNING.
ARE YOU OKAY WITH A TUNA-MAYO ONIGIRI FOR BREAKFAST?
SURE.
SEIICHI.

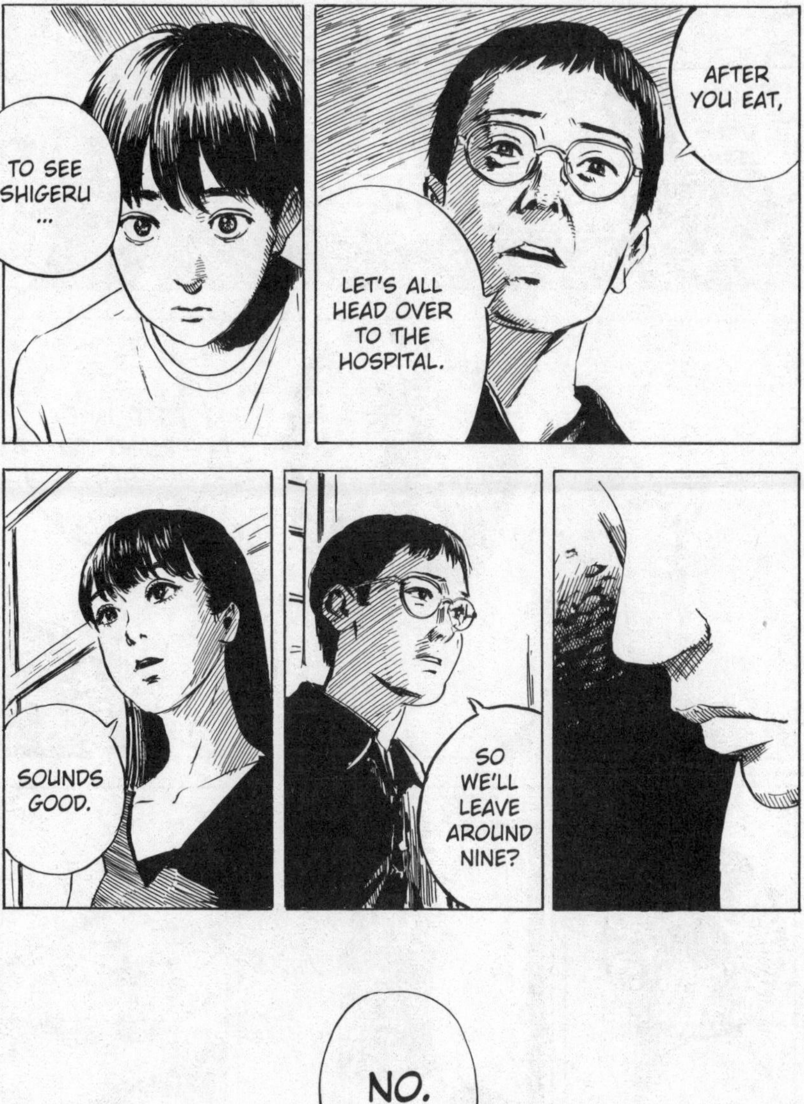
AFTER YOU EAT,
LET'S ALL HEAD OVER TO THE HOSPITAL.
TO SEE SHIGERU ...
SO WE'LL LEAVE AROUND NINE?
SOUNDS GOOD.
NO.

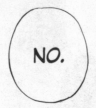

I DON'T WANT TO GO.

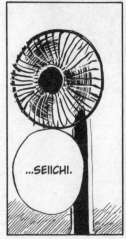

...SEIICHI.

116

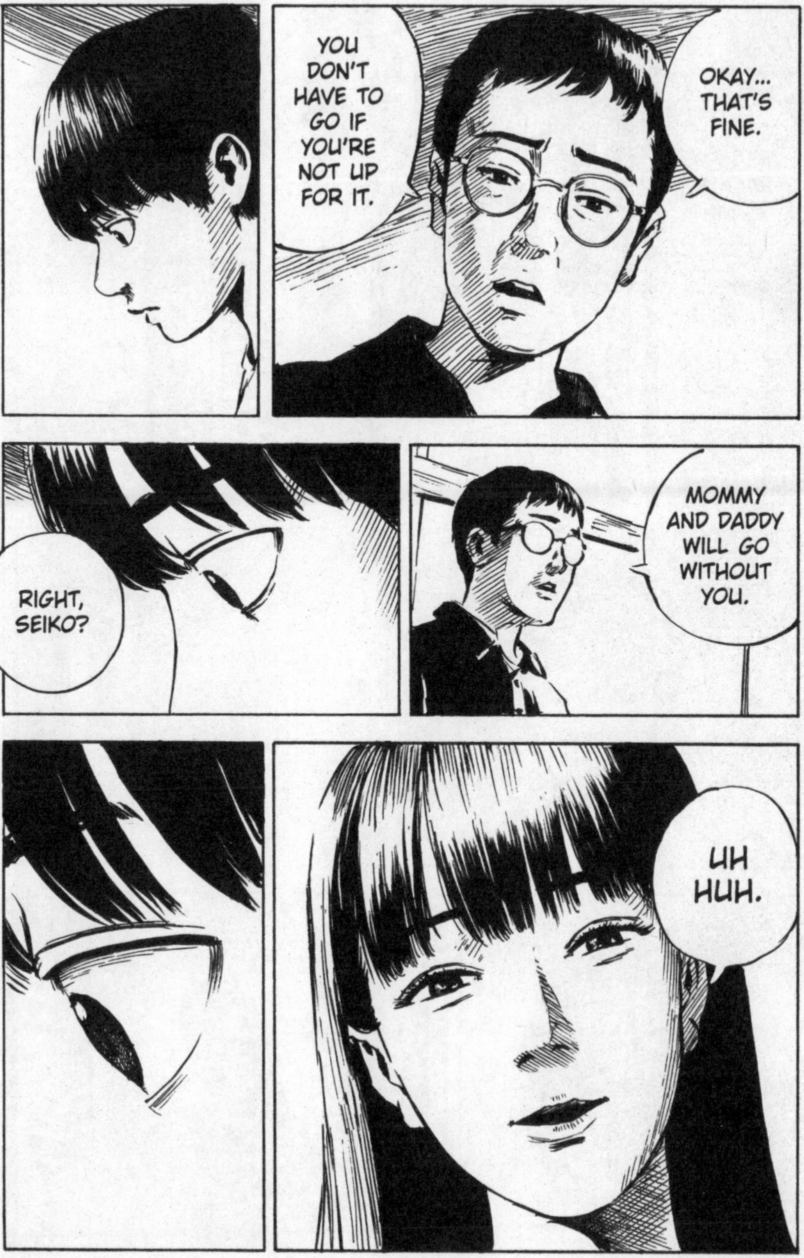
OKAY... THAT'S FINE.
YOU DON'T HAVE TO GO IF YOU'RE NOT UP FOR IT.
MOMMY AND DADDY WILL GO WITHOUT YOU.
RIGHT, SEIKO?
UH HUH.

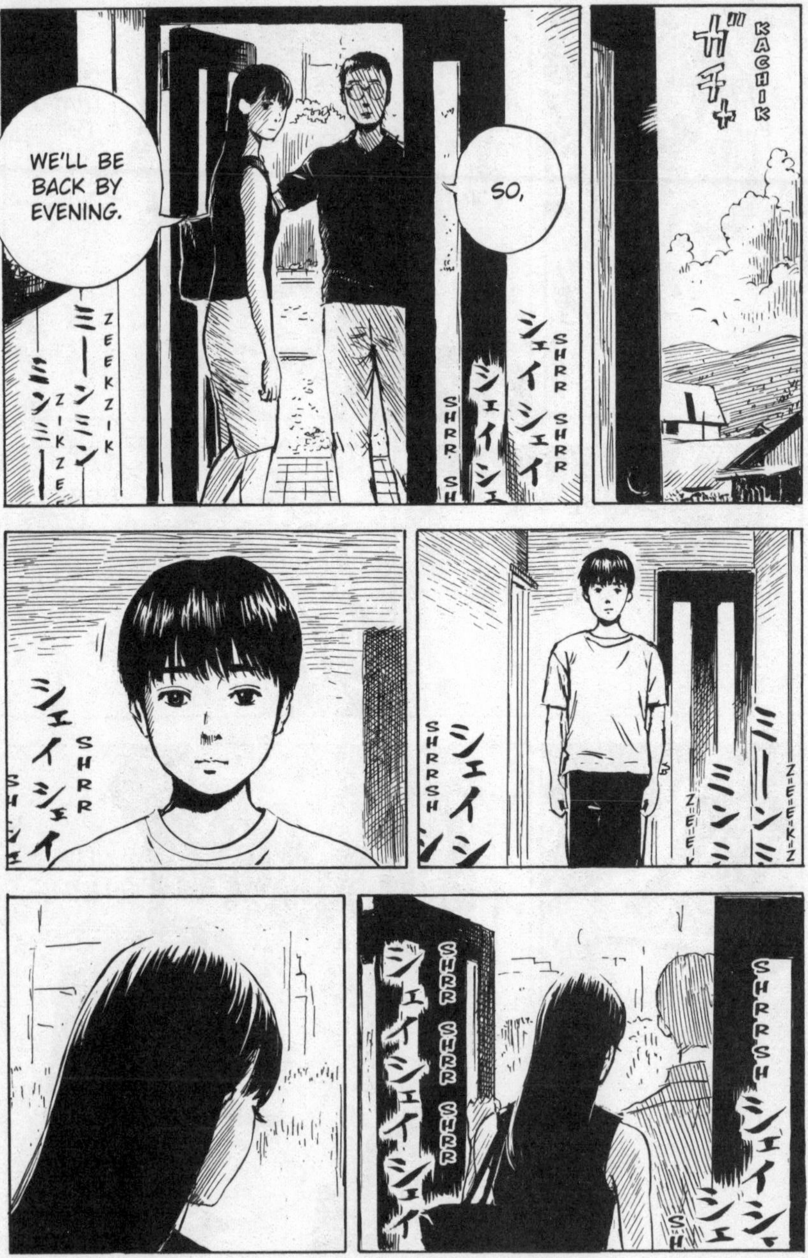
ガチャ
KACHIK
SO,
WE'LL BE BACK BY EVENING.
シェイシェイシェ
SHRR SHRR
SHRR. SH
ミーンミン
ZEEKZIK
ミンミー
ZIKZE
ミーンミ
ZEEKZ
ミンミ
ZEEK
シェイシ
SHRRSH
シェイシェイ
SHRR
SH
SHRRSH
シェイシェ
SH
シェイシェイシェイ
SHRR SHRR SHRR

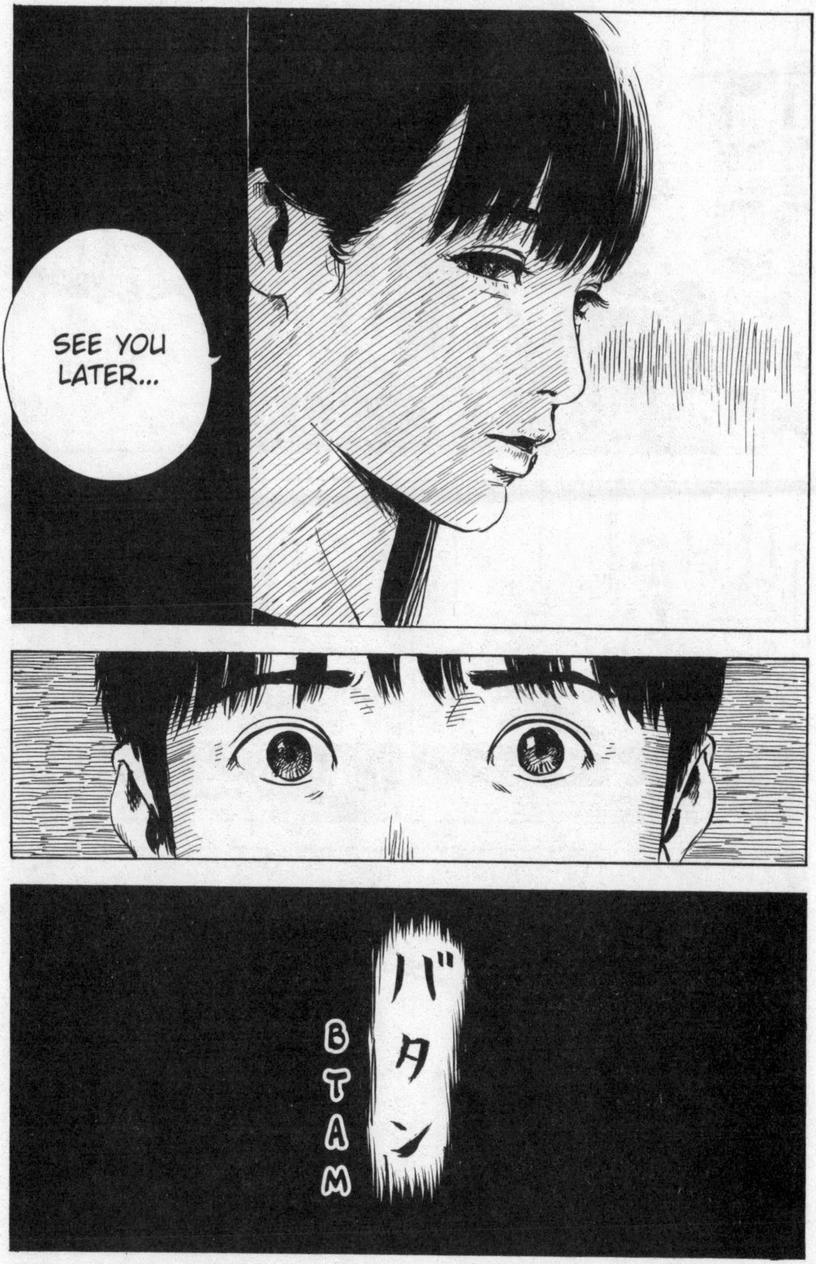
SEE YOU LATER...
バタン
BTAM

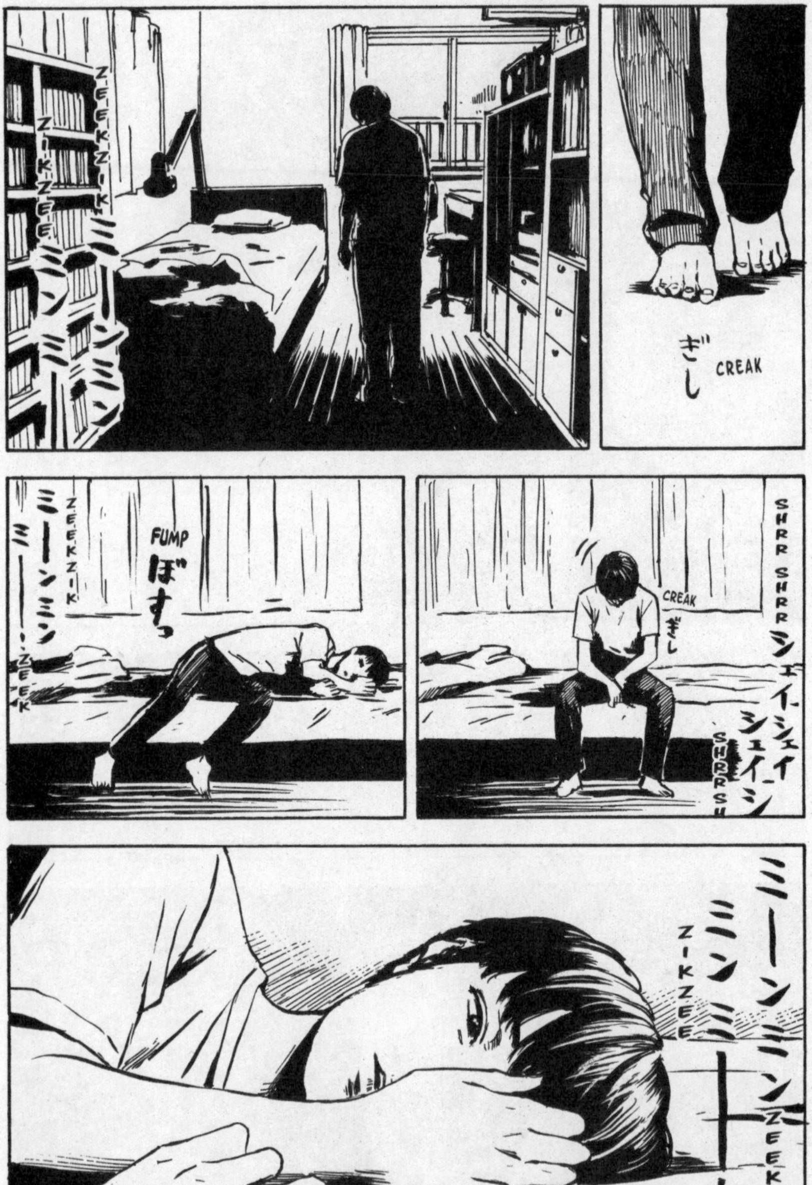
ぎし
CREAK
ZEEK ZIK ZIK ZEE
ミーンミンミン
ミンミン
SHRR SHRR
シェイシェイ
シェイシ
SHRR SH
CREAK
ぎし
FUMP
ぼすっ
ZEEK ZIK
ミーンミン
ミー
ZEEK
ミーンミンミンミー!!
ZIK ZEE
ZEEK ZIK

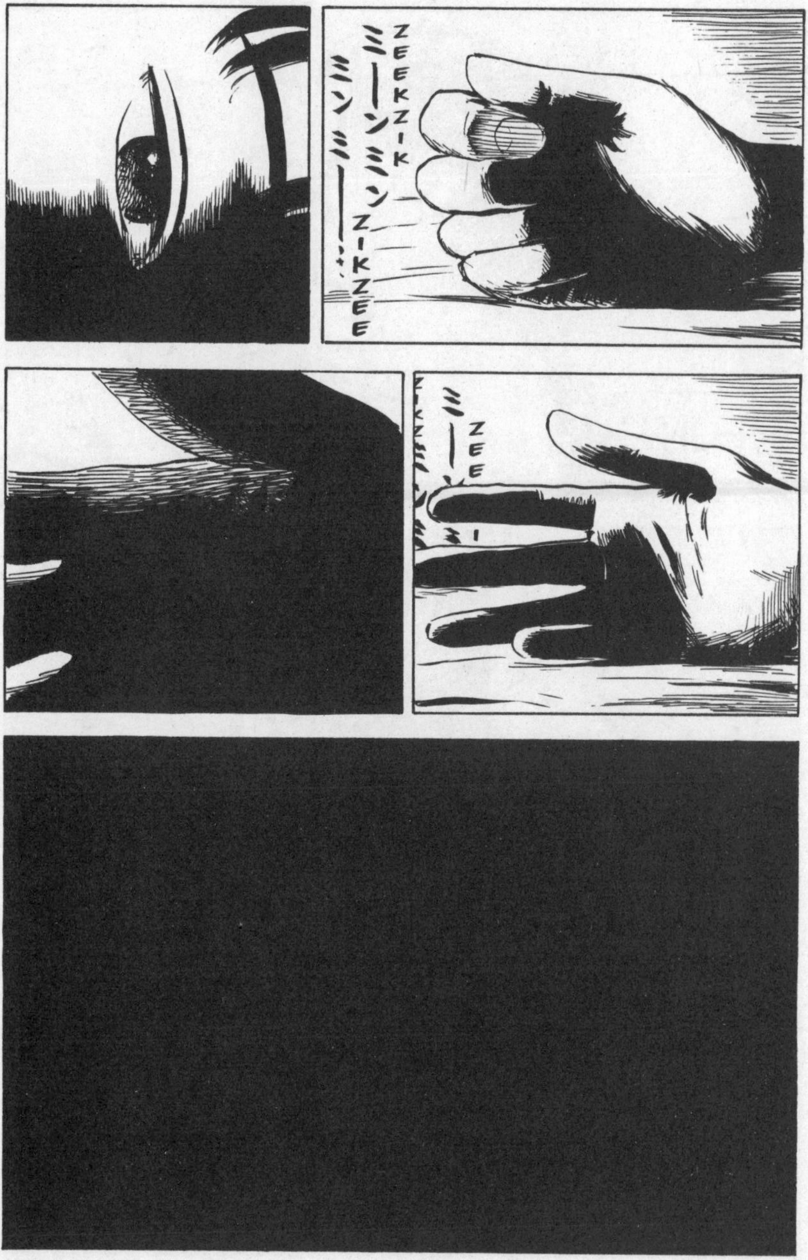
ZEEKZIK
ミーンミン
ZIKZEE
ミンミー…
ZEE
ミー

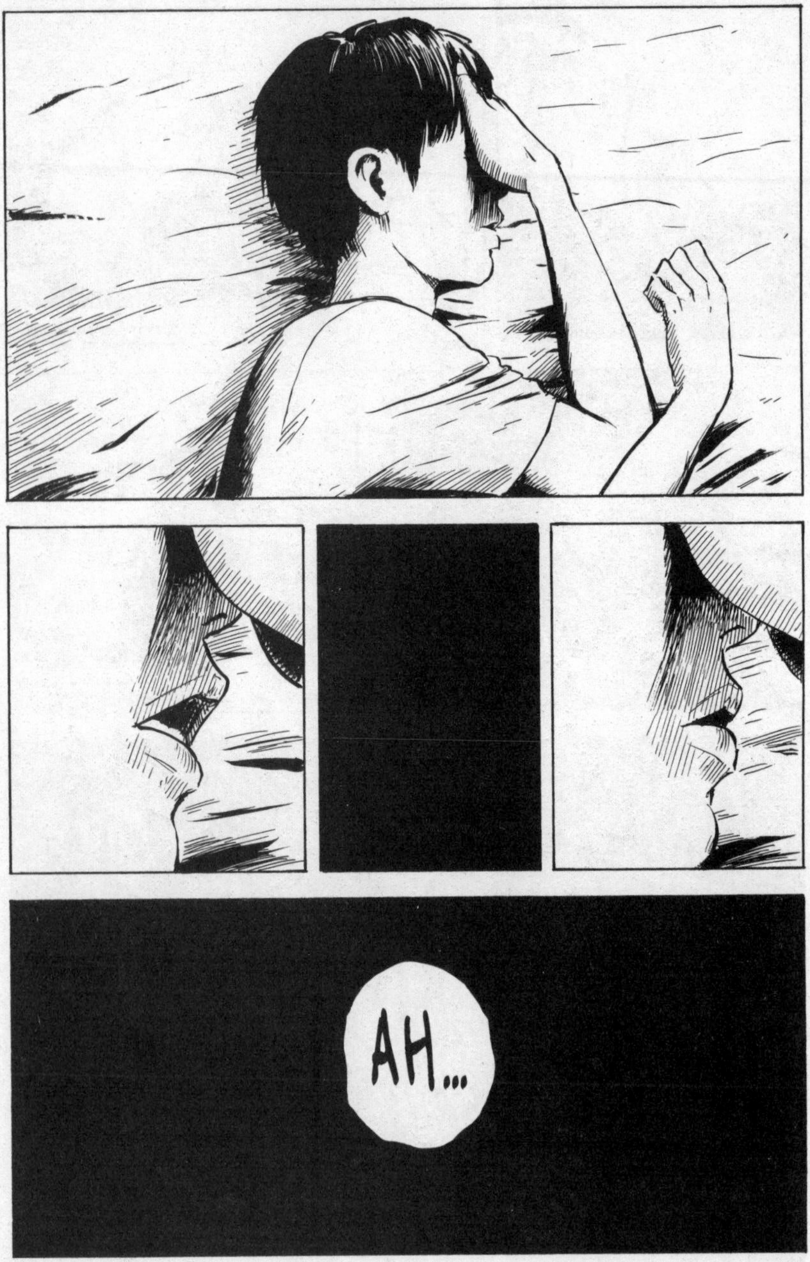
AH...

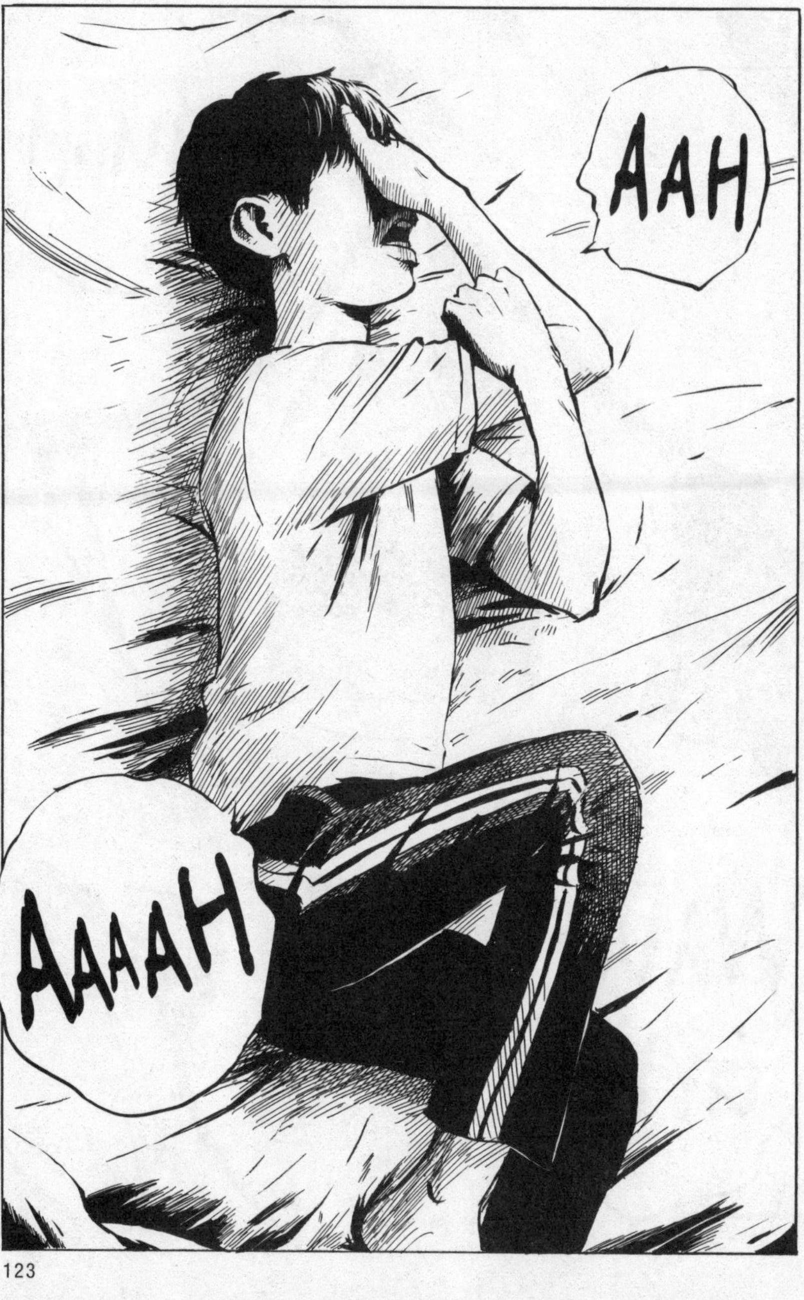
AAH
AAAAH

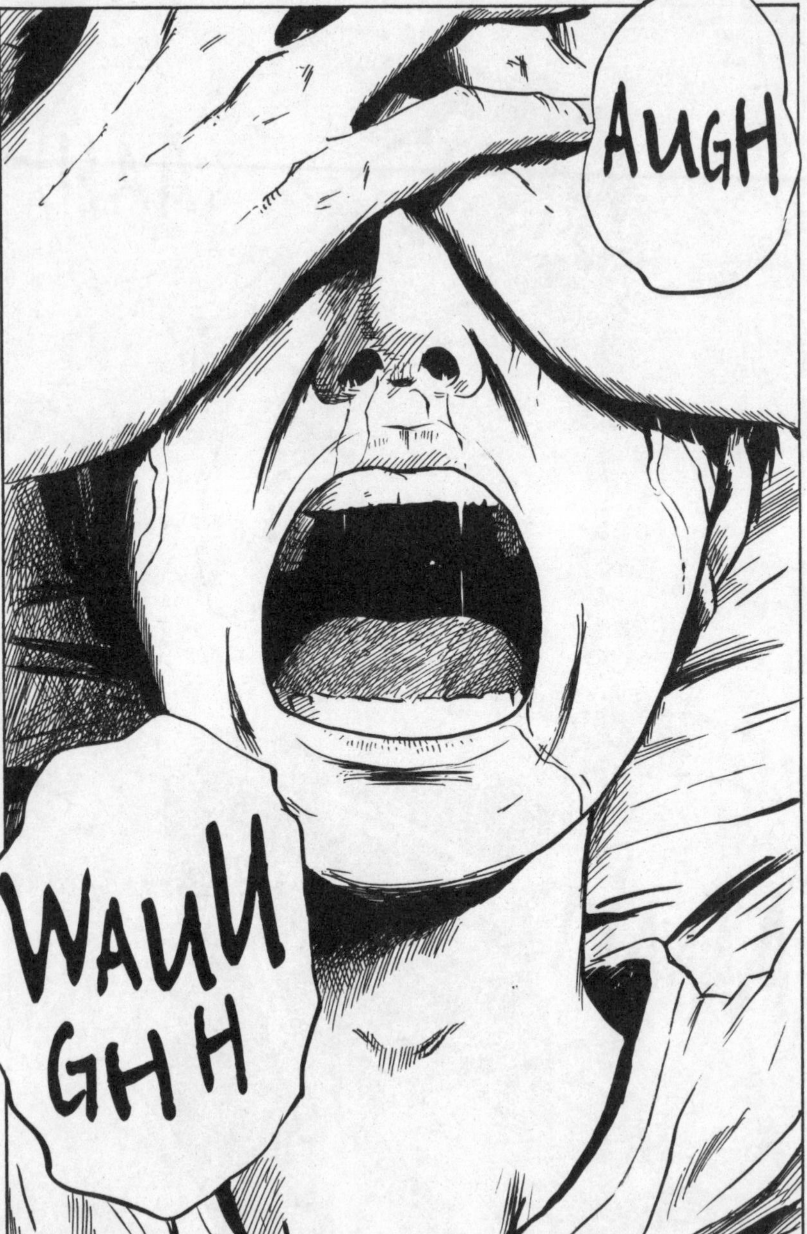
AUGH
WAUU GHH

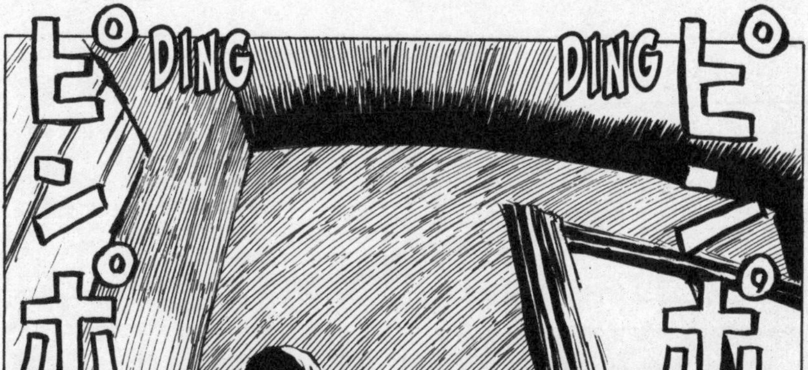
ピンポーン
DING DONG
ピンポーン
DING DONG

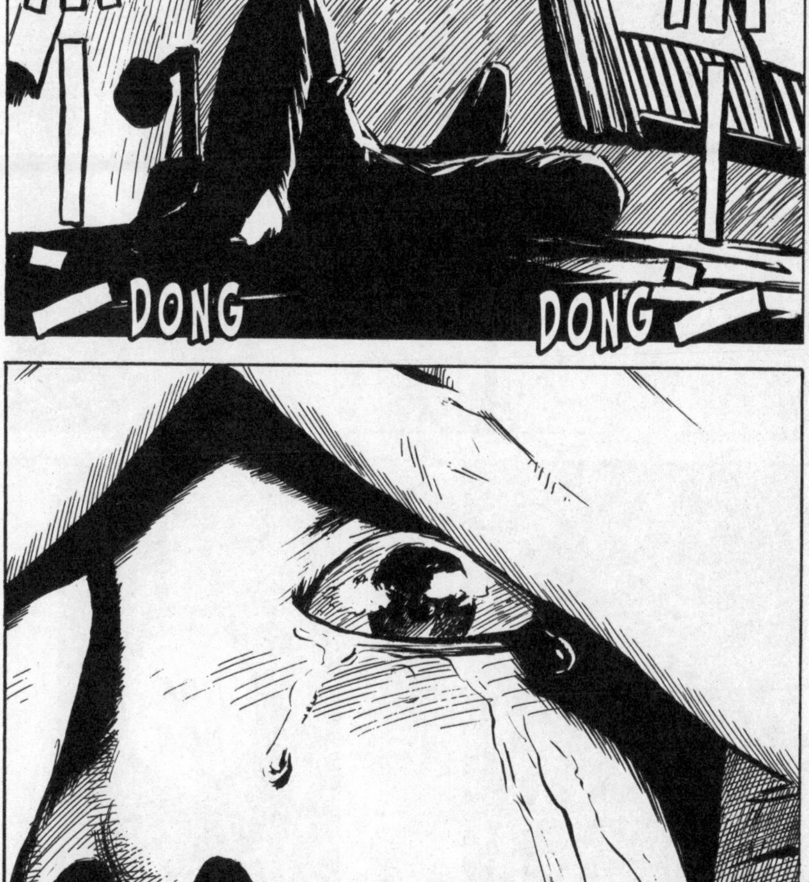

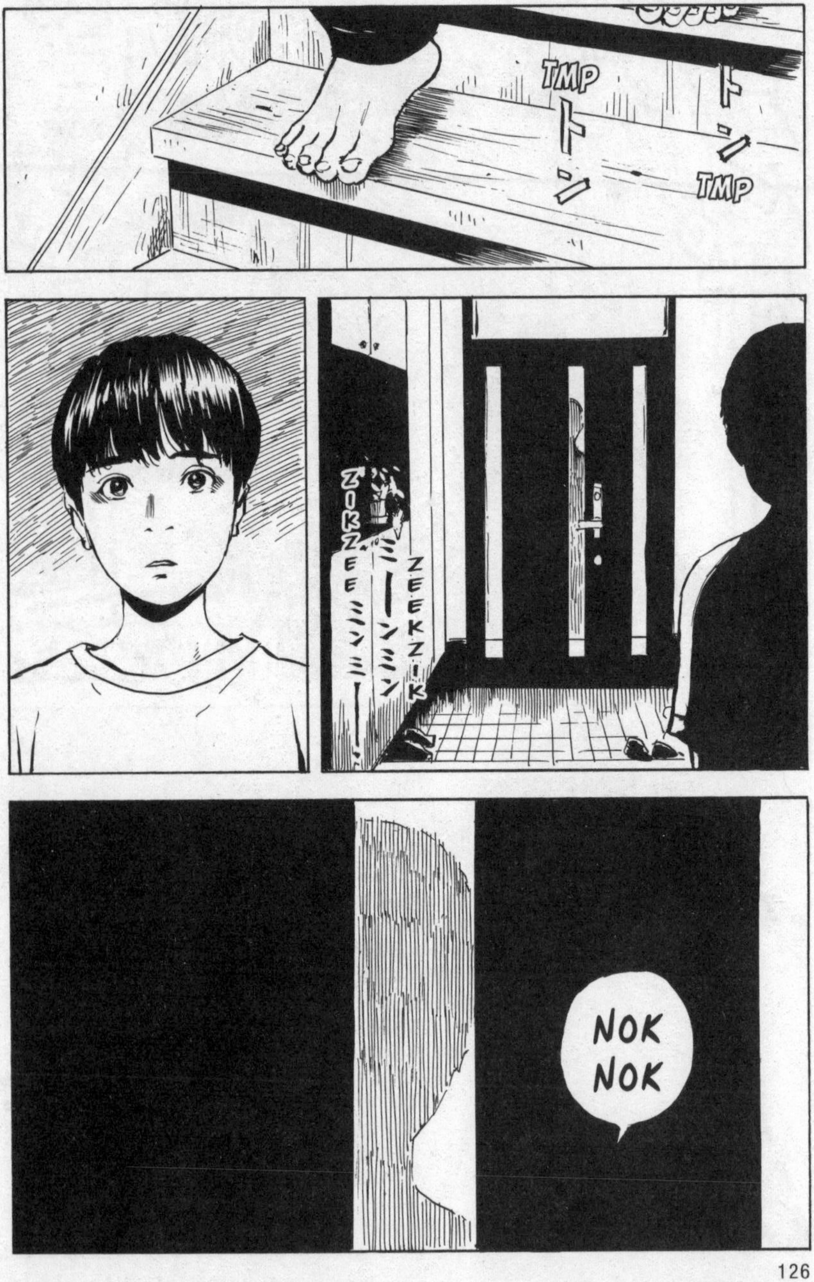
トン
TMP
TMP
トン
ZEEKZIK
ミーンミン
ZIKZEE
ミンミー
NOK NOK

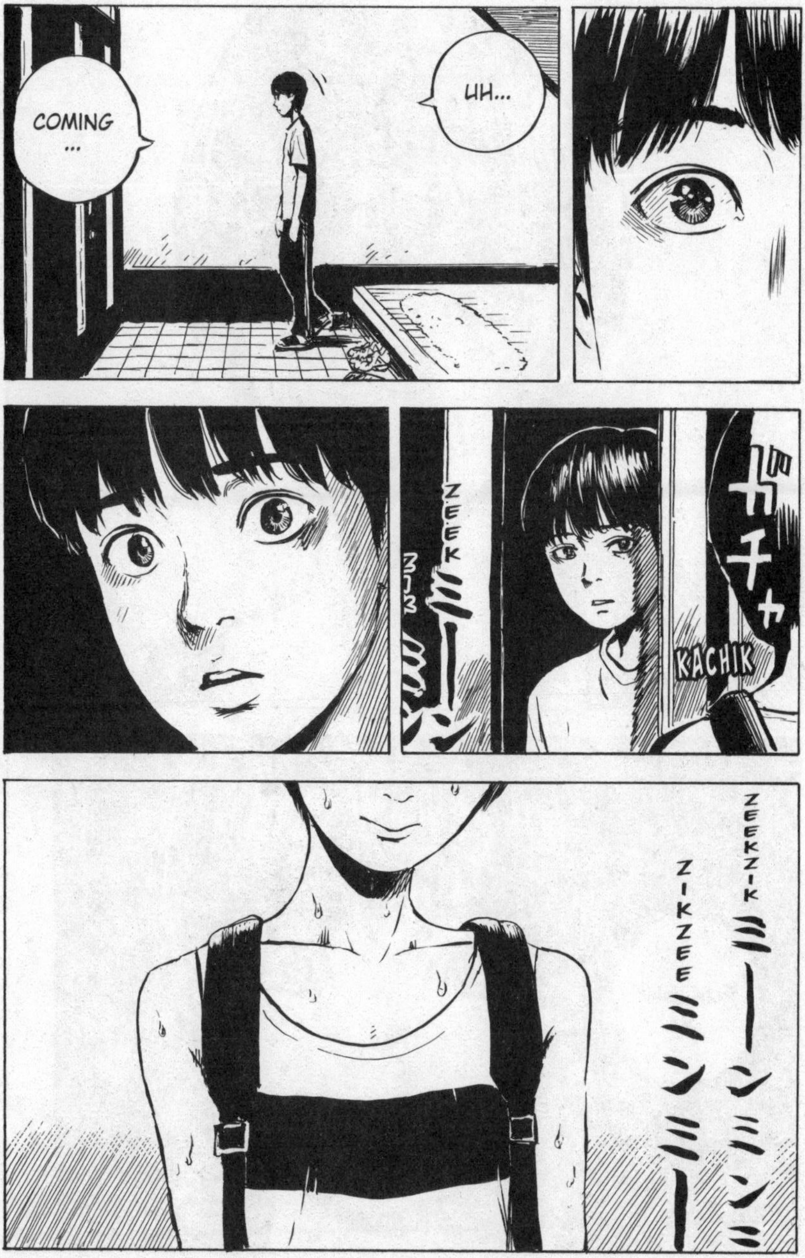
UH...
COMING ...
ガチャ
KACHIK
ZEEK
ミーン
ZIK
ミン
ZEEKZIK
ミーンミンミ
ZIKZEE
ミンミー

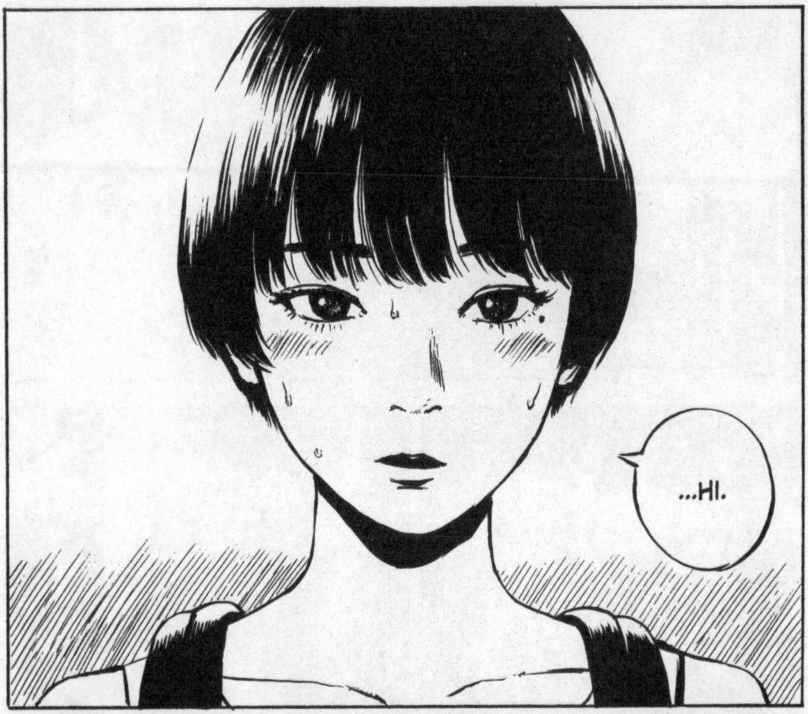
...HI.

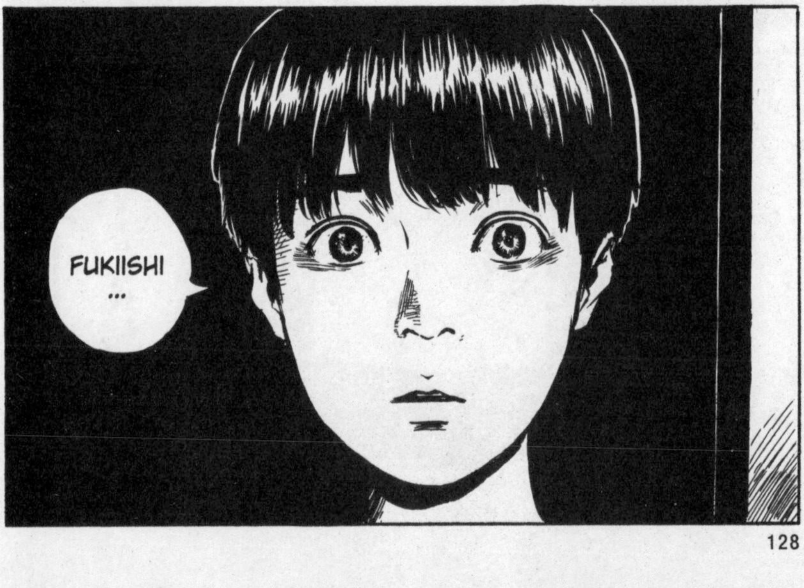
FUKIISHI
...

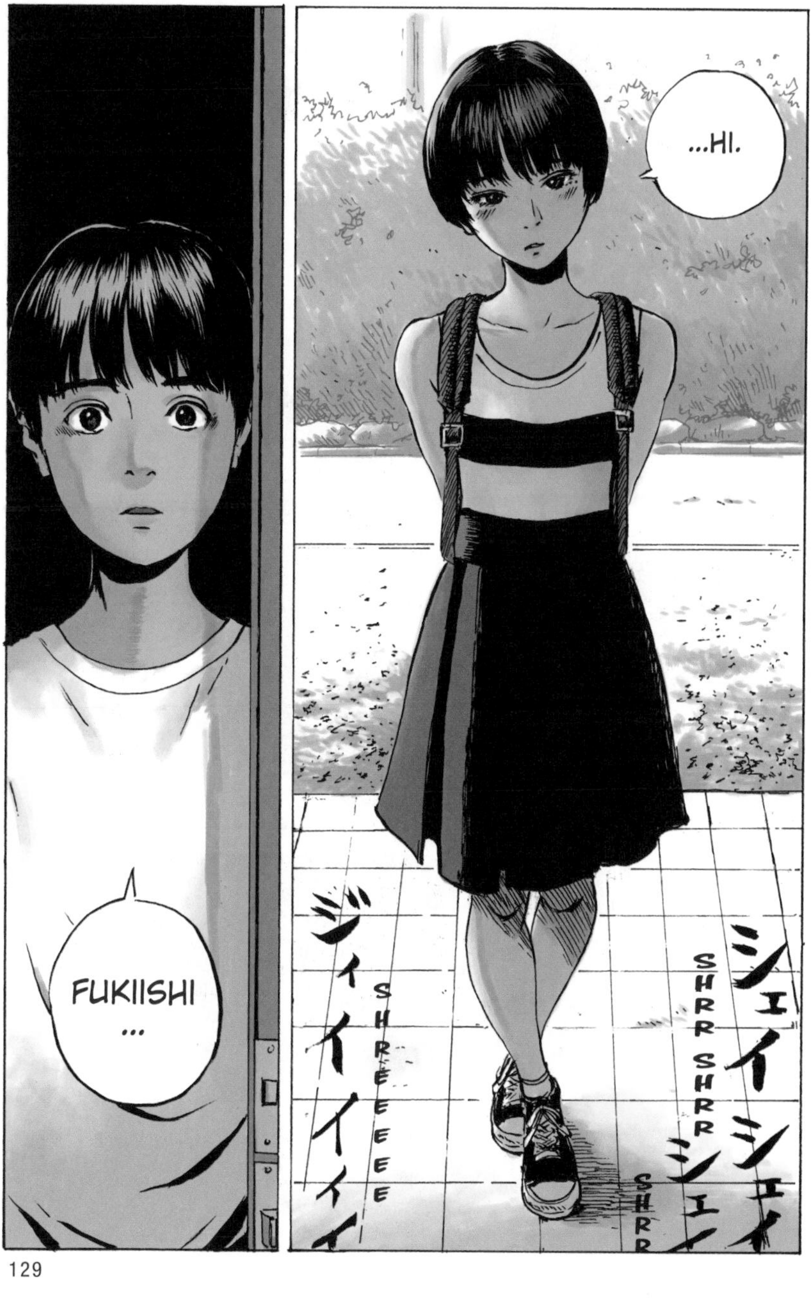
...HI.
SHRR SHRR SHRR
SHREEEEE
FUKIISHI ...

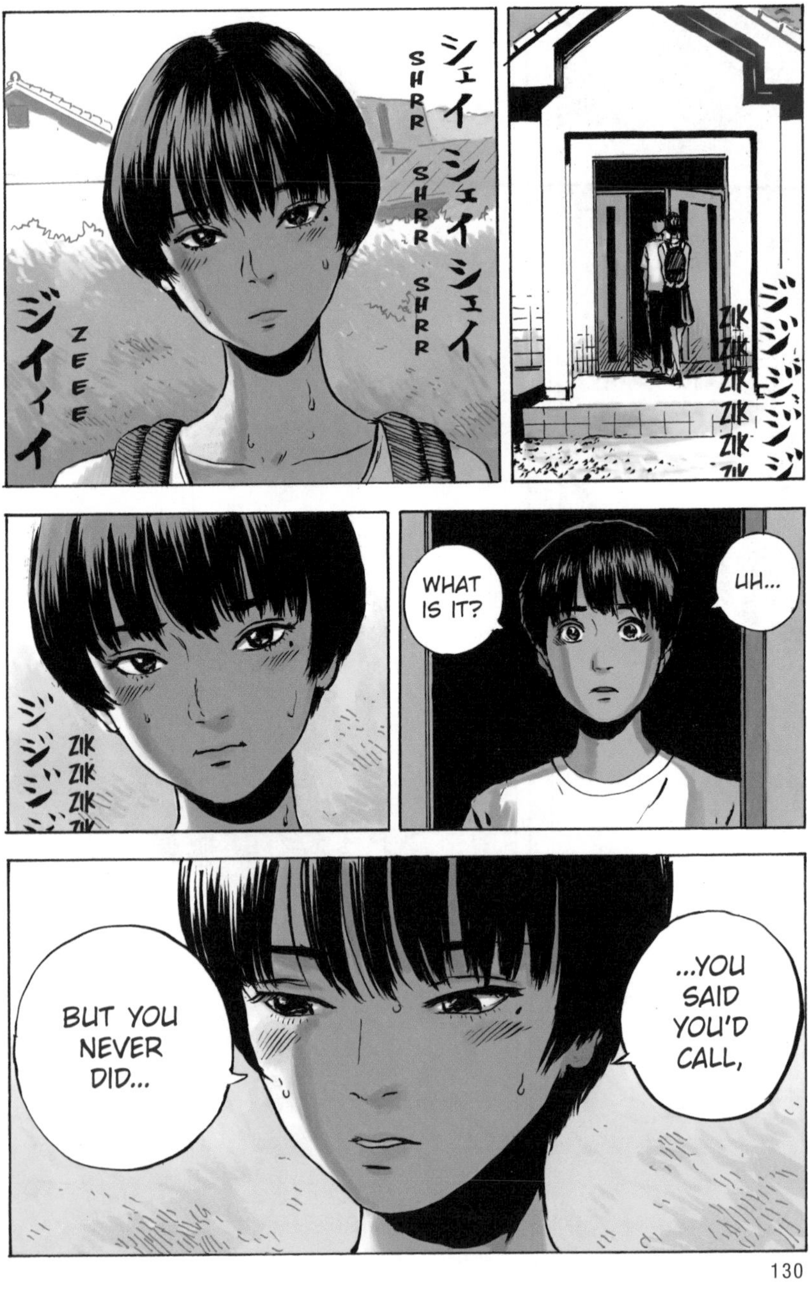
ジジジジ
ZIK ZIK ZIK ZIK ZIK
シェイシェイシェイシェイ
SHRR SHRR SHRR SHRR
ジイイ
ZEEE
WHAT IS IT?
UH...
ジジジジ
ZIK ZIK ZIK
...YOU SAID YOU'D CALL,
BUT YOU NEVER DID...

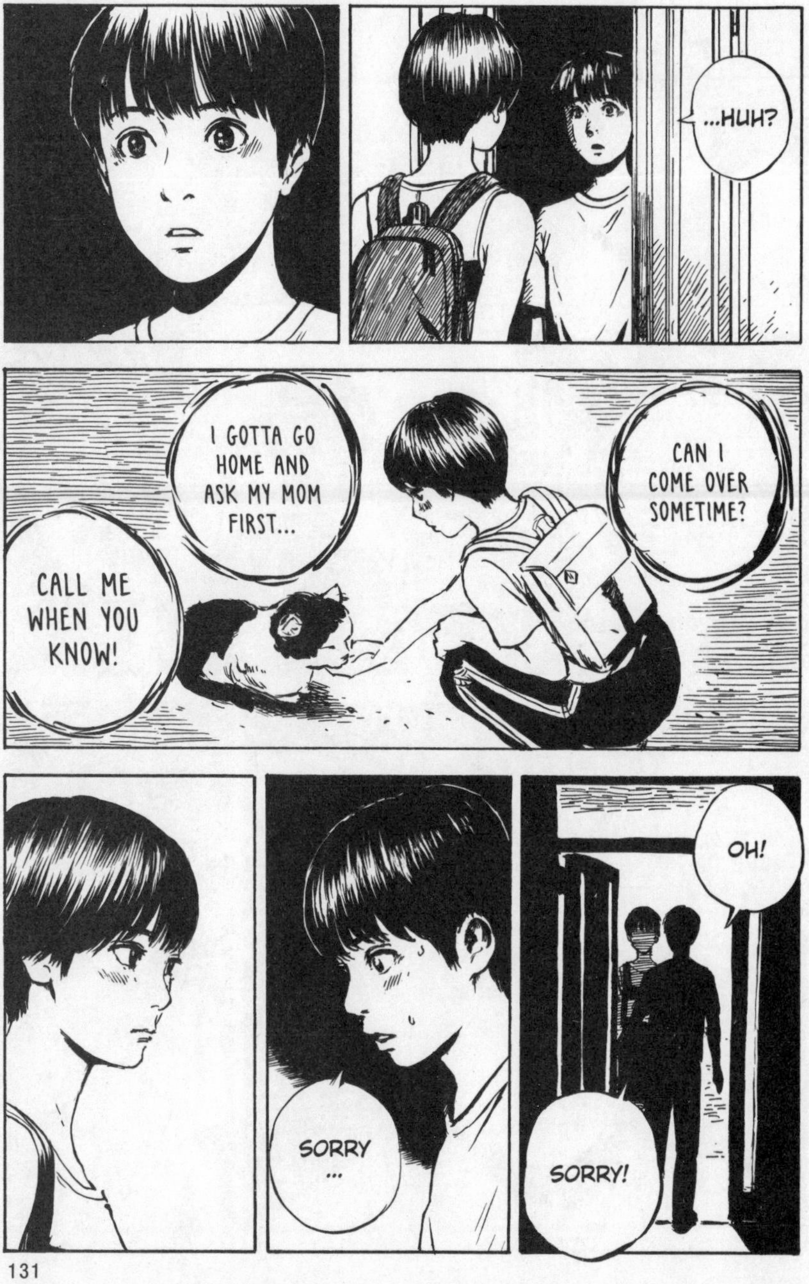
...HUH?
CAN I COME OVER SOMETIME?
I GOTTA GO HOME AND ASK MY MOM FIRST...
CALL ME WHEN YOU KNOW!
OH!
SORRY!
SORRY ...

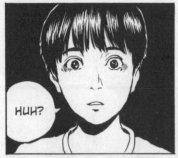

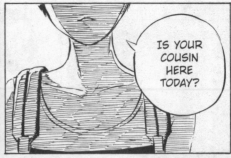

IS YOUR COUSIN HERE TODAY?
HUH?
YOU SAID YOU COULDN'T HANG OUT IF YOUR COUSIN WAS HERE, RIGHT?
SO IS HE HERE TODAY?
UH...
NO... NO ONE'S HERE RIGHT NOW...

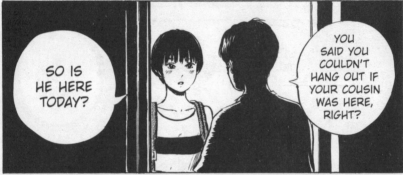

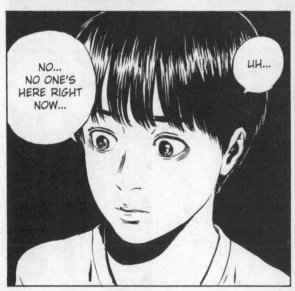

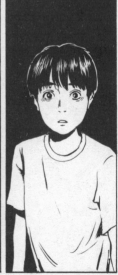

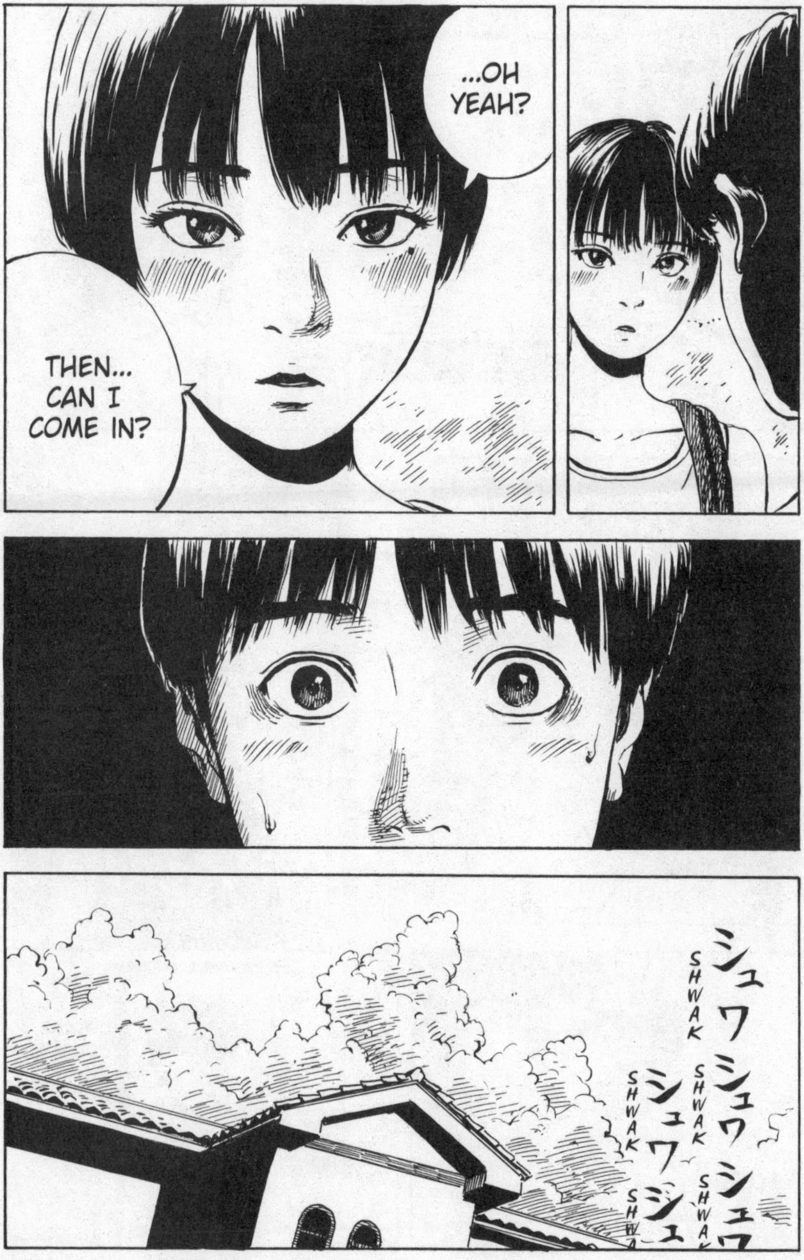
...OH YEAH?
THEN... CAN I COME IN?
シュワシュワシュワ
SHWAK SHWAK SHWAK
シュワシュ
SHWAK SHWA

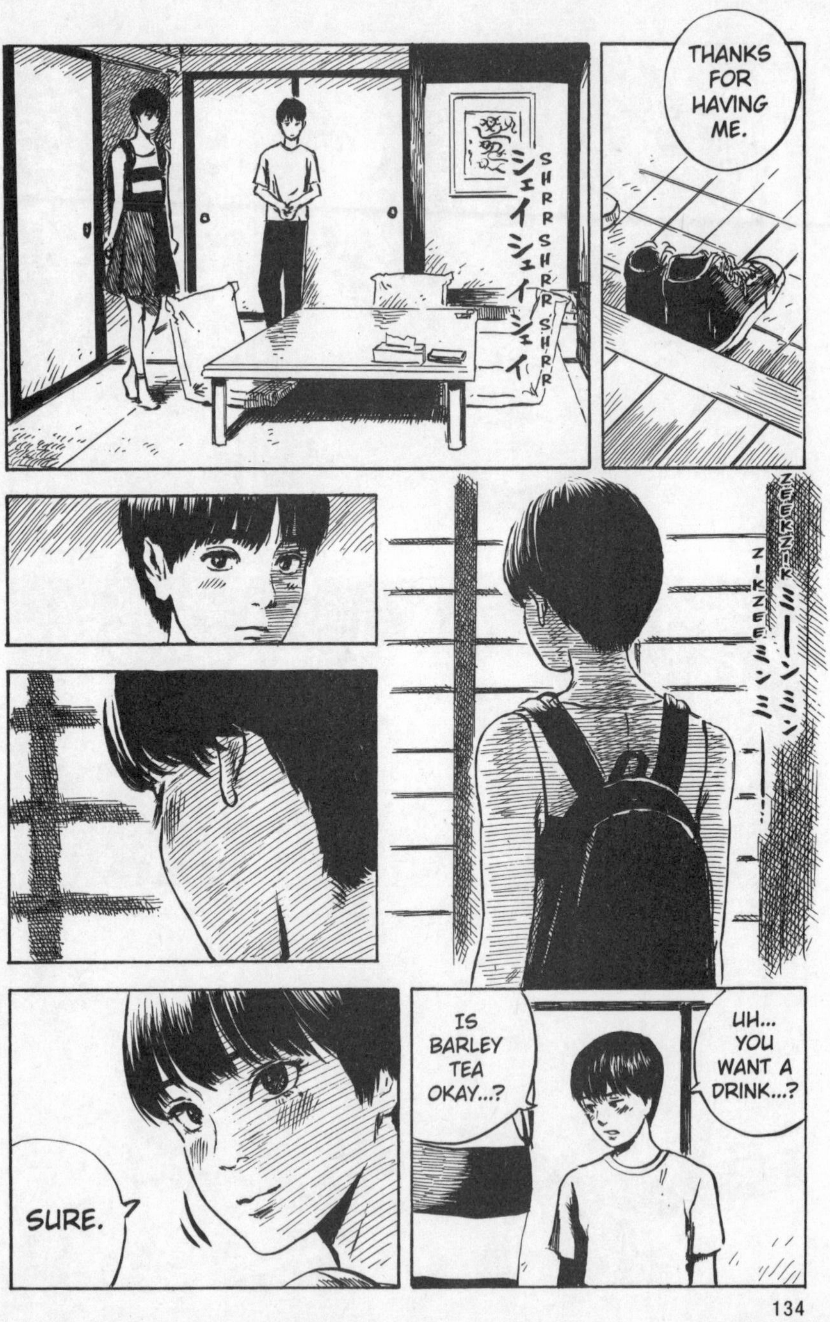
THANKS FOR HAVING ME.
SHRR SHRR SHRR SHRR
シェイシェイ
ZEEKZIK ZIKZEE
ミーンミン ミンミ
UH... YOU WANT A DRINK...?
IS BARLEY TEA OKAY...?
SURE.

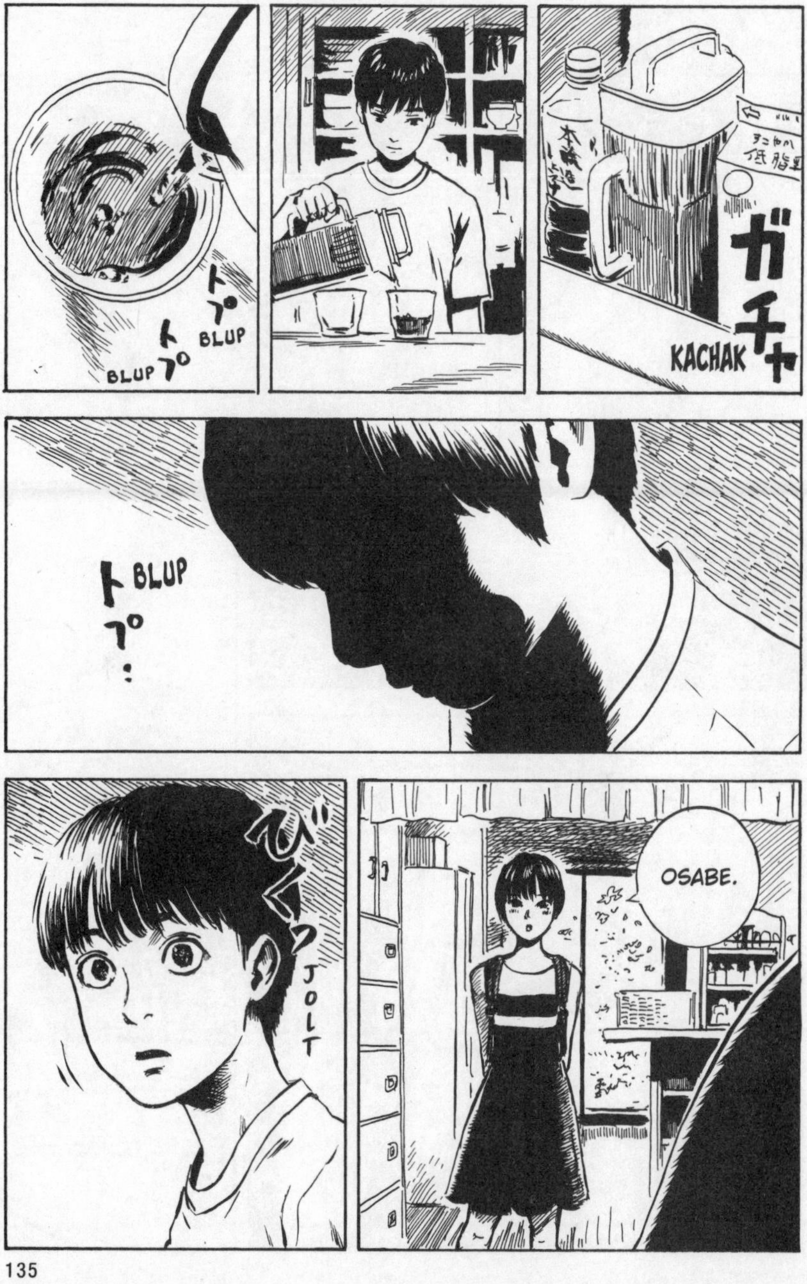
ガチャ
KACHAK
トプ
BLUP
トプ
BLUP
トプ…
BLUP
OSABE.
びくっ
JOLT

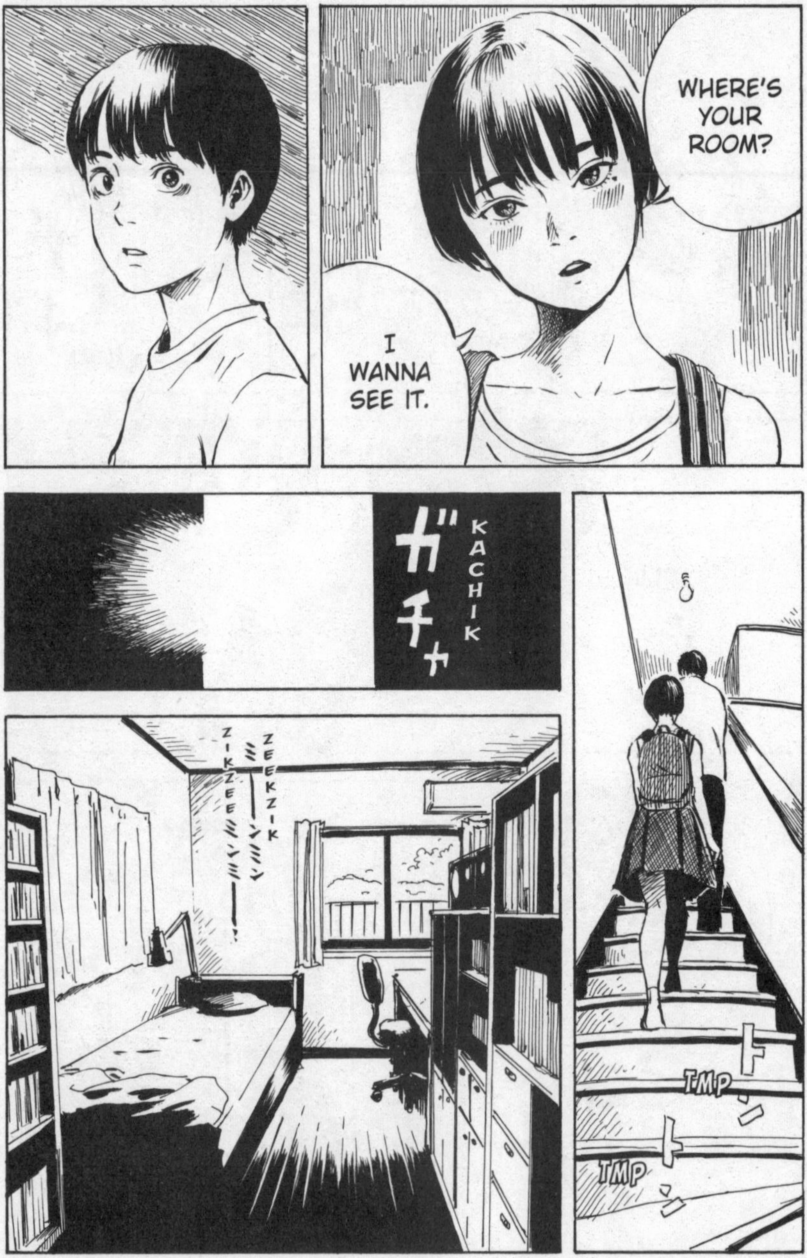
WHERE'S YOUR ROOM?
I WANNA SEE IT.
TMP
TMP
ガチャ
KACHIK
ZEEKZIK
ZIKZEEE

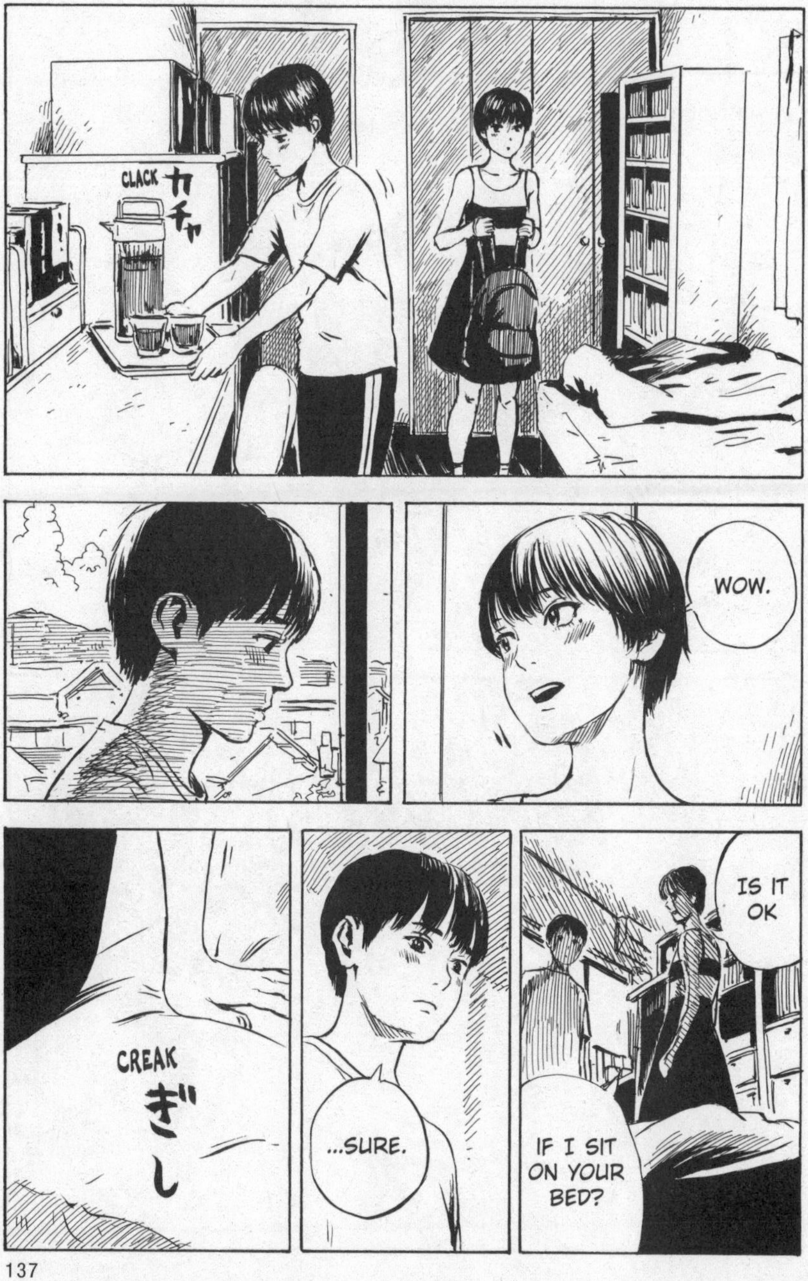
CLACK
カチャ
WOW.
IS IT OK
IF I SIT ON YOUR BED?
...SURE.
CREAK
ぎし

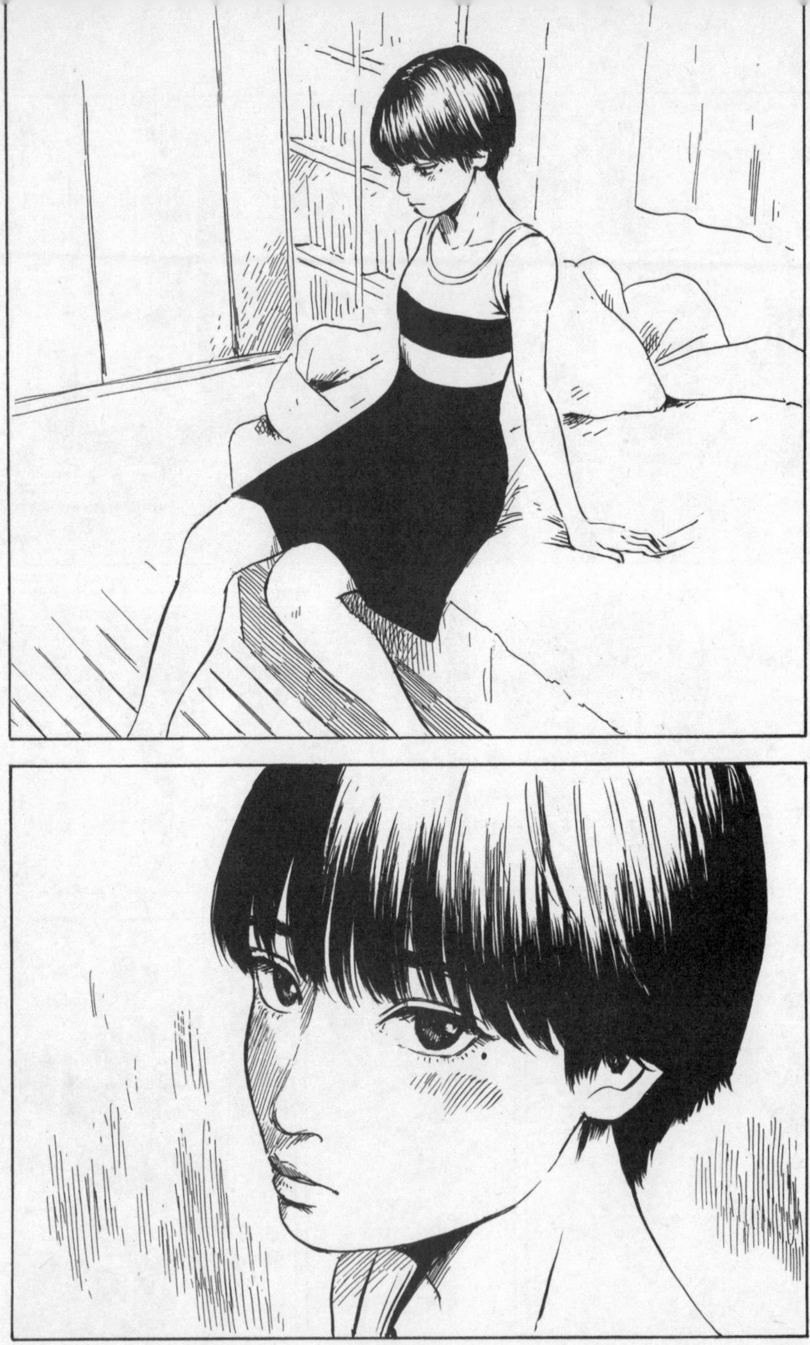

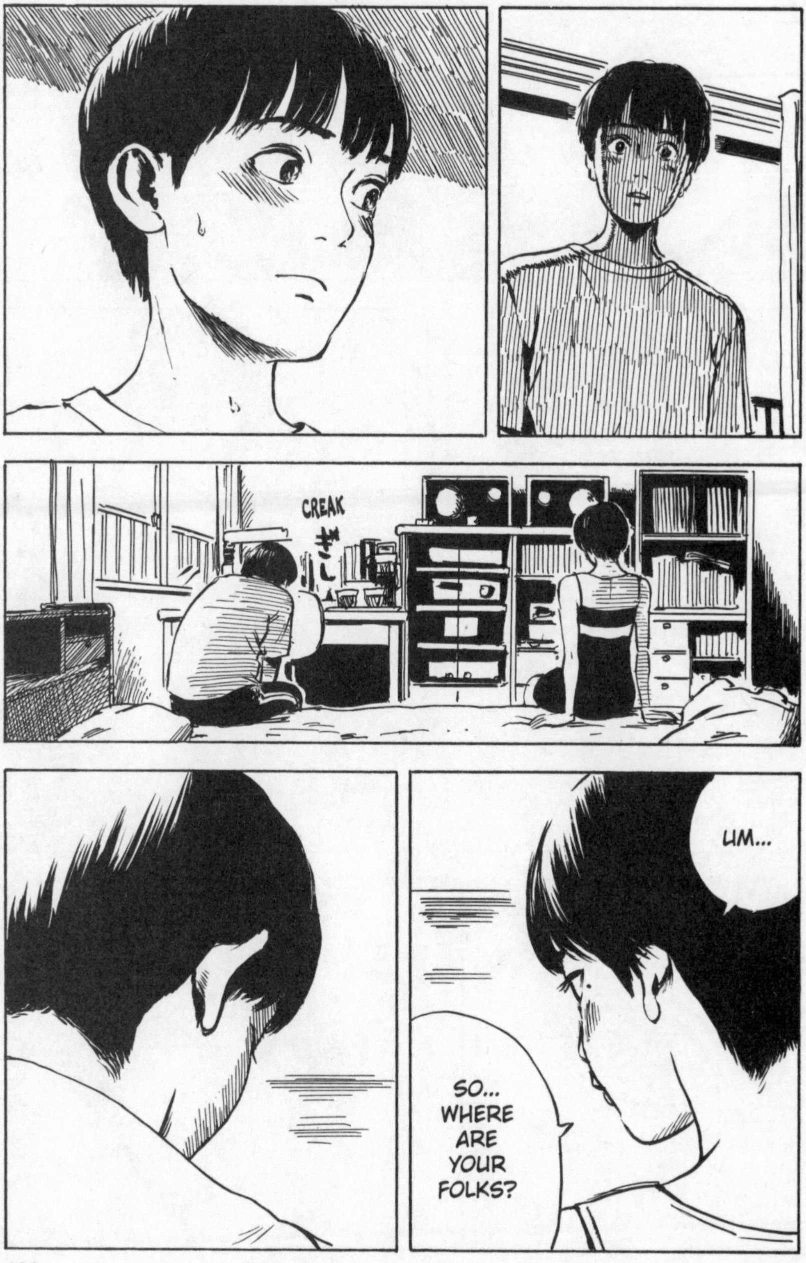
CREAK
ぎし
UM...
SO... WHERE ARE YOUR FOLKS?

...OH...
THEY'RE... AT THE HOSPITAL...
THE HOSPI-TAL?
VISITING SOME-ONE?
MY COUSIN ...
GOT HURT...
REALLY?
IS HE OKAY?

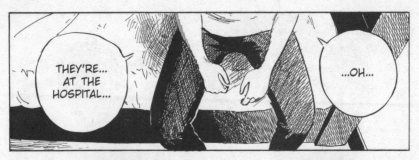

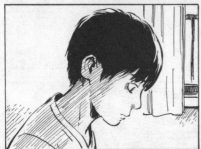

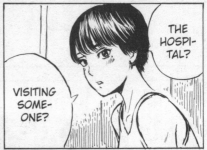

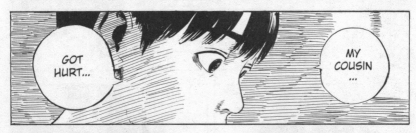

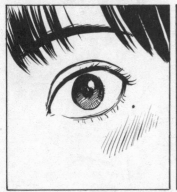

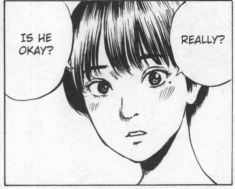

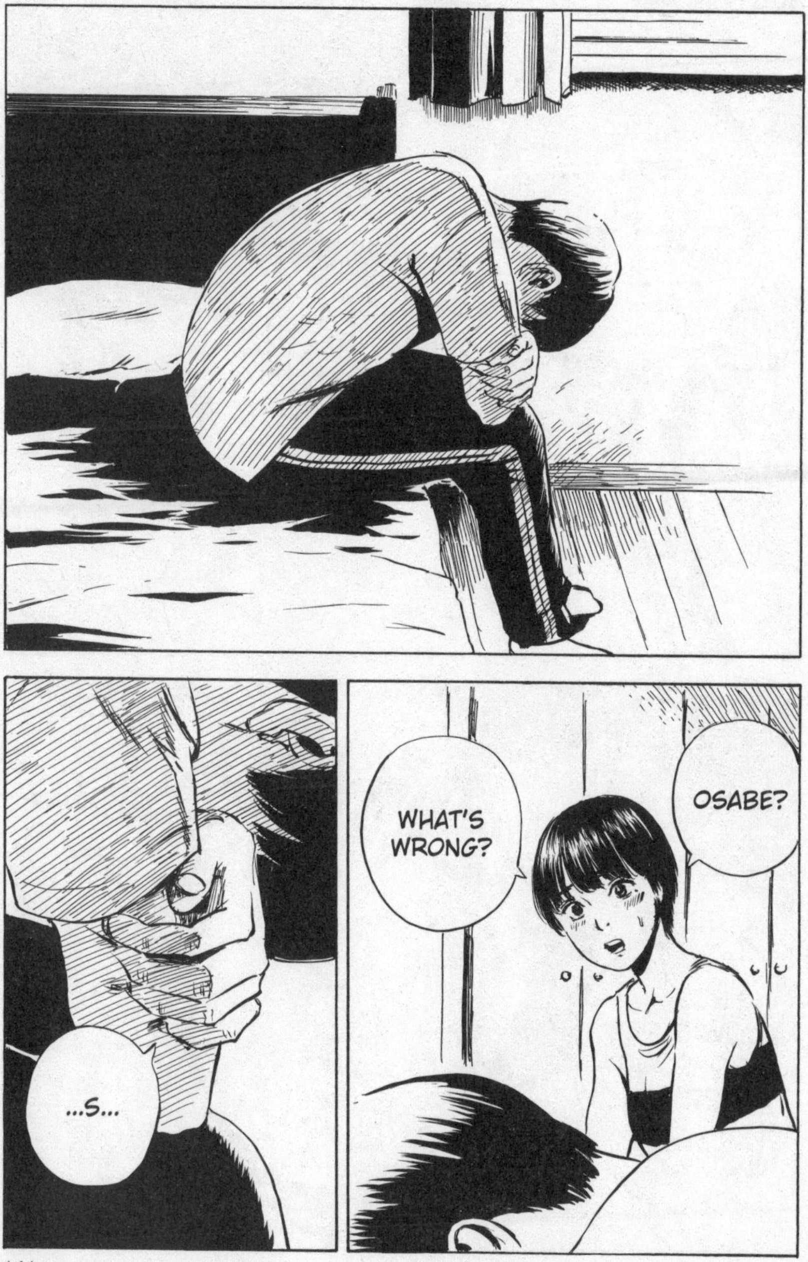
OSABE?
WHAT'S WRONG?
...S...

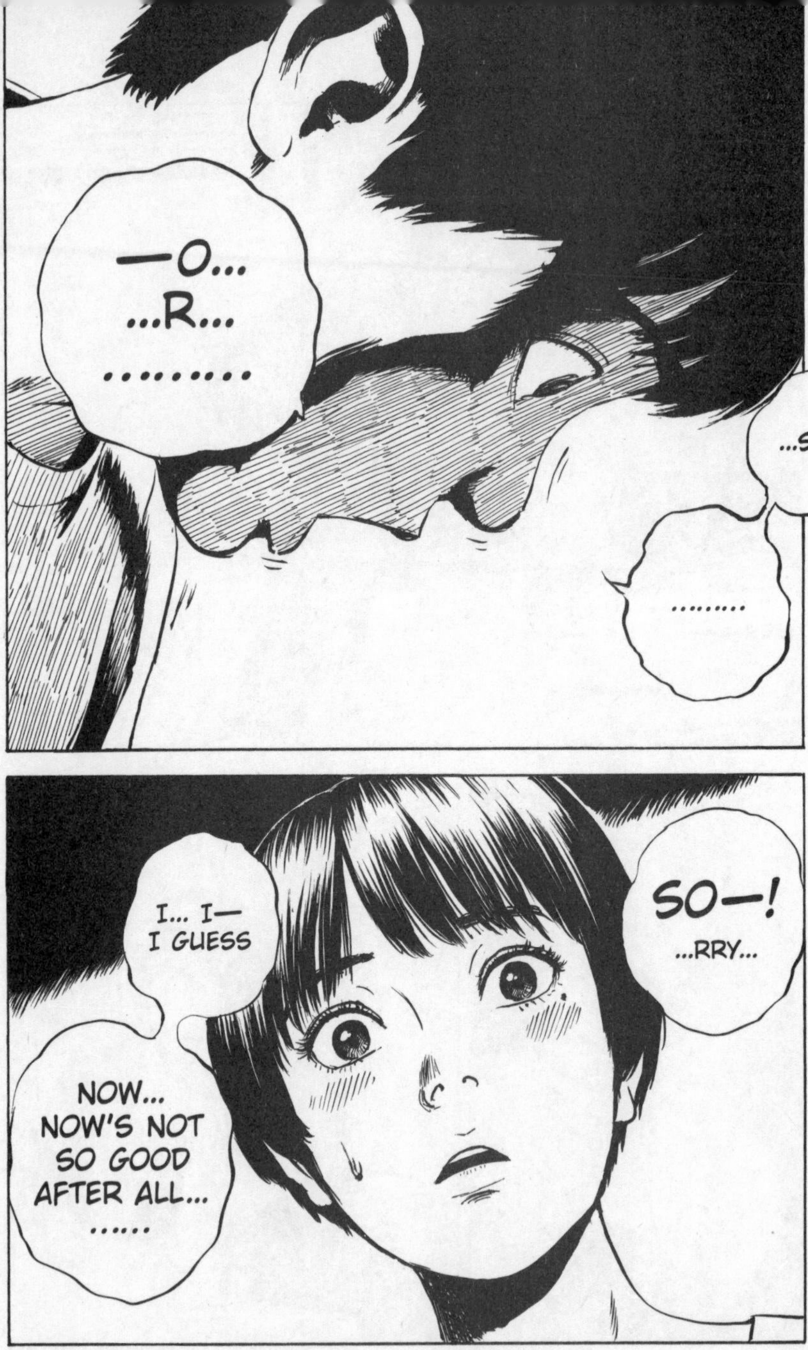

...S—
....
—O... ...R... ....
SO—! ...RRY...
I... I— I GUESS
NOW... NOW'S NOT SO GOOD AFTER ALL... ......

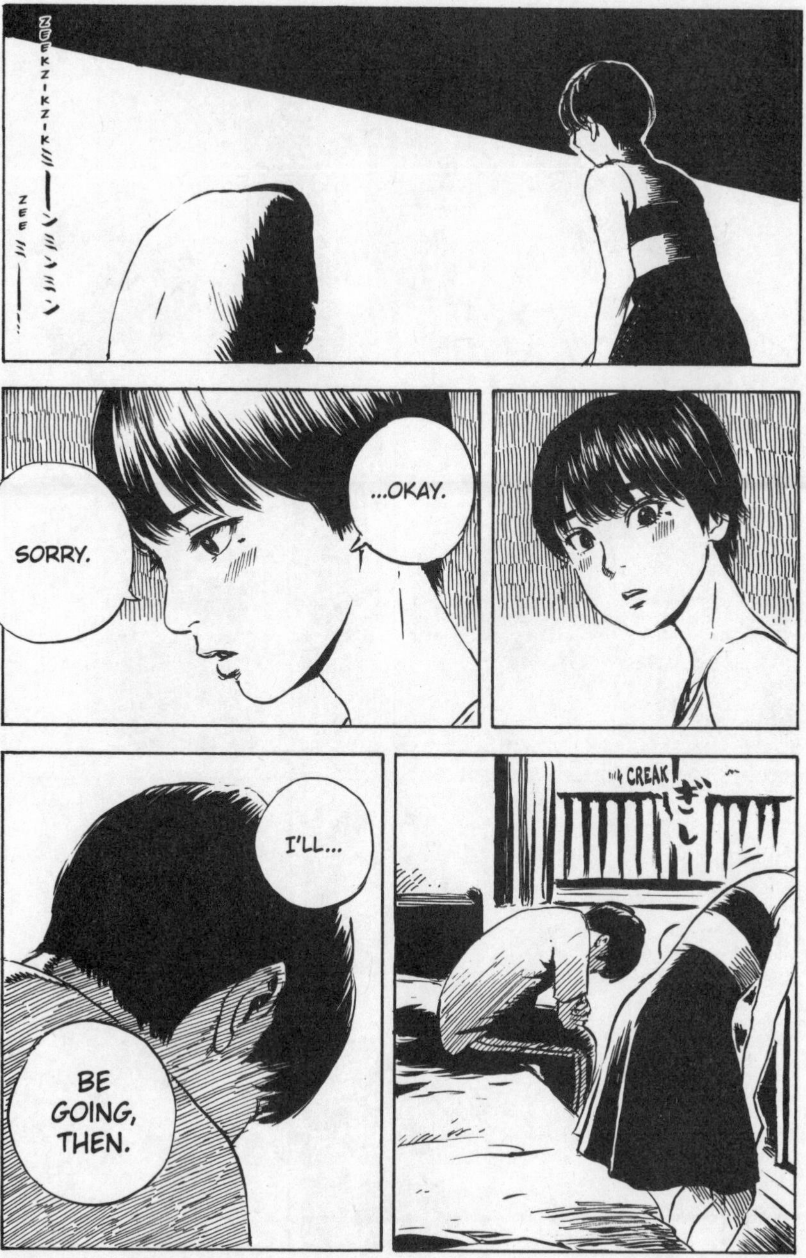
ZEEKZIKZIK
ミーンミンミン
ZEE
ミー…
...OKAY.
SORRY.
CREAK
ぎし
I'LL...
BE GOING, THEN.

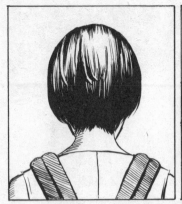

RUSTLE
ごそ ごそ
RUSTLE

ZEE
ジィィィ

ZHP
ズ ザ

HERE.

TP とと
TP とと

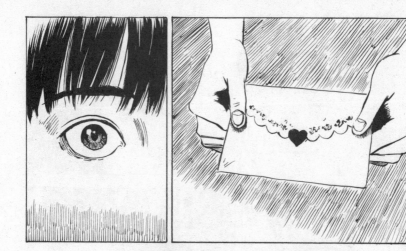

READ IT LATER...

...UH...

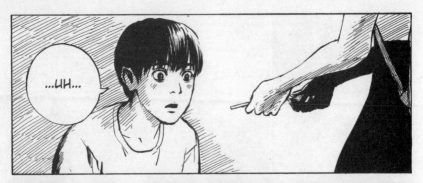

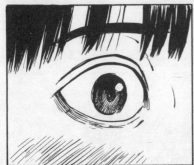

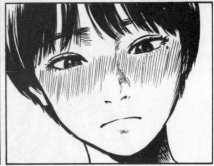

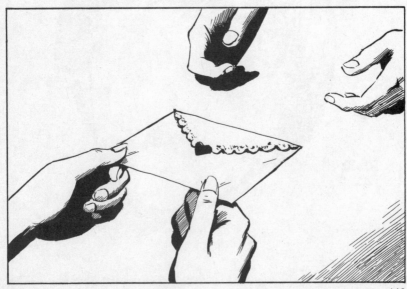

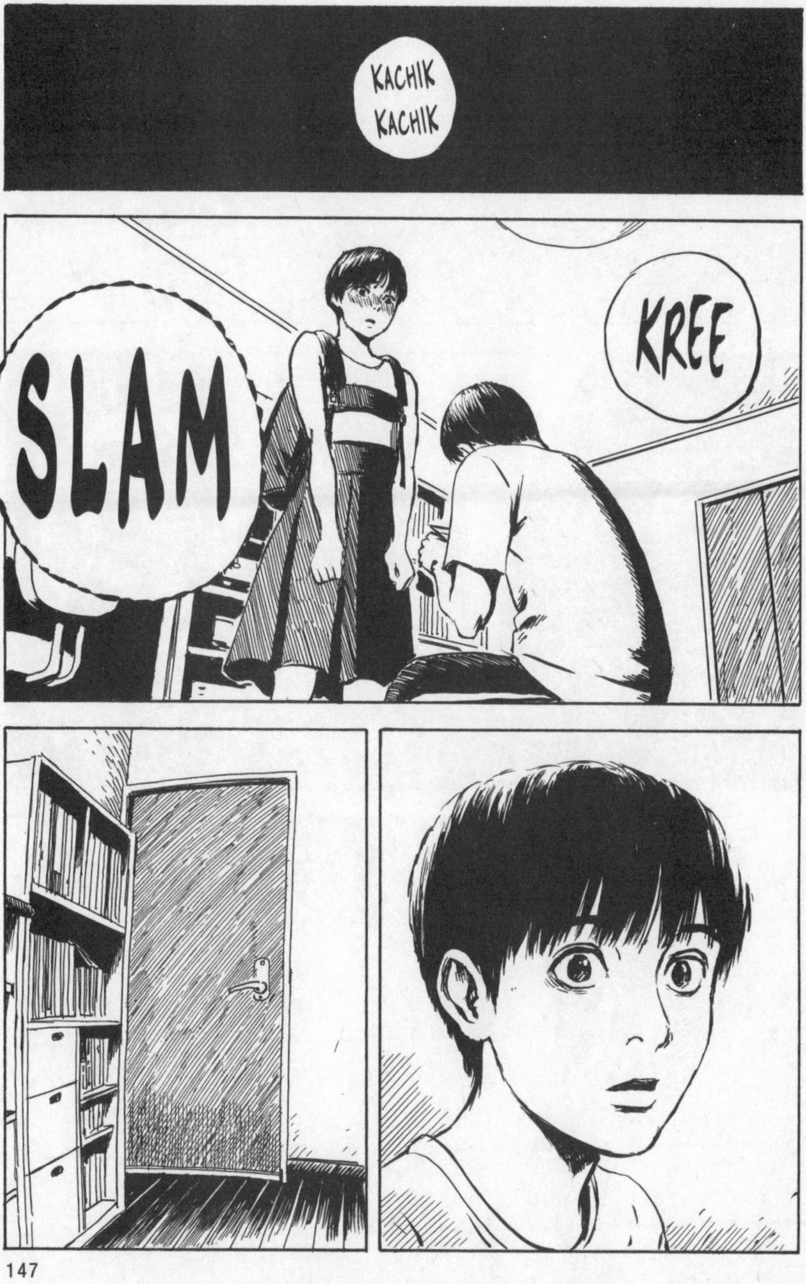
KACHIK KACHIK
KREE
SLAM

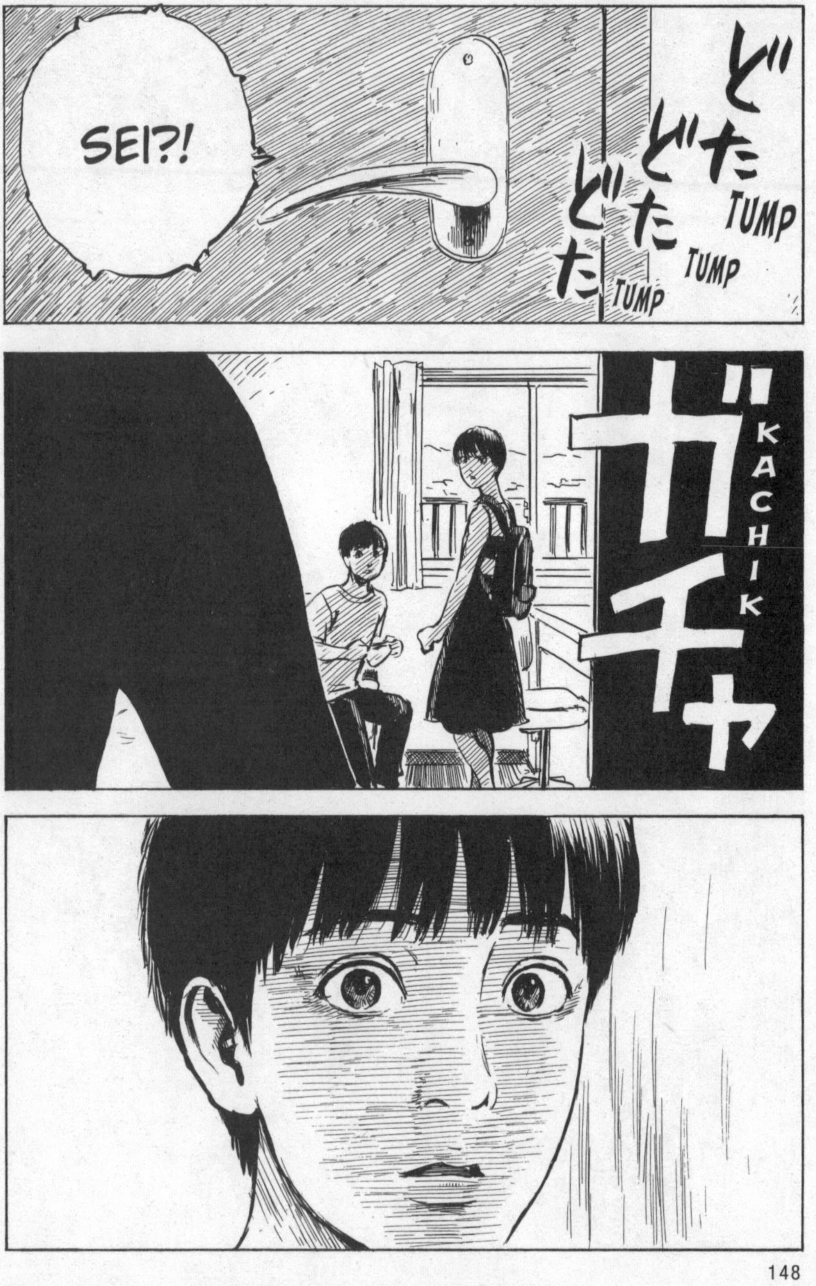

SEI?!
どた
TUMP
どた
TUMP
どた
TUMP
ガチャ
KACHIK

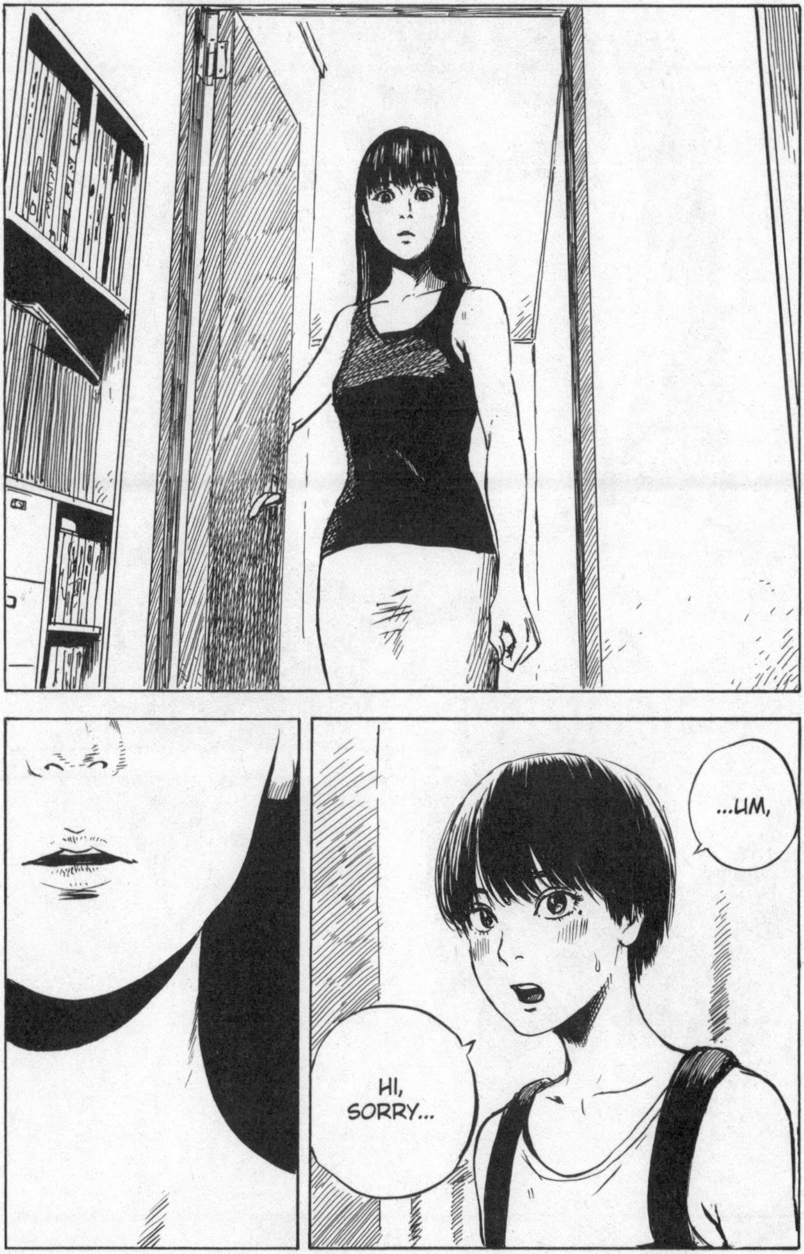
...UM,
HI, SORRY...

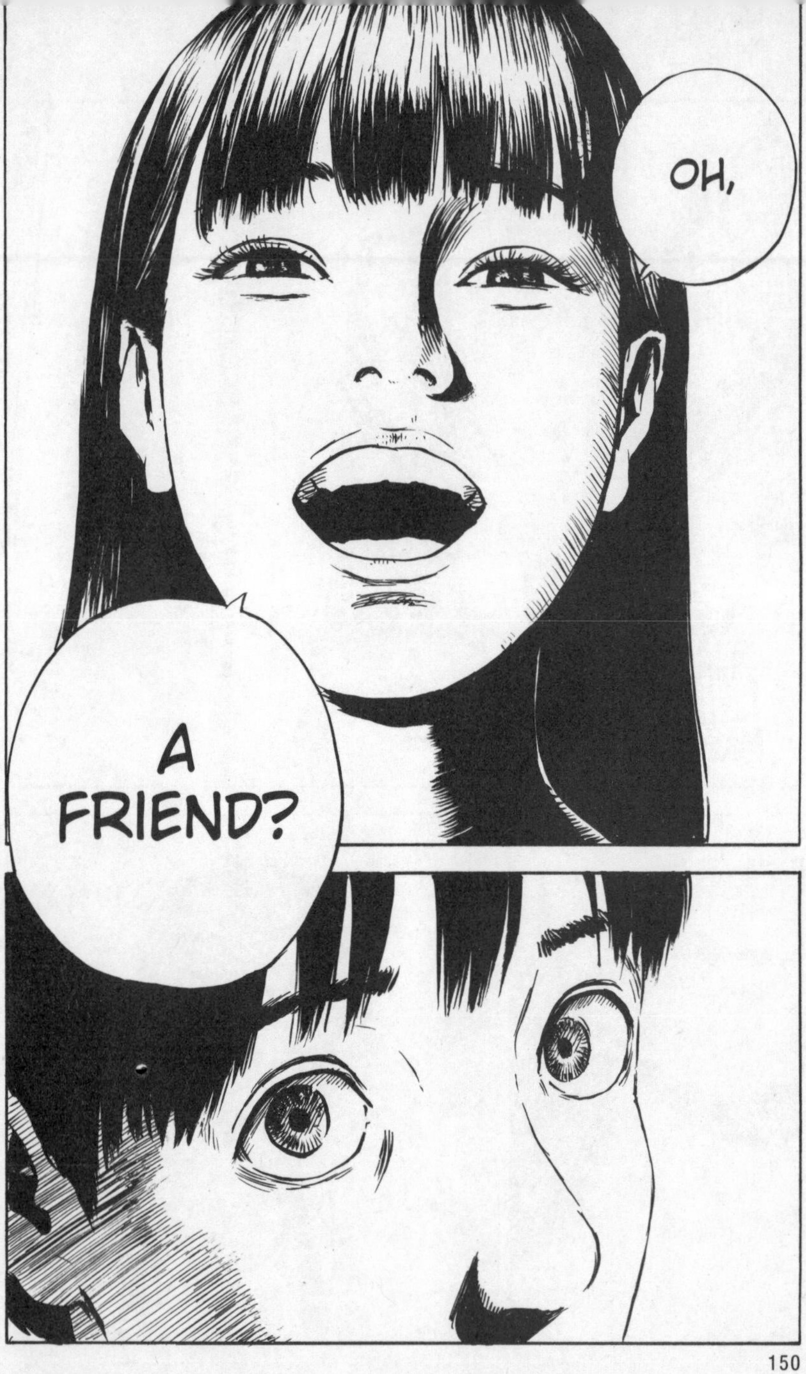
OH,
A FRIEND?

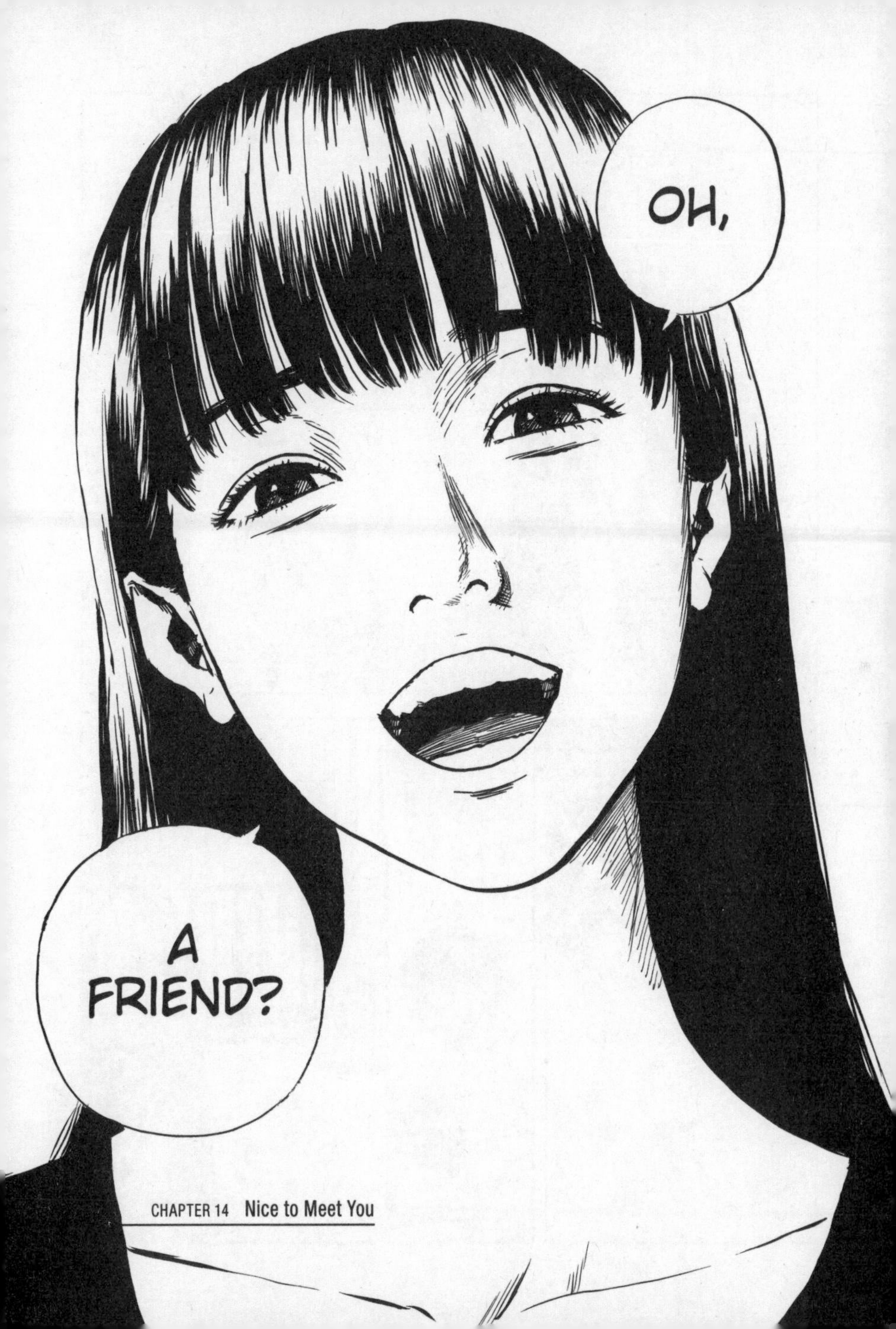
OH,
A FRIEND?

CHAPTER 14 Nice to Meet You

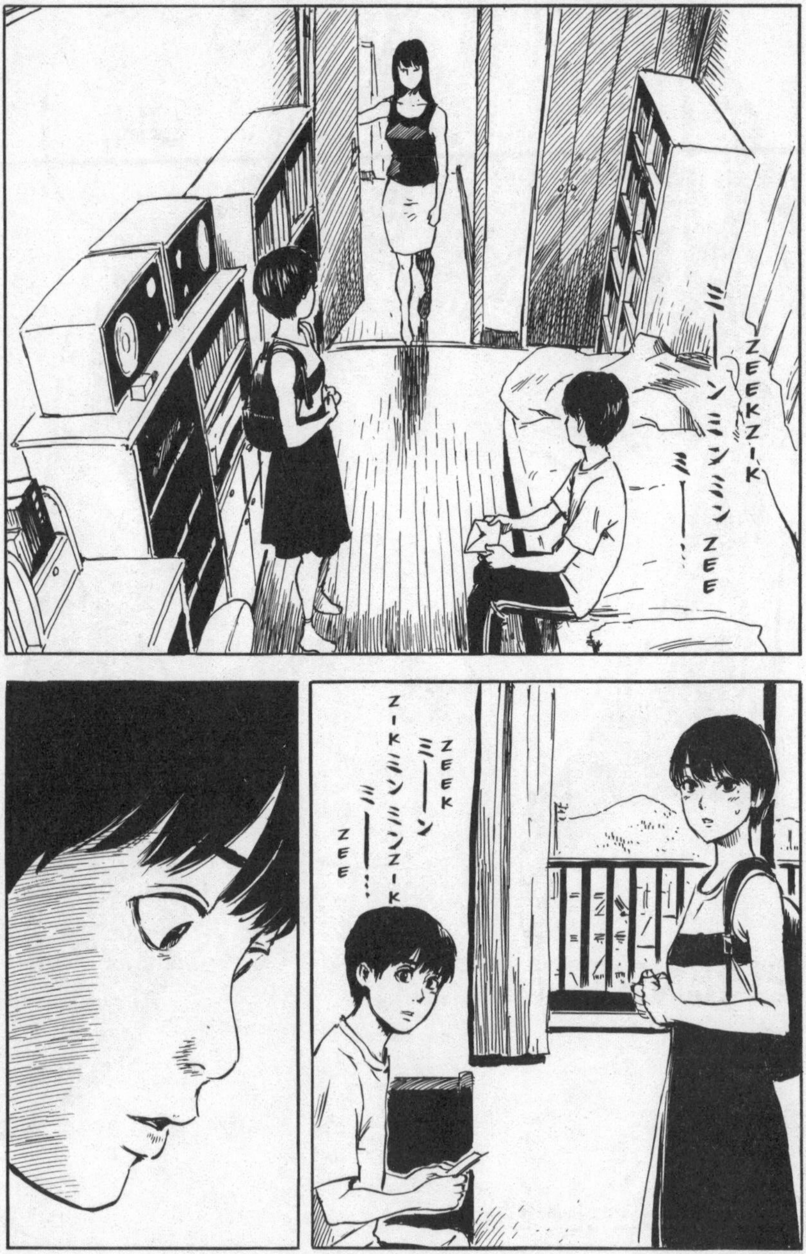
ZEEKZI-K
ミーンミンミン ZEE
ミー…
ZEEK
ミーン
ZI-KミンミンZI-K
ミー…
ZEE

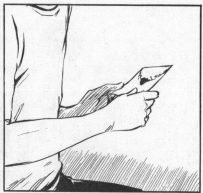

FFP

UM...

...UH
...

AH...

...MM
...

WHUH!
- UT...

HAP-
PENED?

WEREN'T
YOU...?

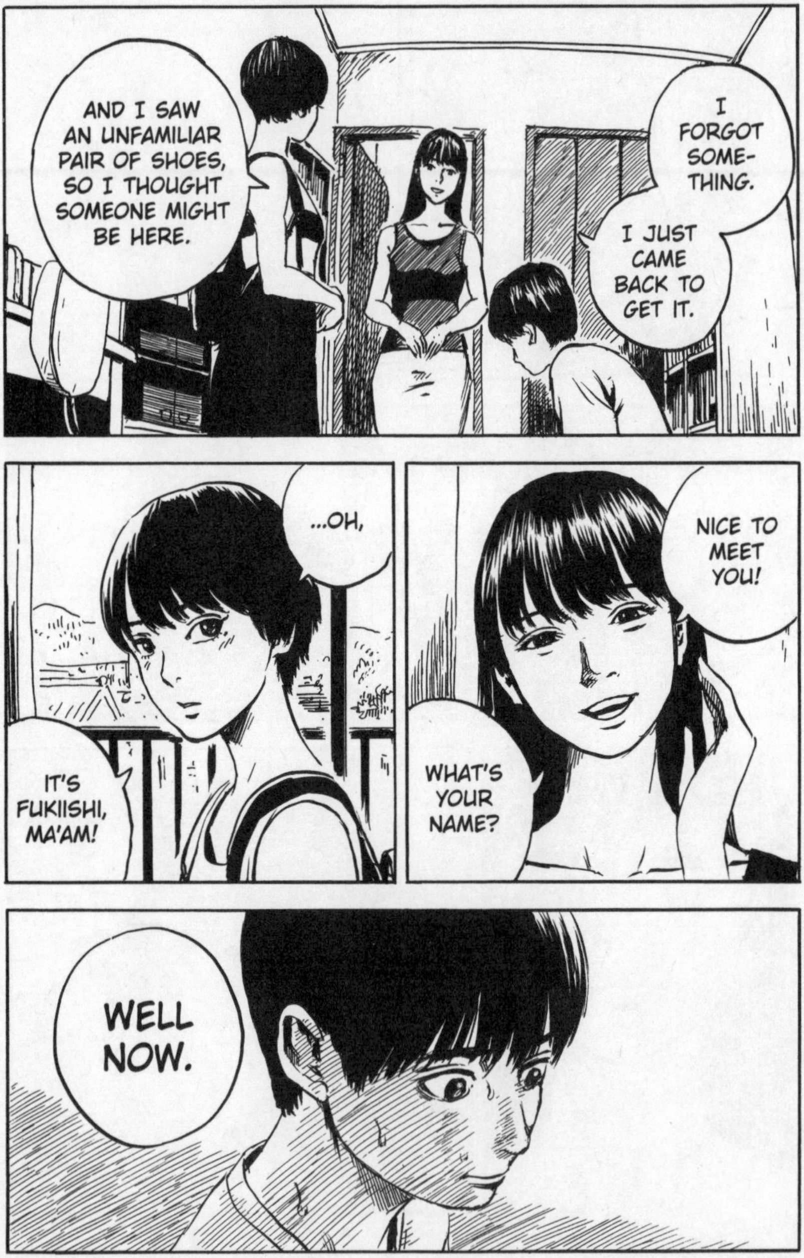
I FORGOT SOME-THING.
I JUST CAME BACK TO GET IT.
AND I SAW AN UNFAMILIAR PAIR OF SHOES, SO I THOUGHT SOMEONE MIGHT BE HERE.
NICE TO MEET YOU!
WHAT'S YOUR NAME?
...OH,
IT'S FUKIISHI, MA'AM!
WELL NOW.

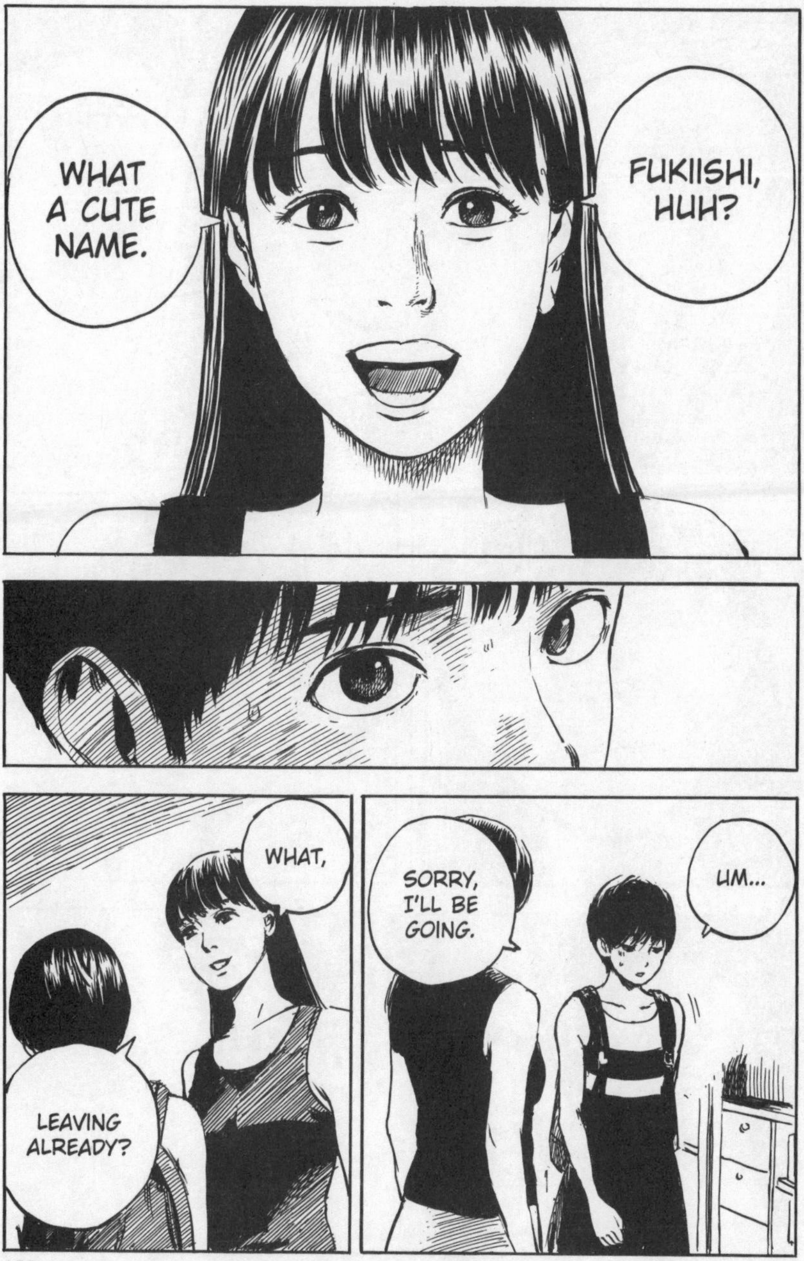
FUKIISHI, HUH?
WHAT A CUTE NAME.
UM...
SORRY, I'LL BE GOING.
WHAT,
LEAVING ALREADY?

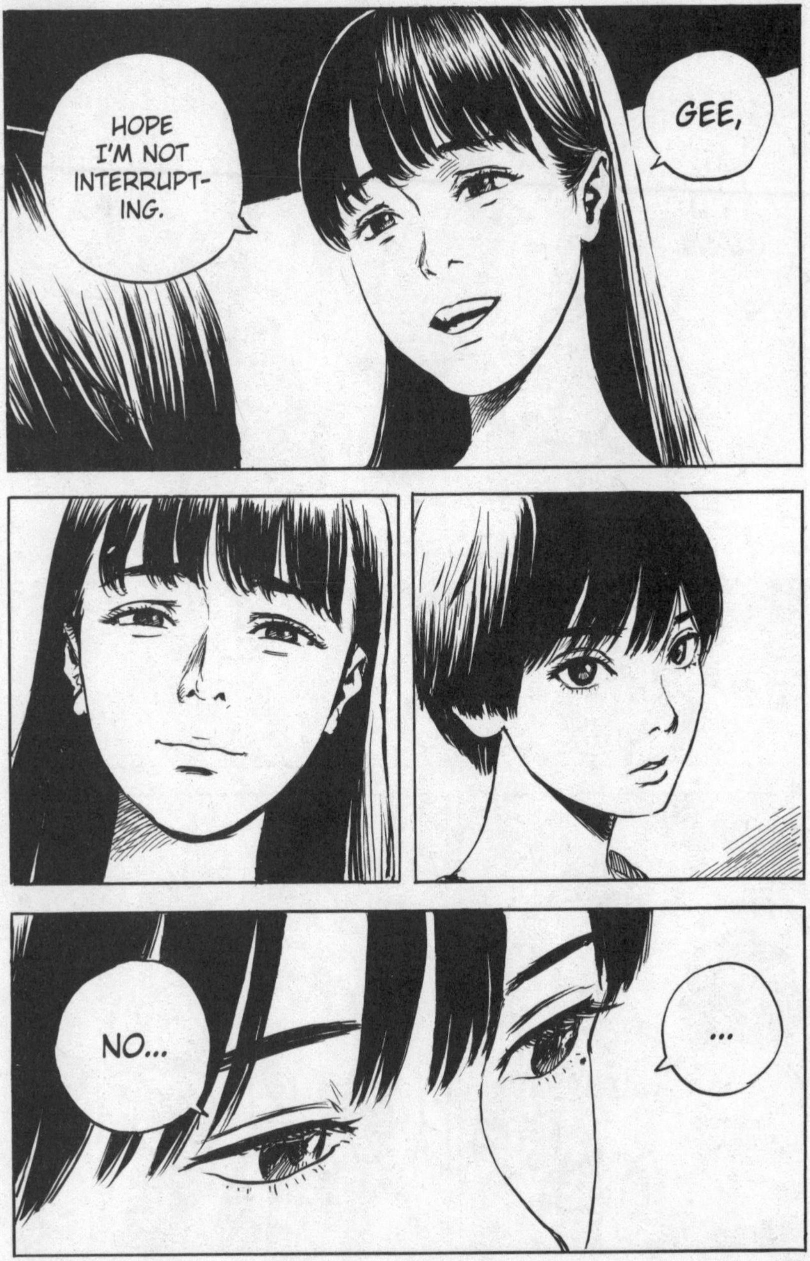
GEE,
HOPE I'M NOT INTERRUPT-ING.
...
NO...

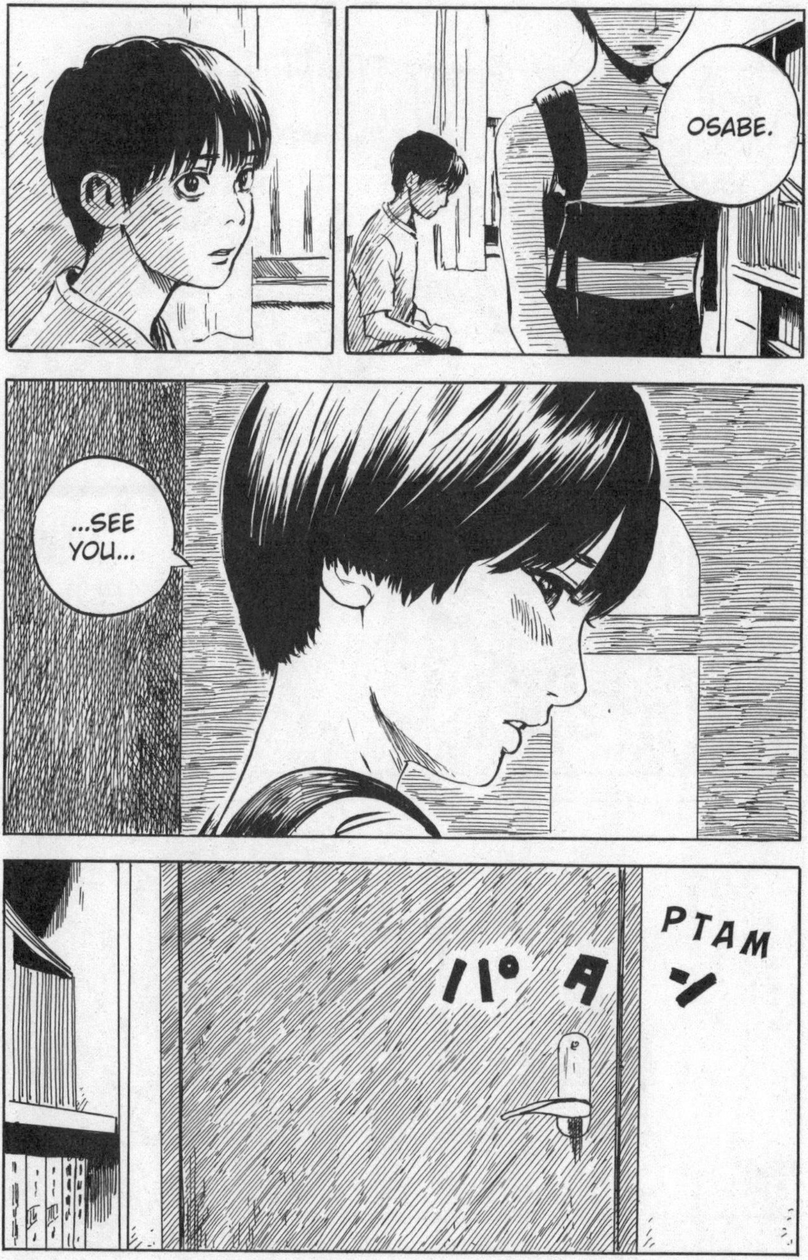
OSABE.
...SEE YOU...
PTAM
パタン

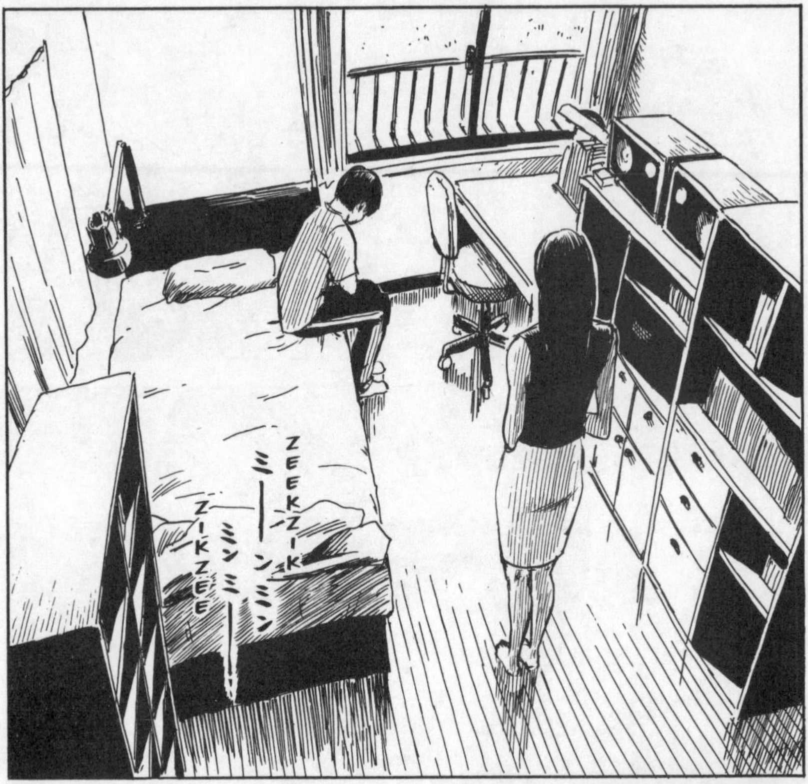
ZEEKZIK
ミーンミン
ミンミー
ZIKZEE

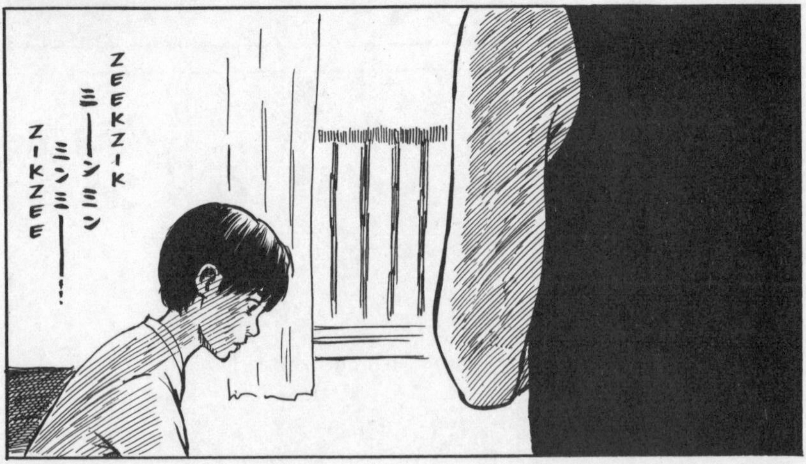
ZEEKZIK
ミーンミン
ミンミー—!!
ZIKZEE

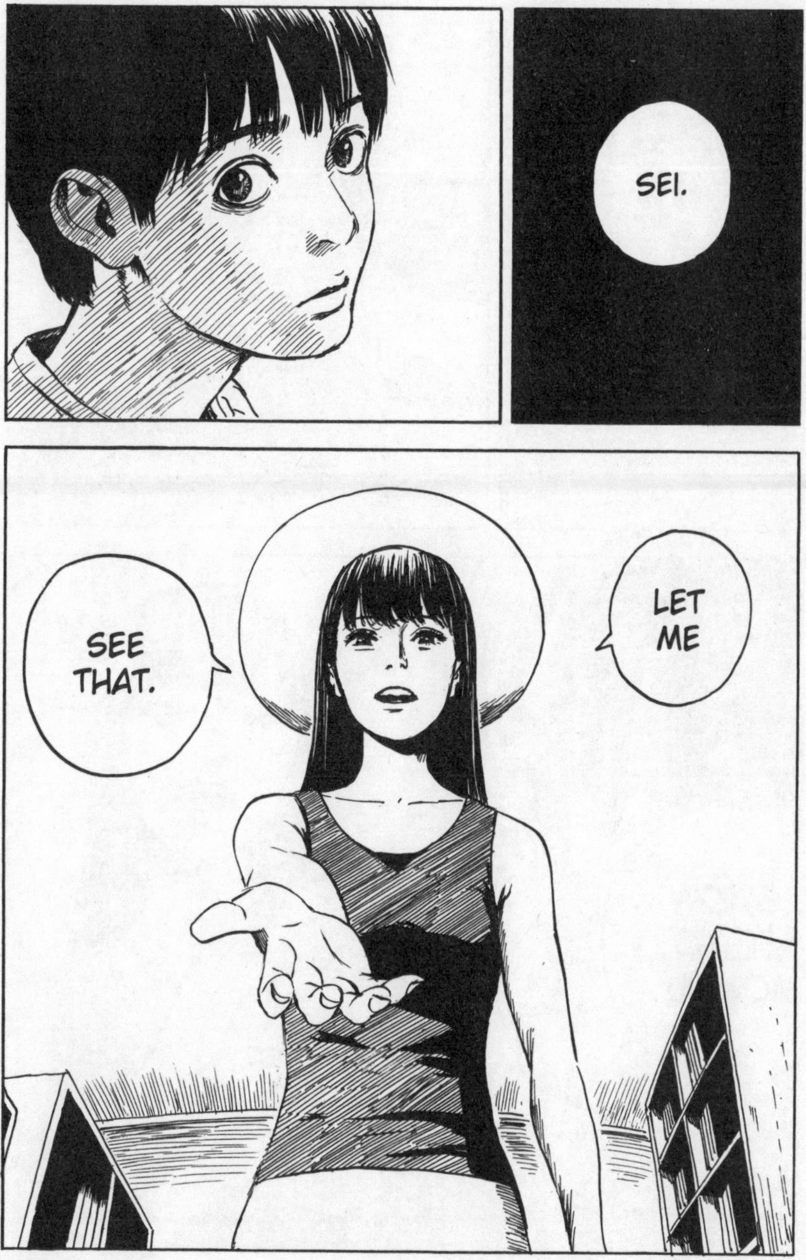
SEI.
LET ME
SEE THAT.

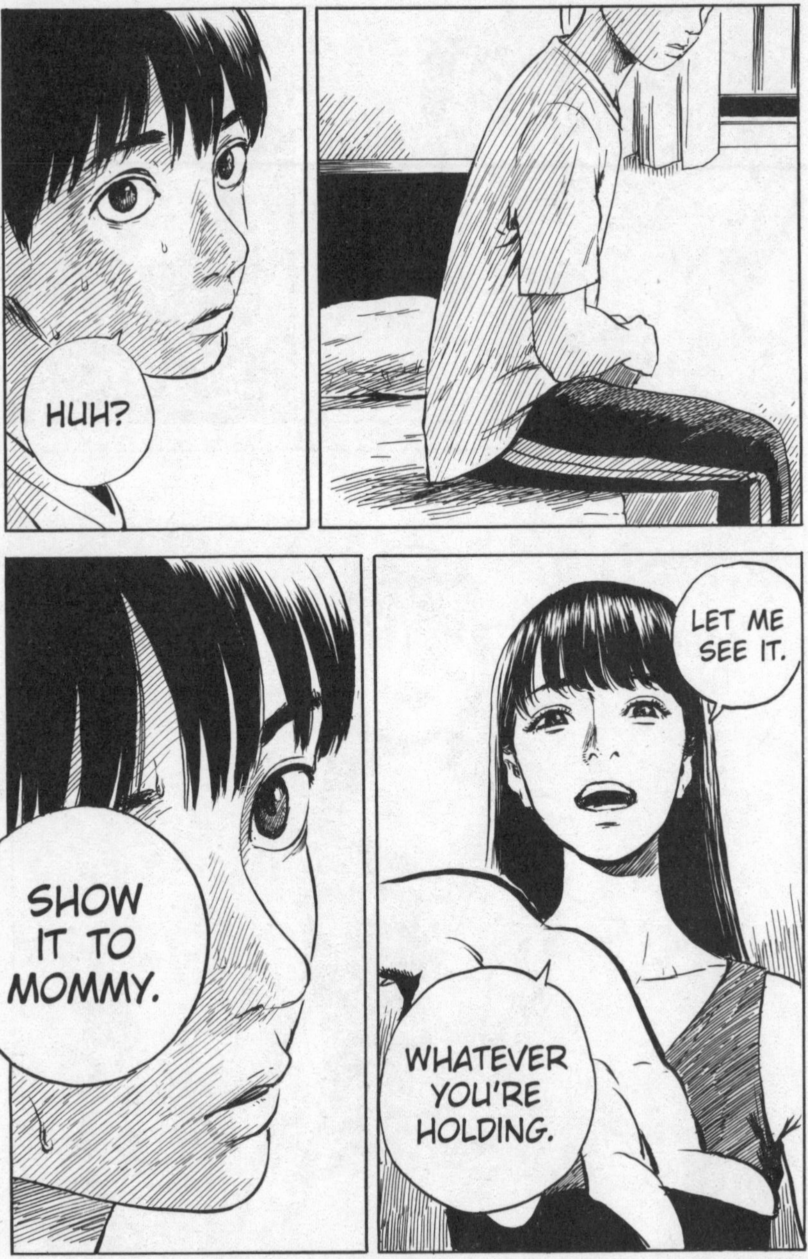
HUH?
LET ME SEE IT.
WHATEVER YOU'RE HOLDING.
SHOW IT TO MOMMY.

NOW.

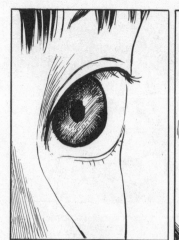

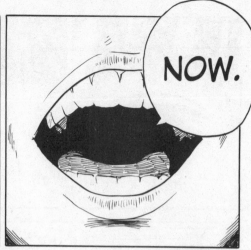

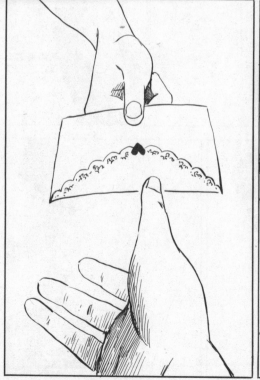

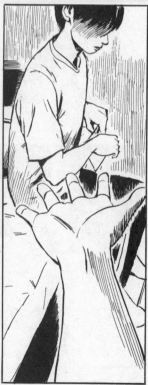

RIP
カサ
FSHK

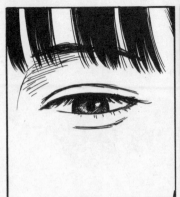

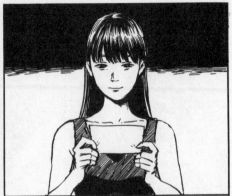

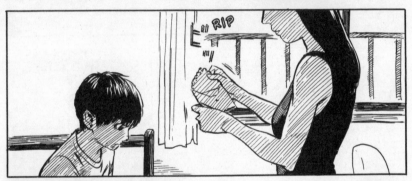

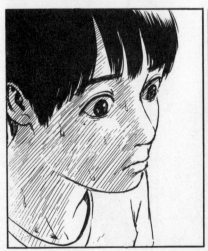

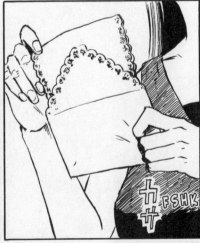

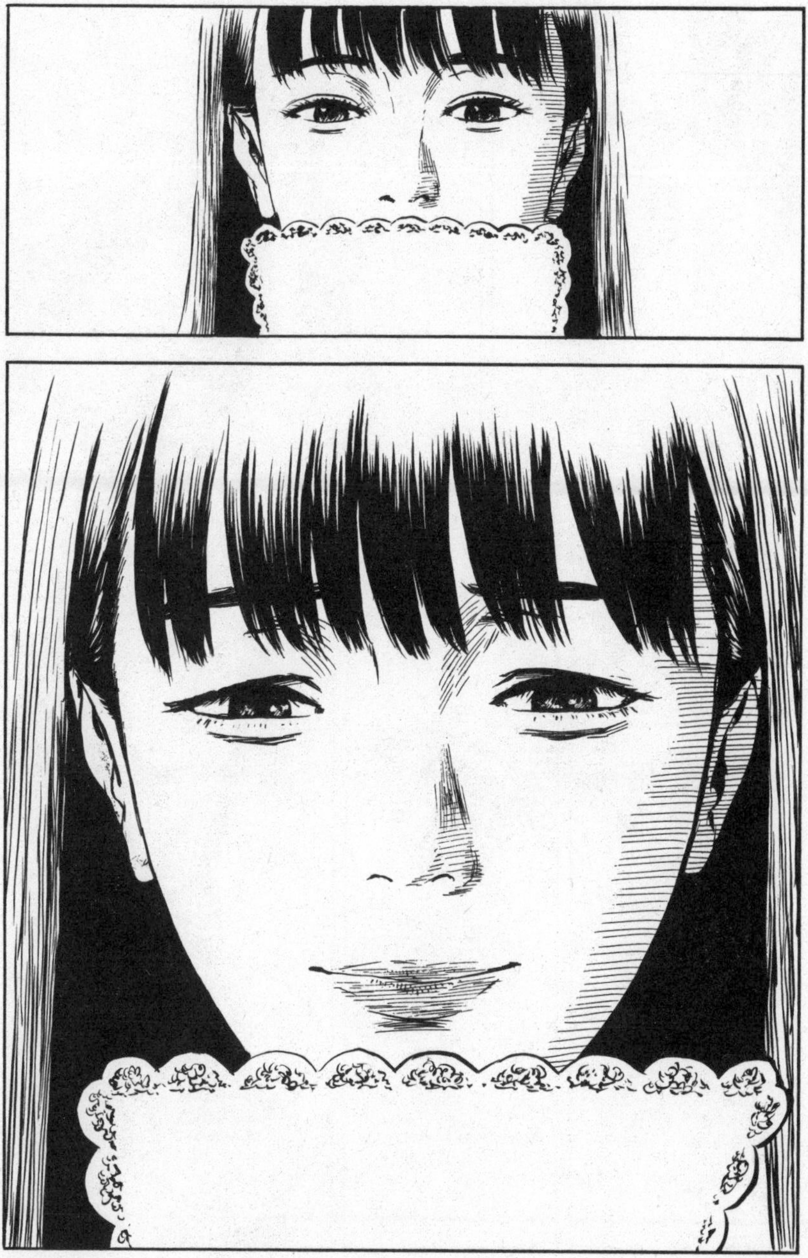

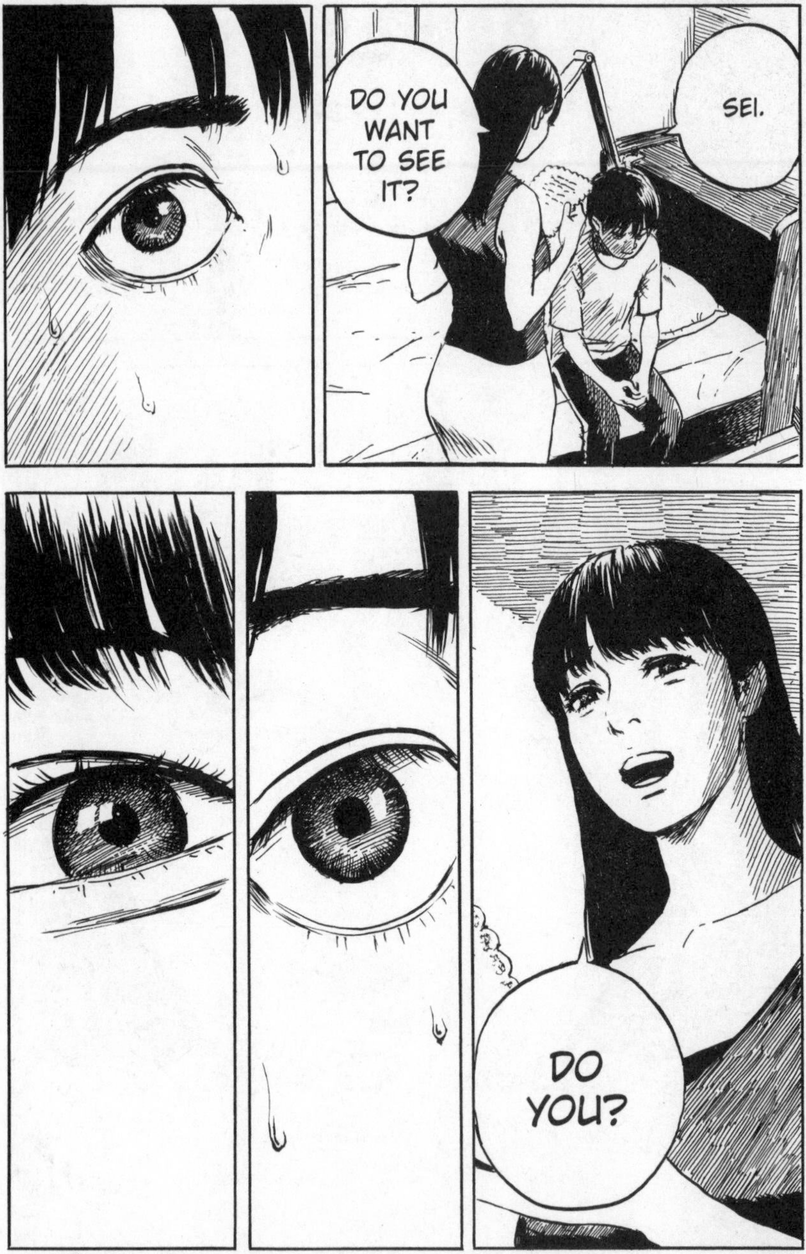
SEI.
DO YOU WANT TO SEE IT?
DO YOU?

HERE.
ぎし
CREAK

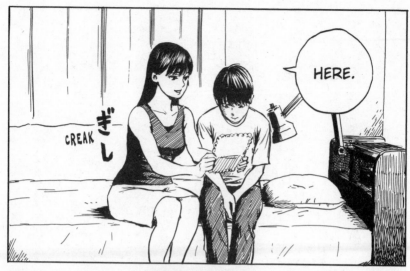

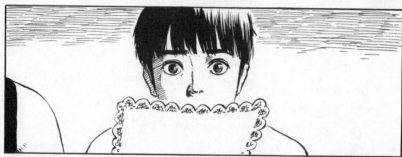

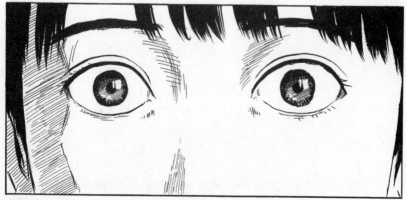

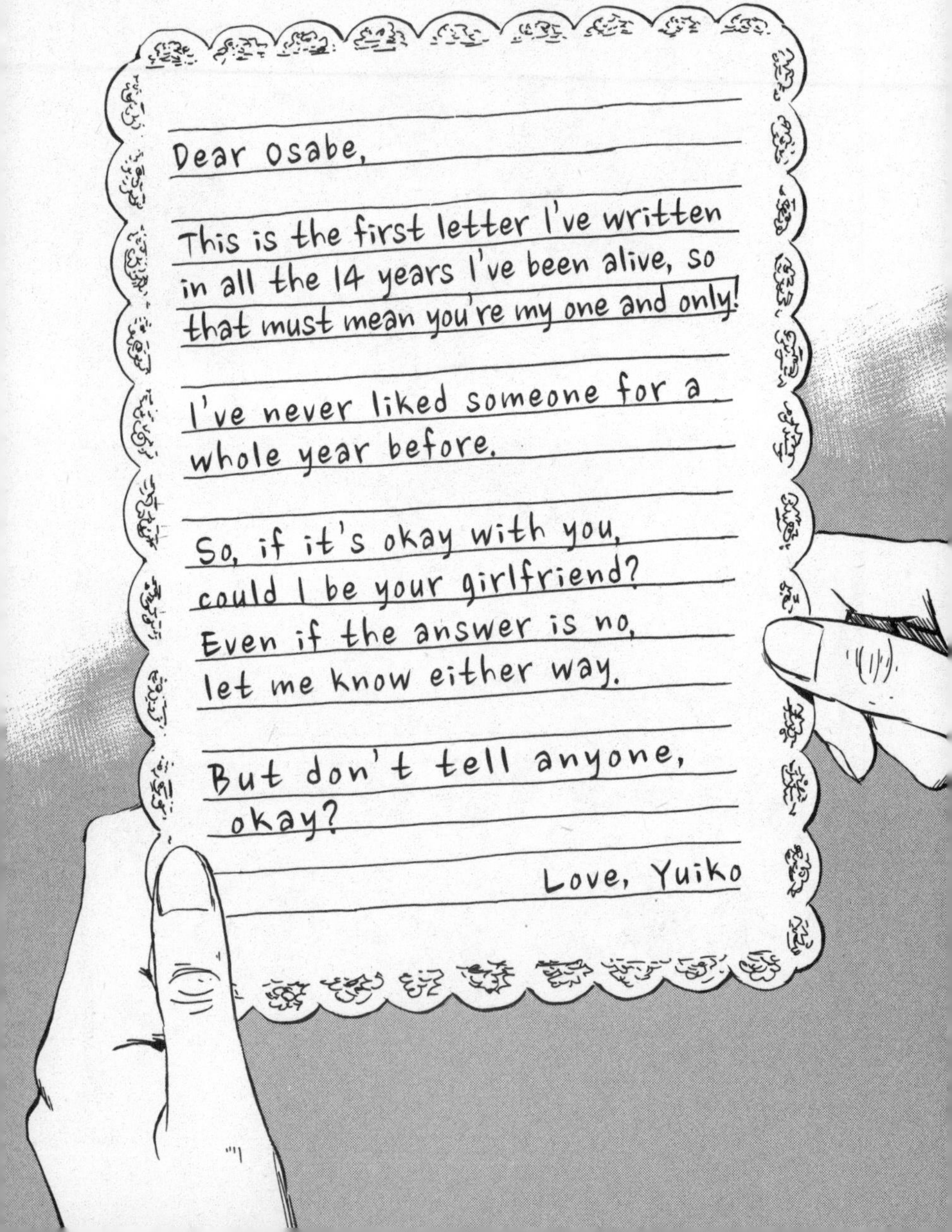
Dear Osabe,

This is the first letter I've written in all the 14 years I've been alive, so that must mean you're my one and only!

I've never liked someone for a whole year before.

So, if it's okay with you, could I be your girlfriend? Even if the answer is no, let me know either way.

But don't tell anyone, okay?

Love, Yuiko

ポタ PLIP

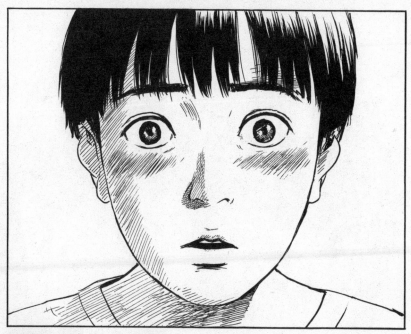

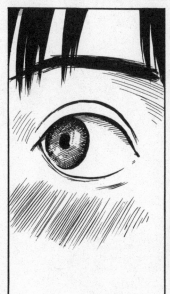

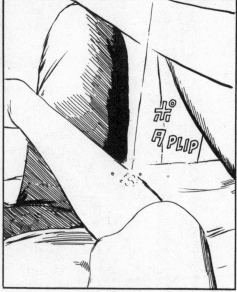

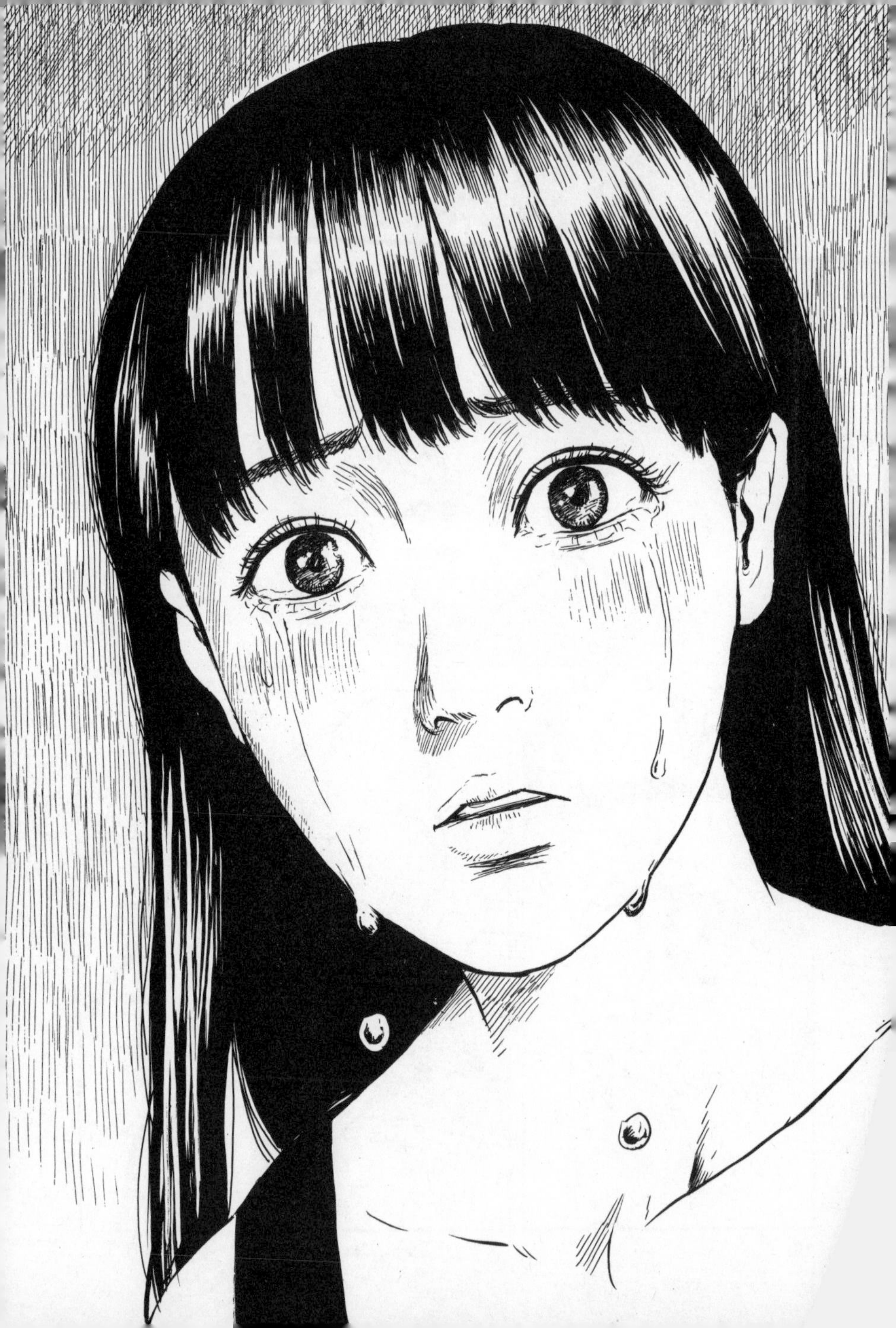

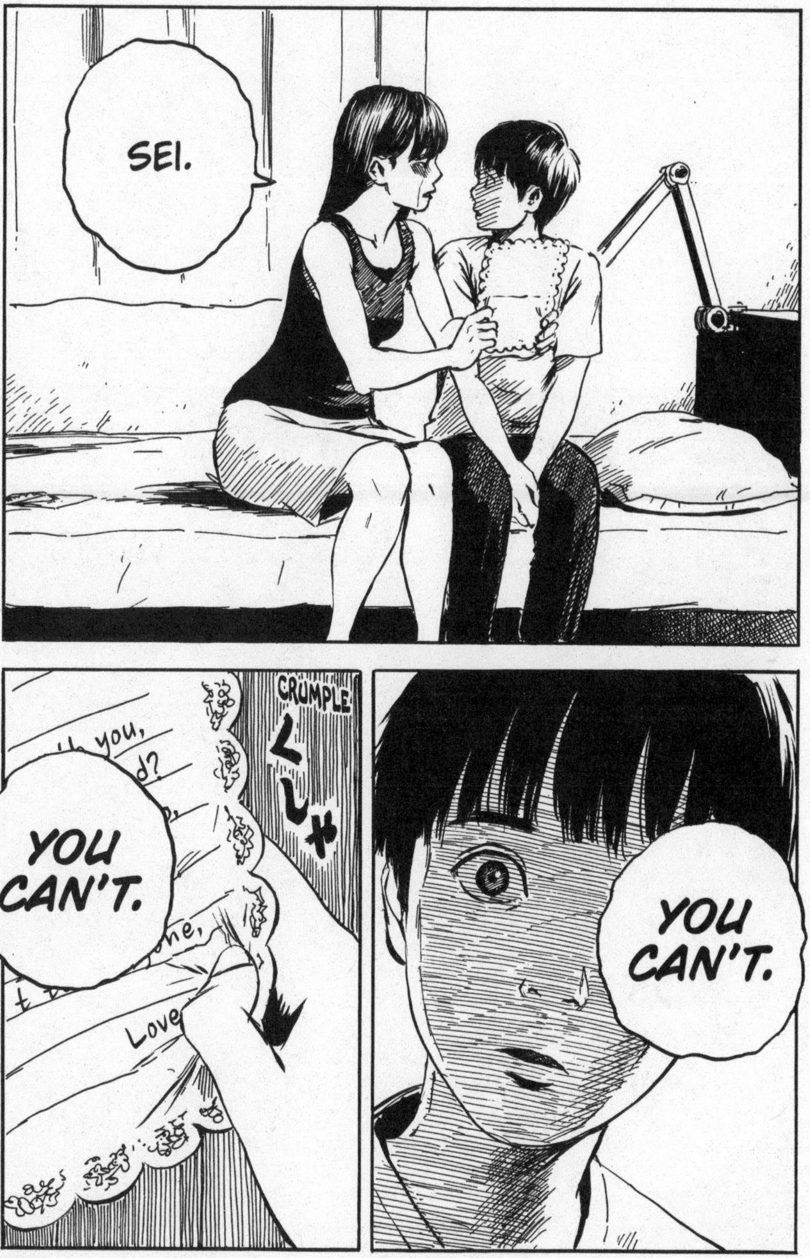
SEI.
YOU CAN'T.
CRUMPLE
くしゃ
YOU CAN'T.

NO.
I WON'T.
I WON'T ACCEPT IT!

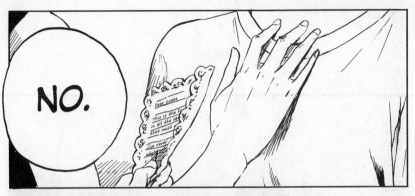

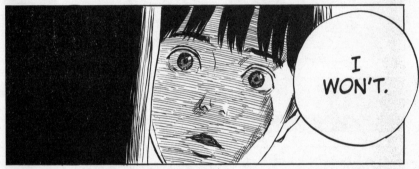

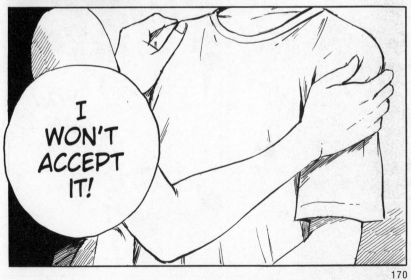

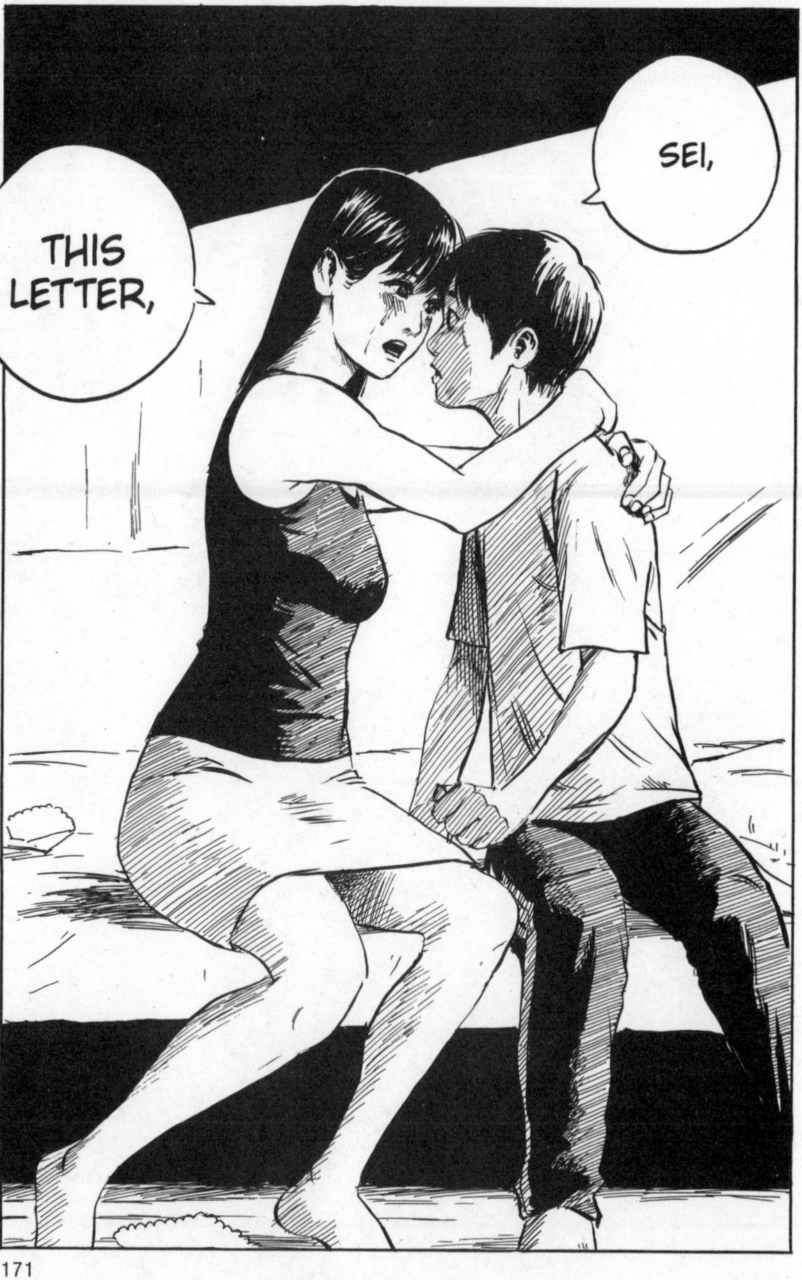
SEI,
THIS LETTER,

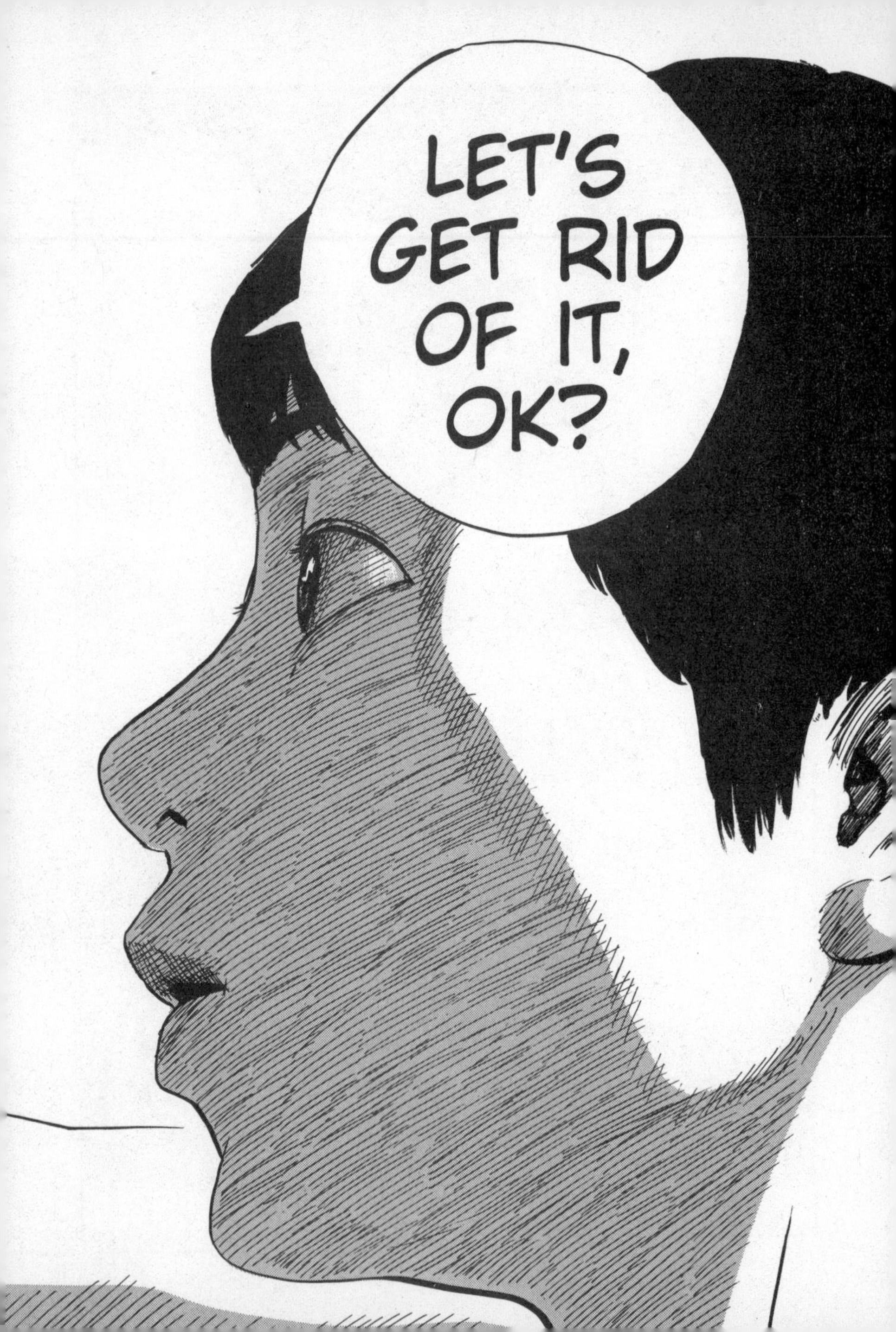
LET'S GET RID OF IT, OK?

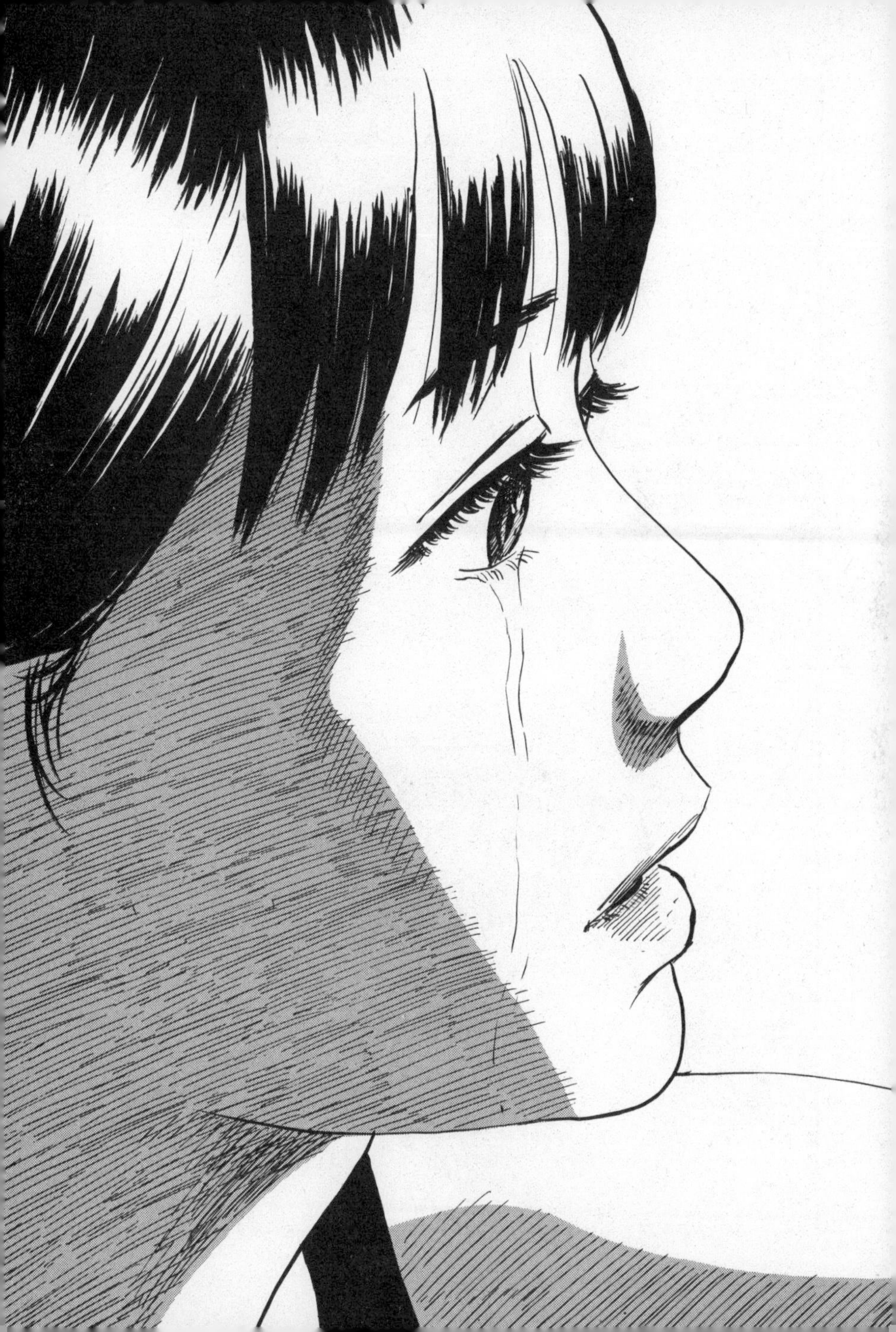

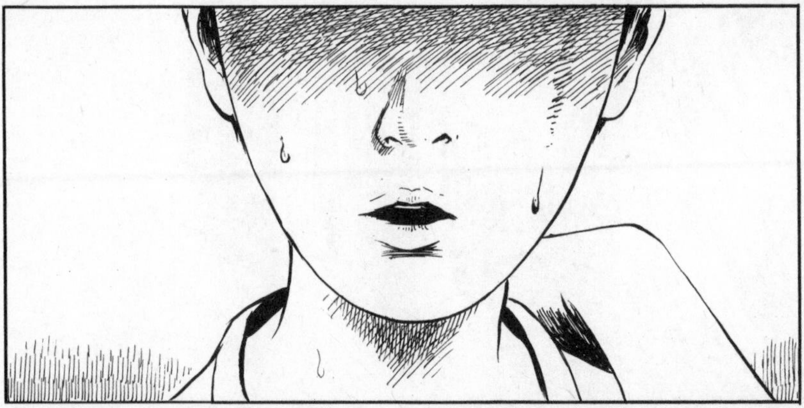
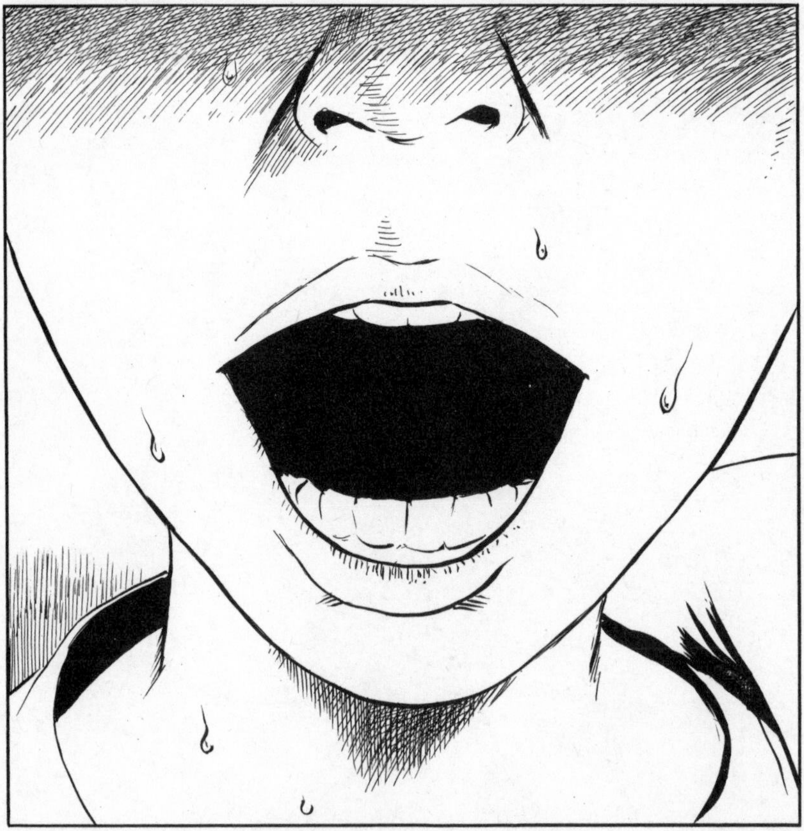

CHAPTER 15 Salvation

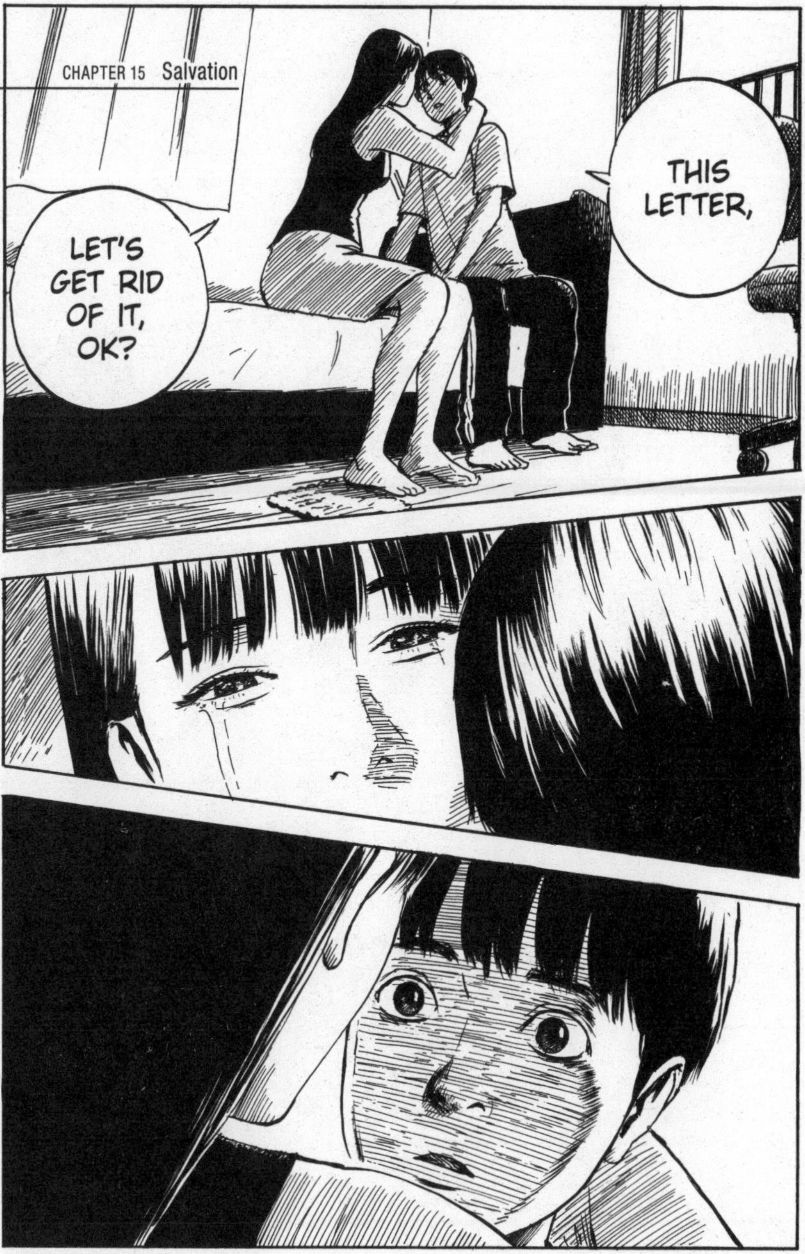
THIS LETTER,
LET'S GET RID OF IT, OK?

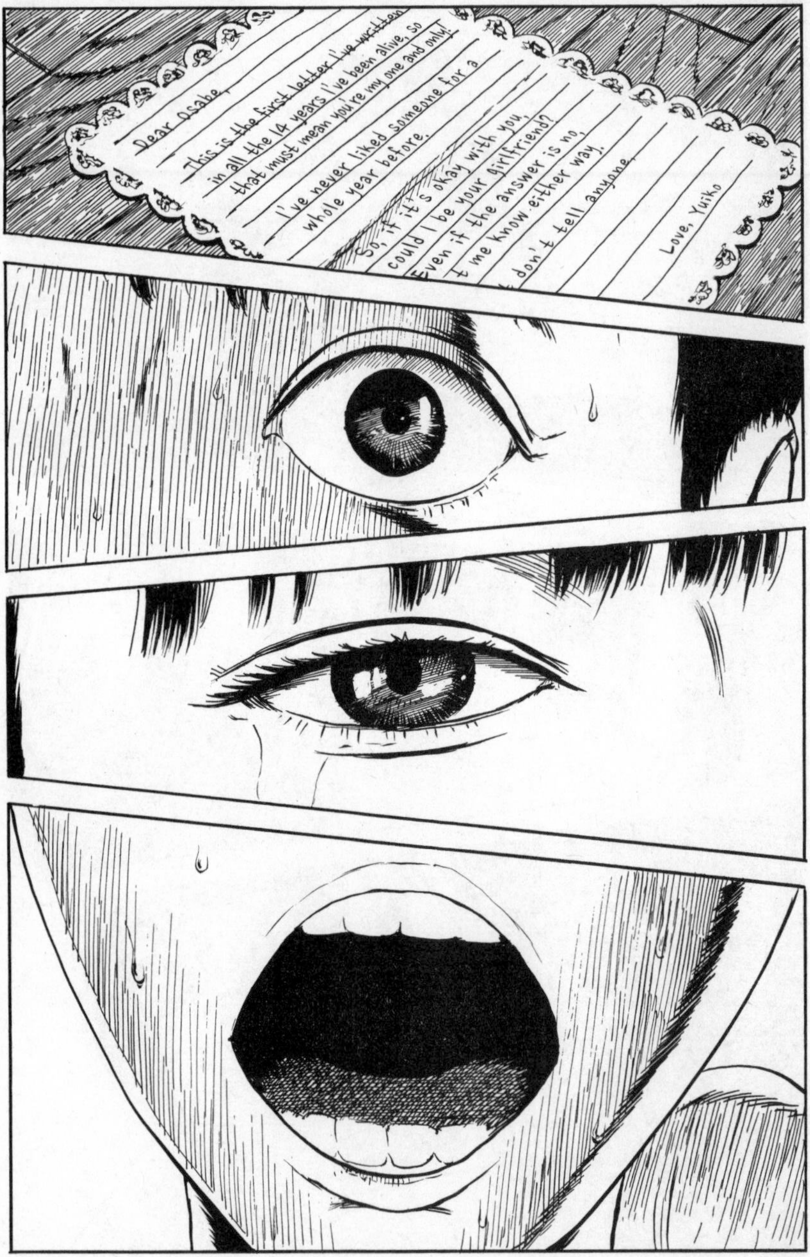

Dear Osabe,
This is the first letter I've written
in all the 14 years I've been alive, so
that must mean you're my one and only!
I've never liked someone for a
whole year before.
So, if it's okay with you,
could I be your girlfriend?
Even if the answer is no,
t me know either way.
don't tell anyone,
Love, Yuiko

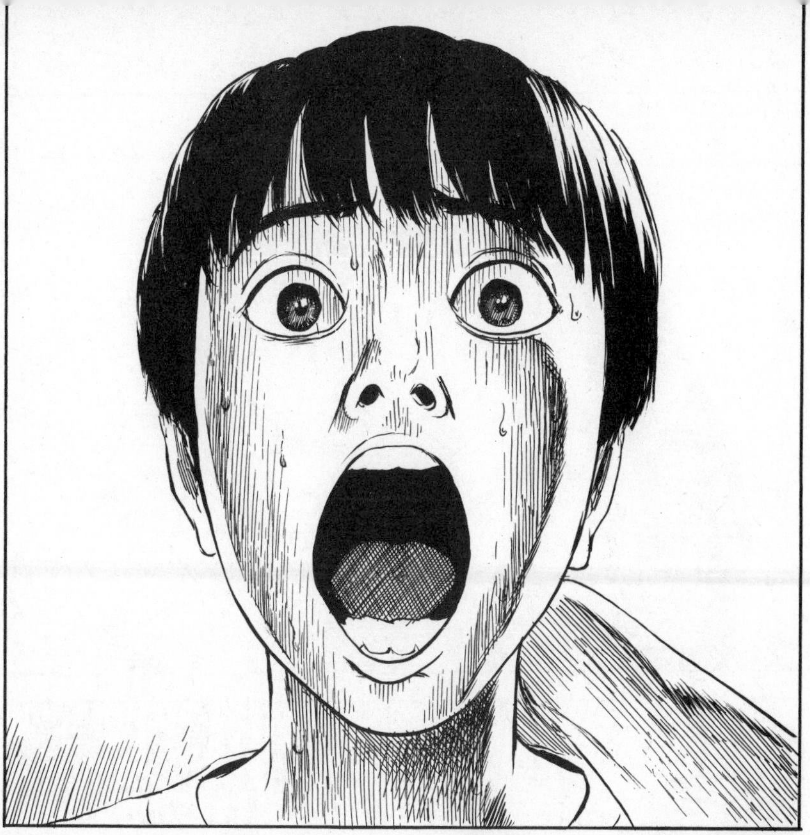

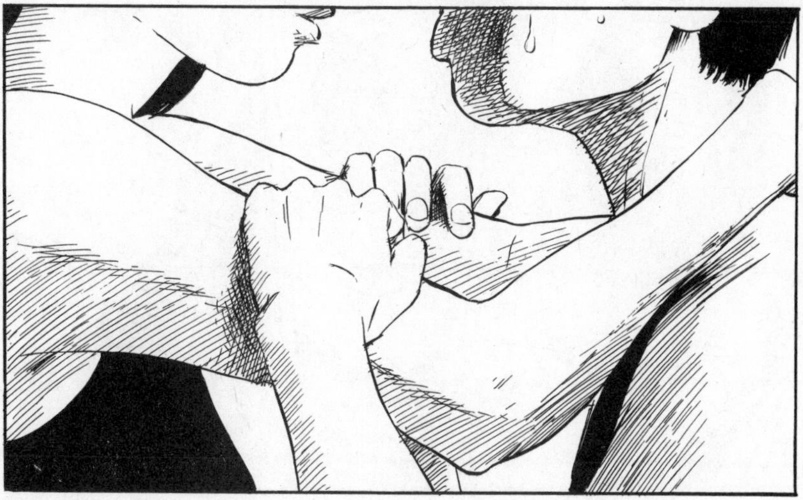

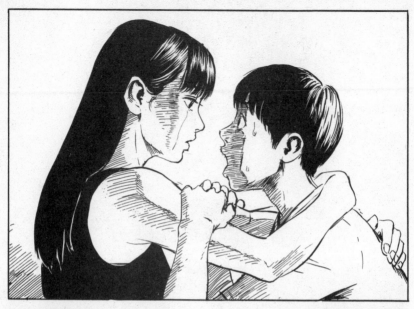

178

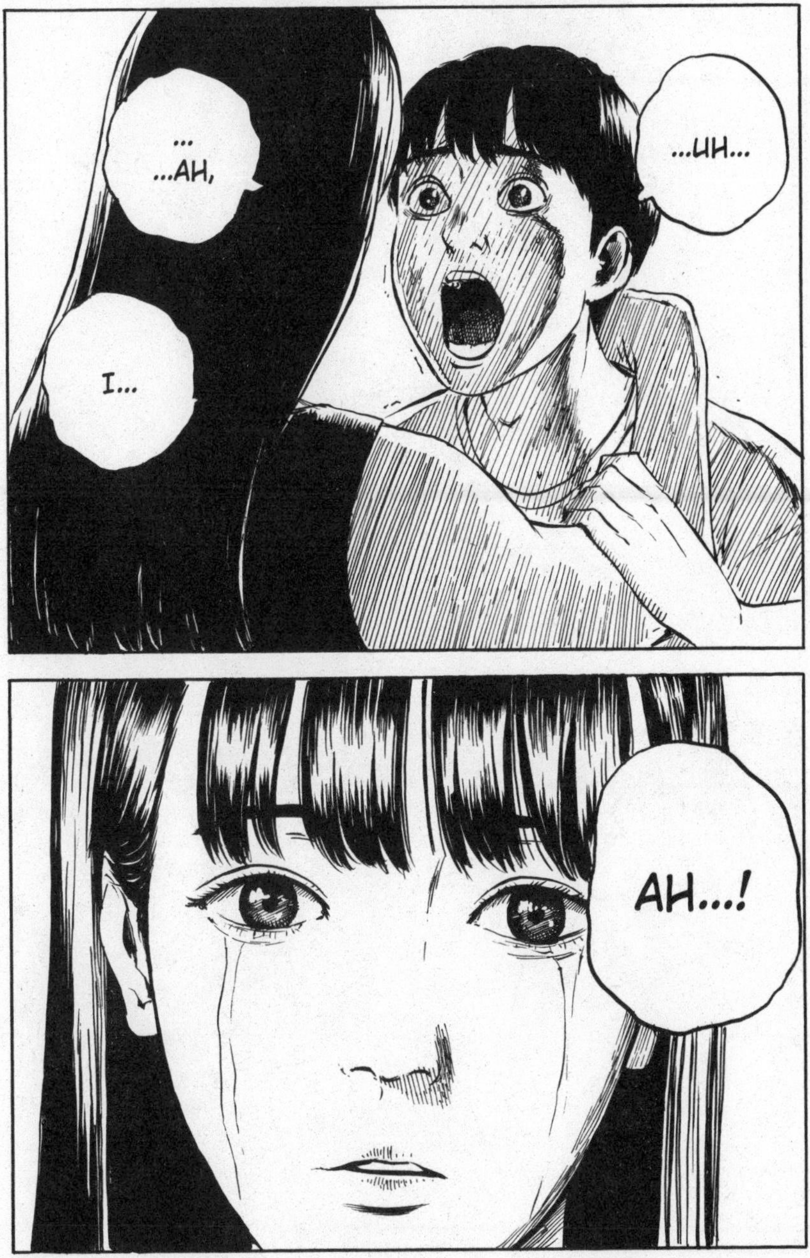
...UH...
... ...AH,
I...
AH...!

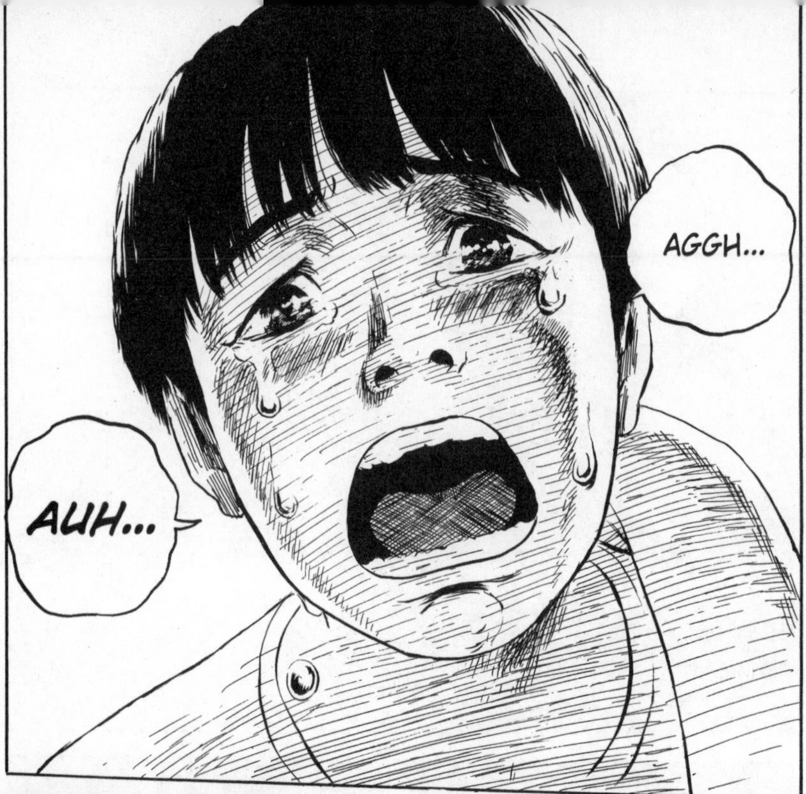
AGGH...
AUH...

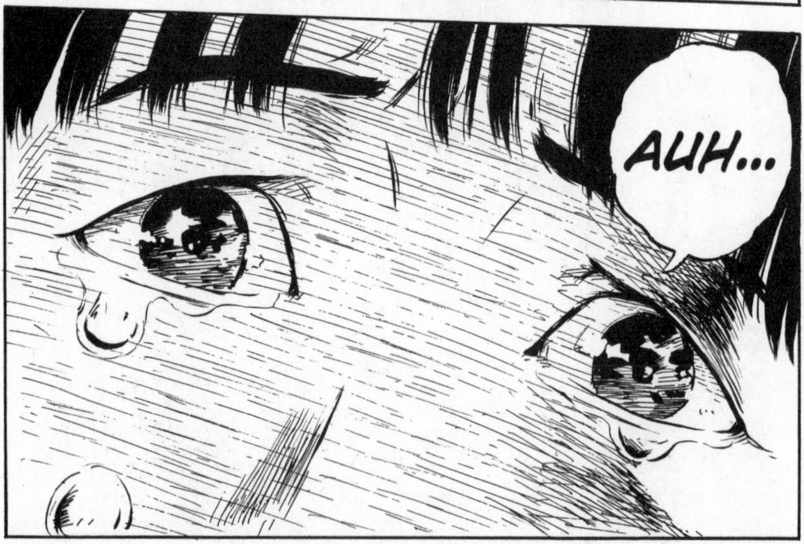
AUH...

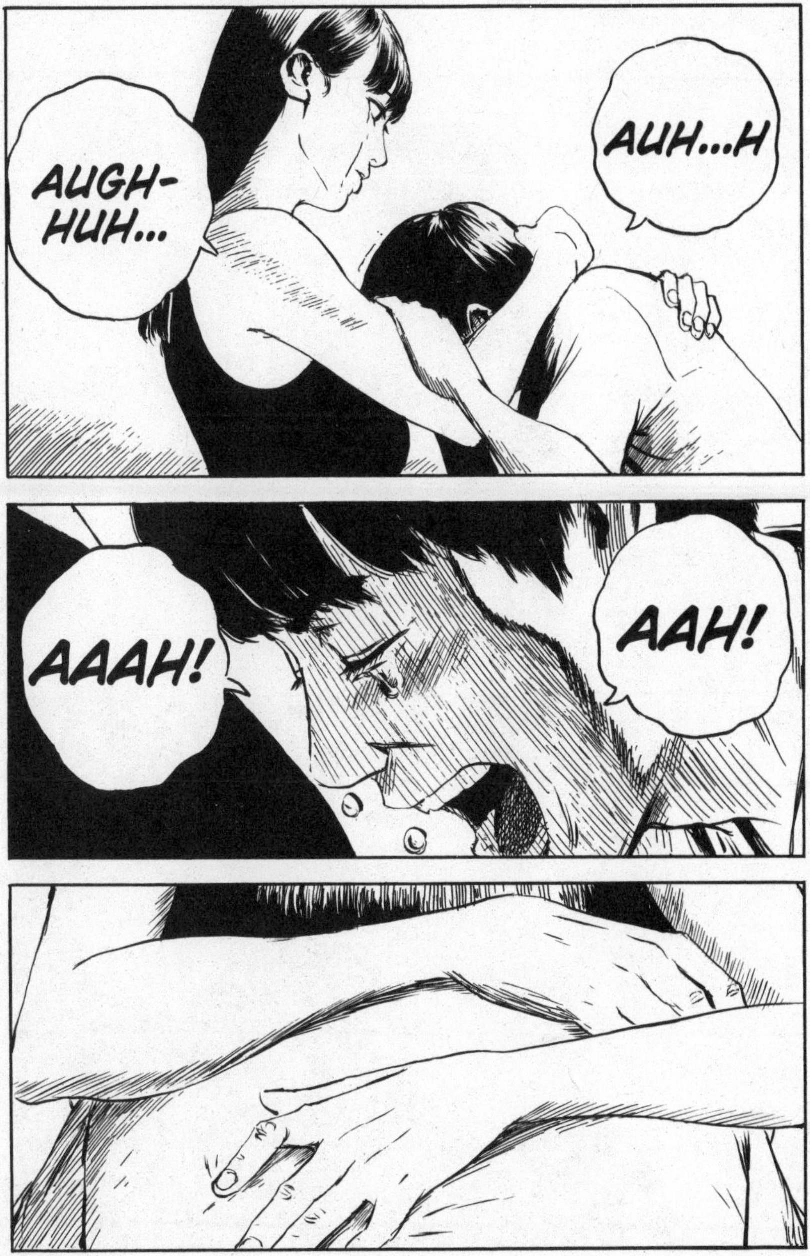
AUH...H
AUGH-HUH...
AAH!
AAAH!

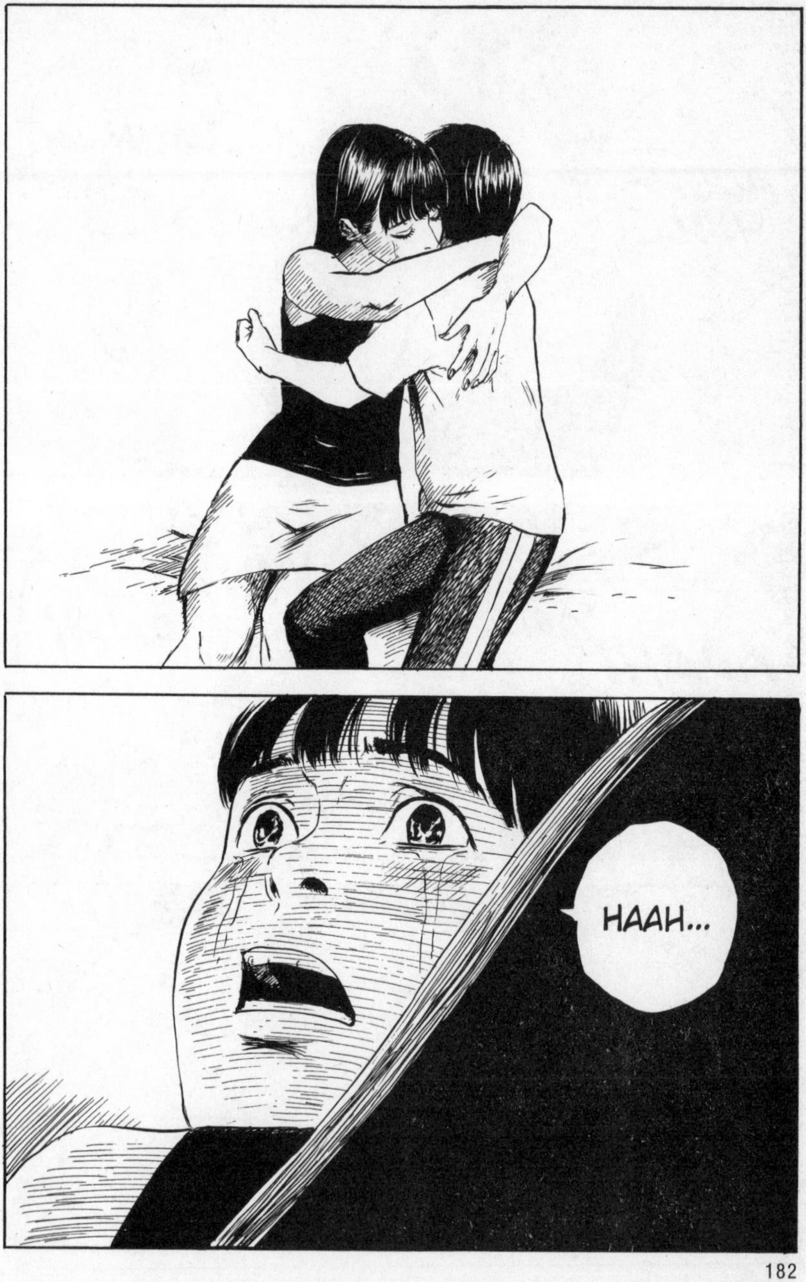
HAAH...

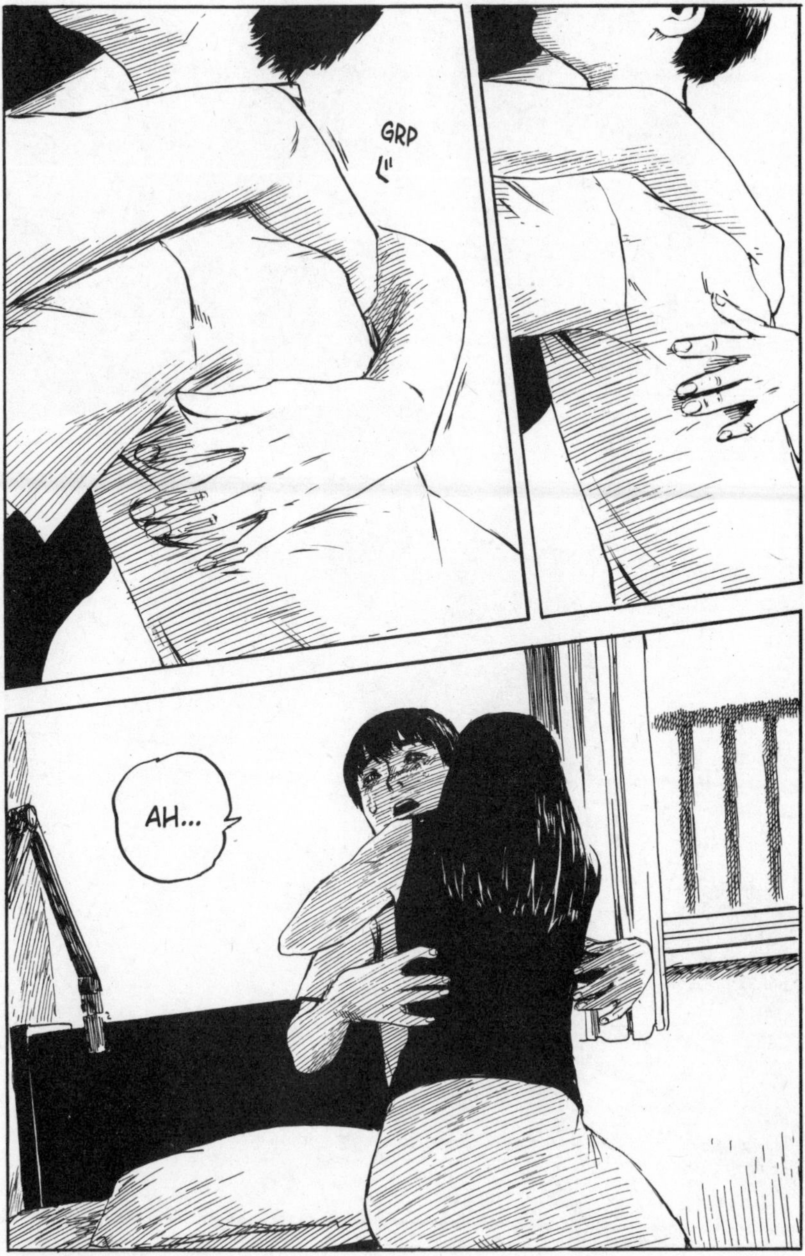
GRP
じ
AH...

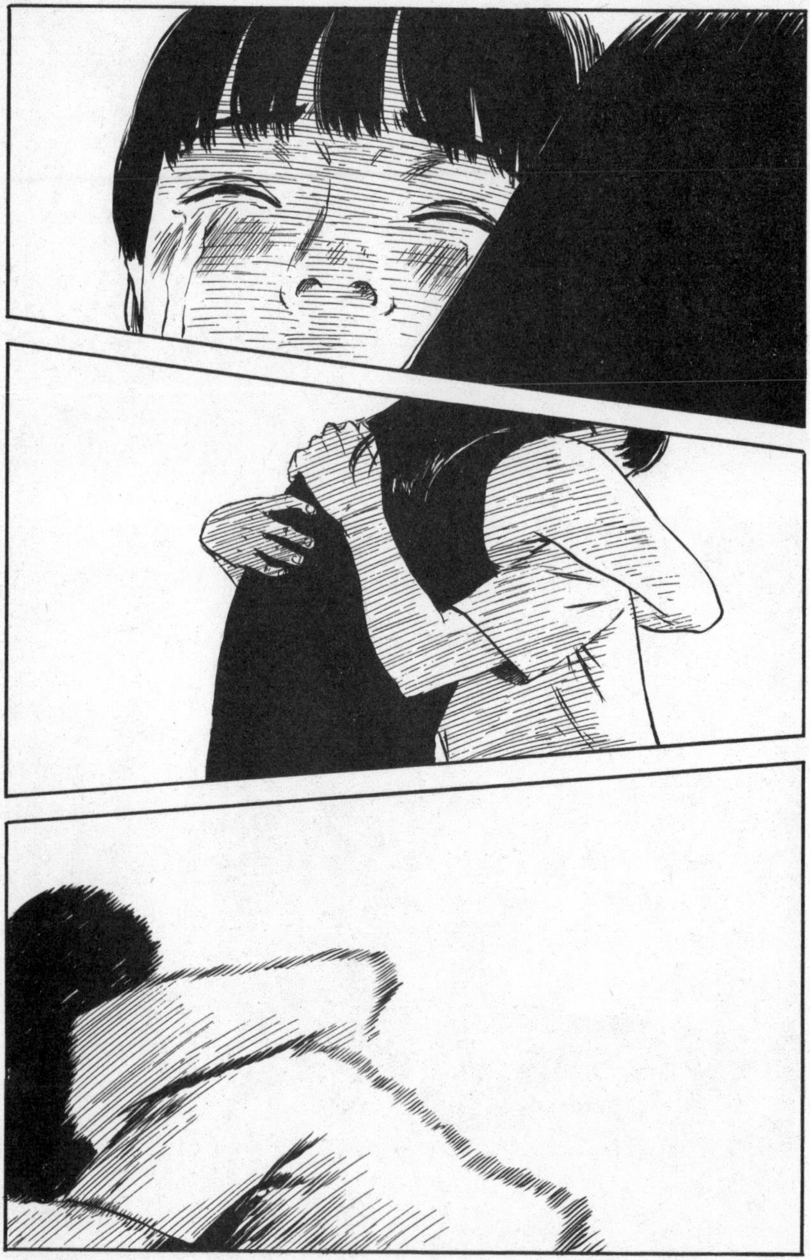

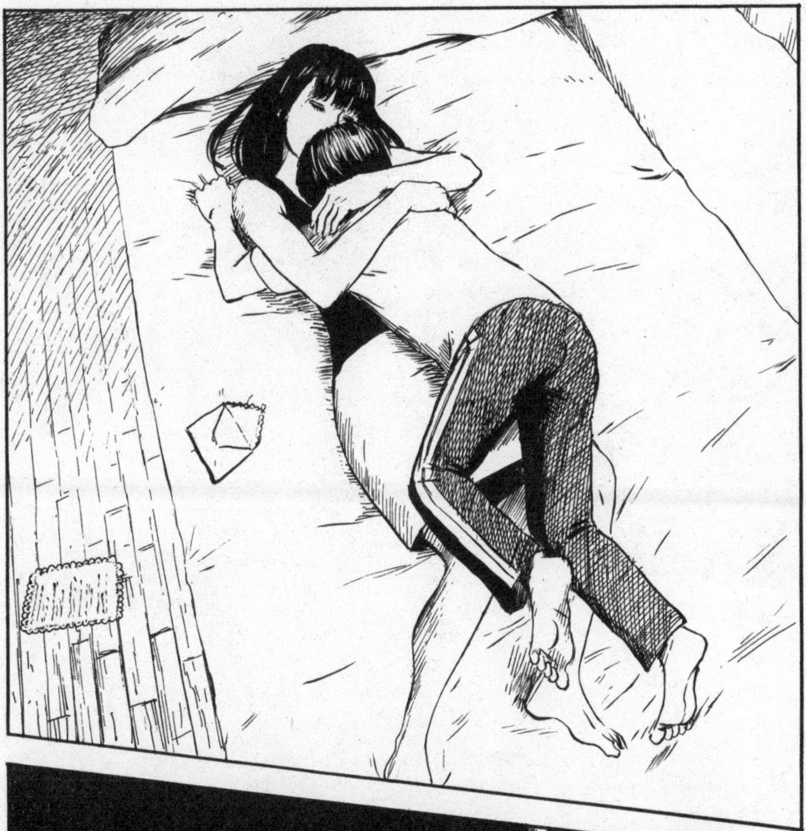
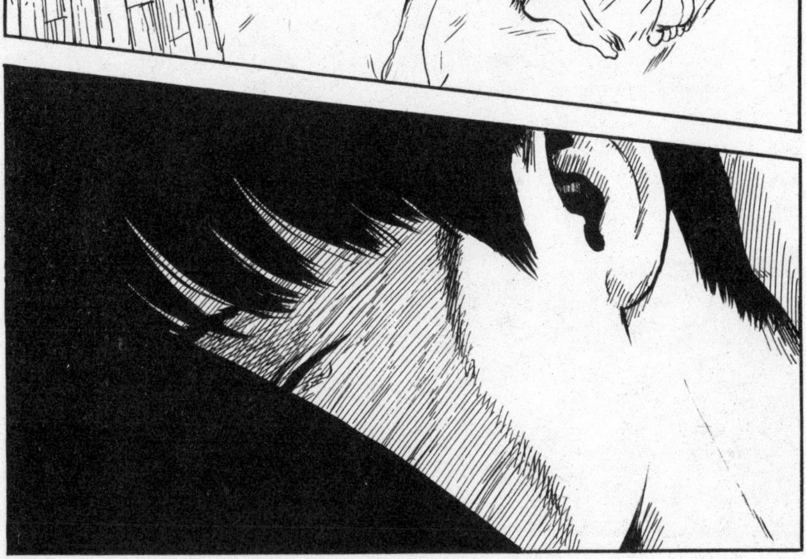

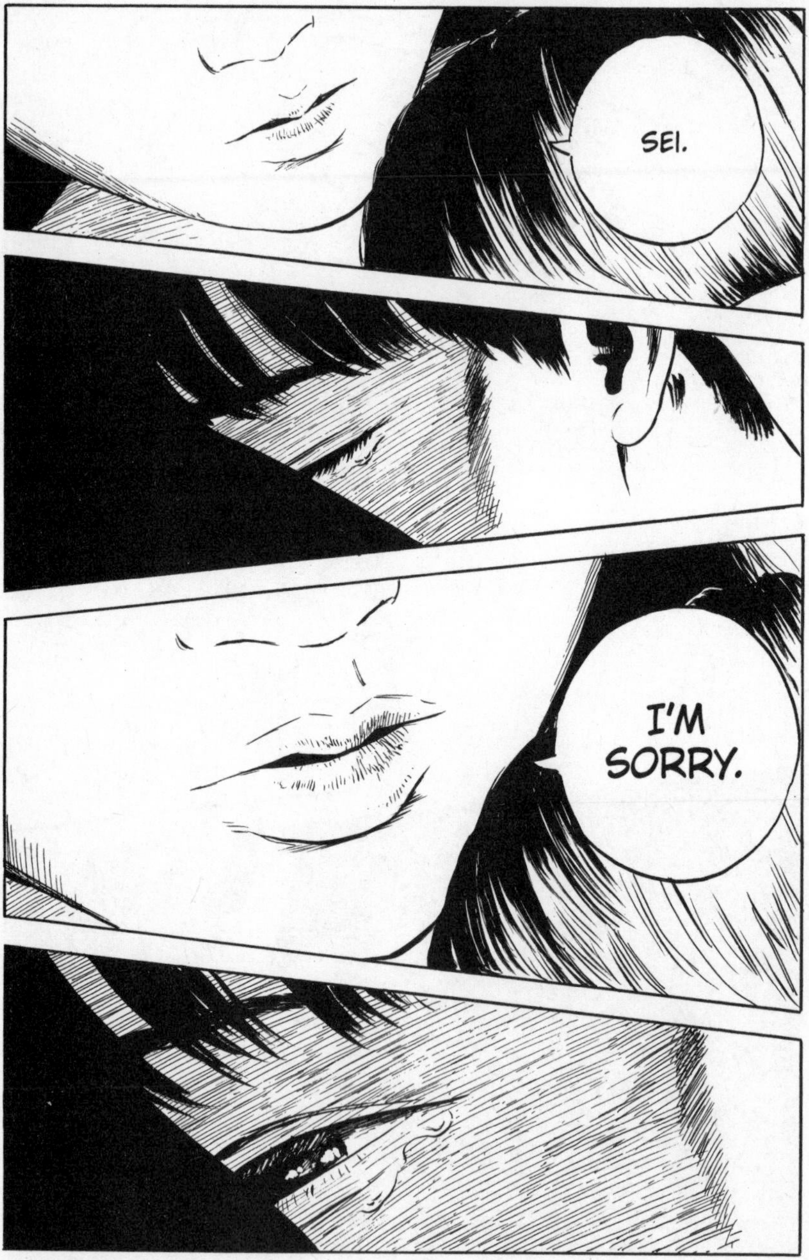
SEI.
I'M SORRY.

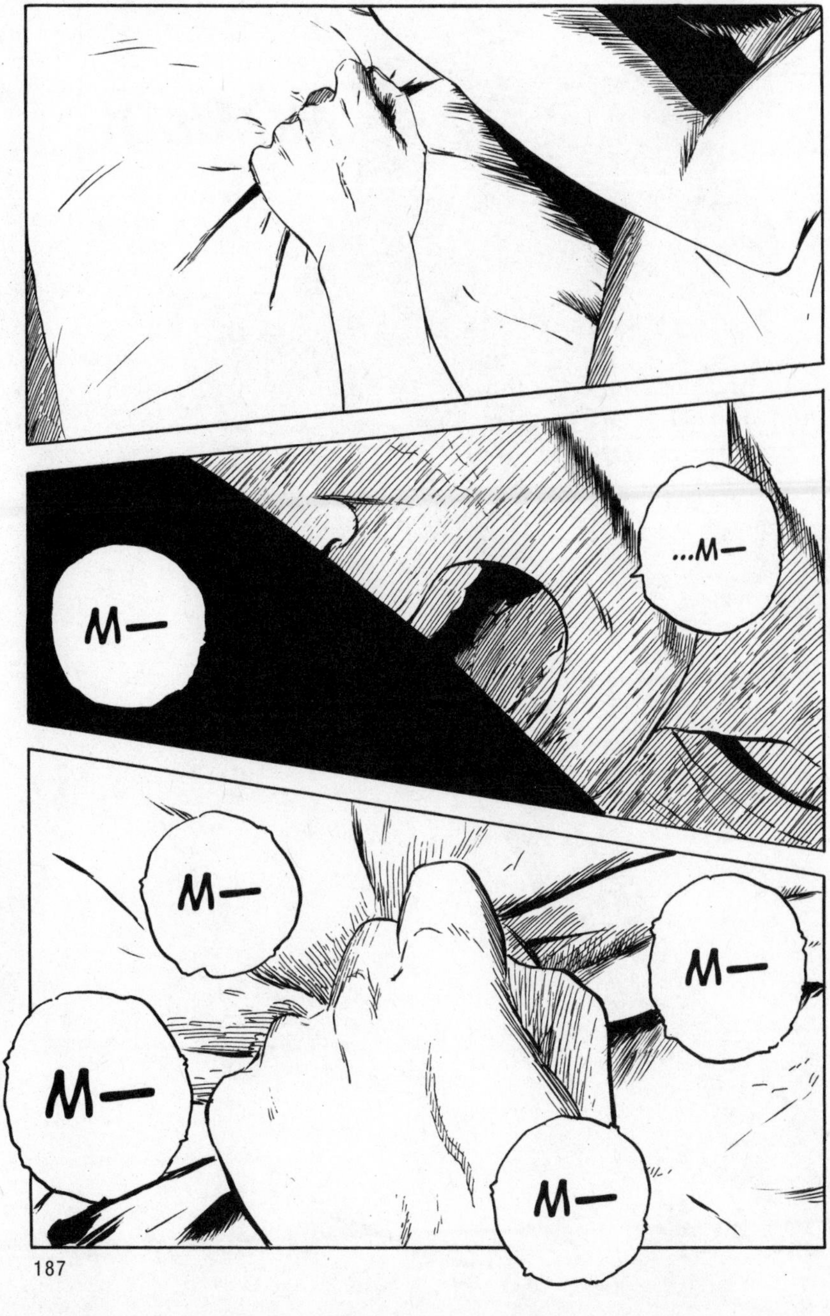
...M—
M—
M—
M—
M—
M—

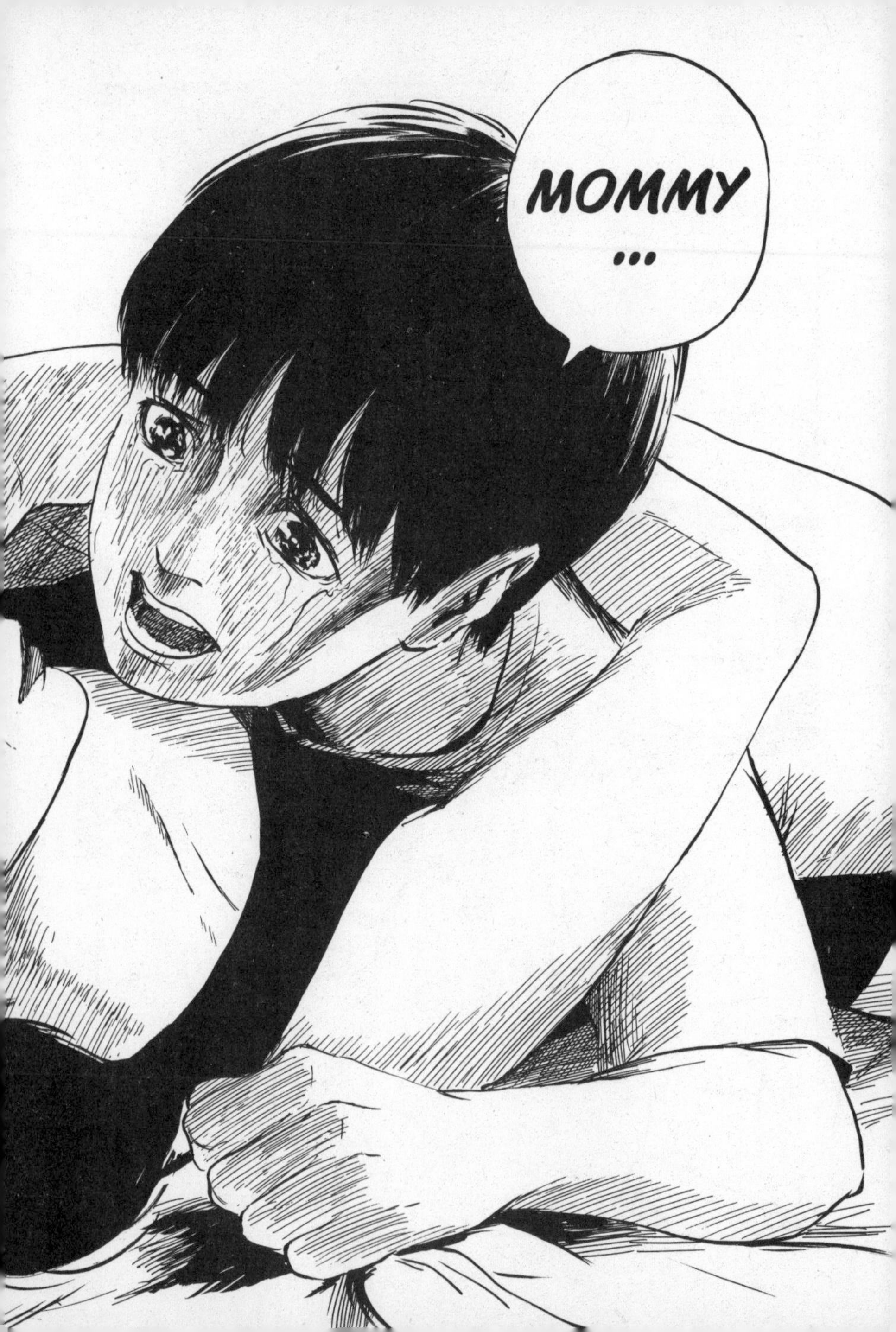
MOMMY ...

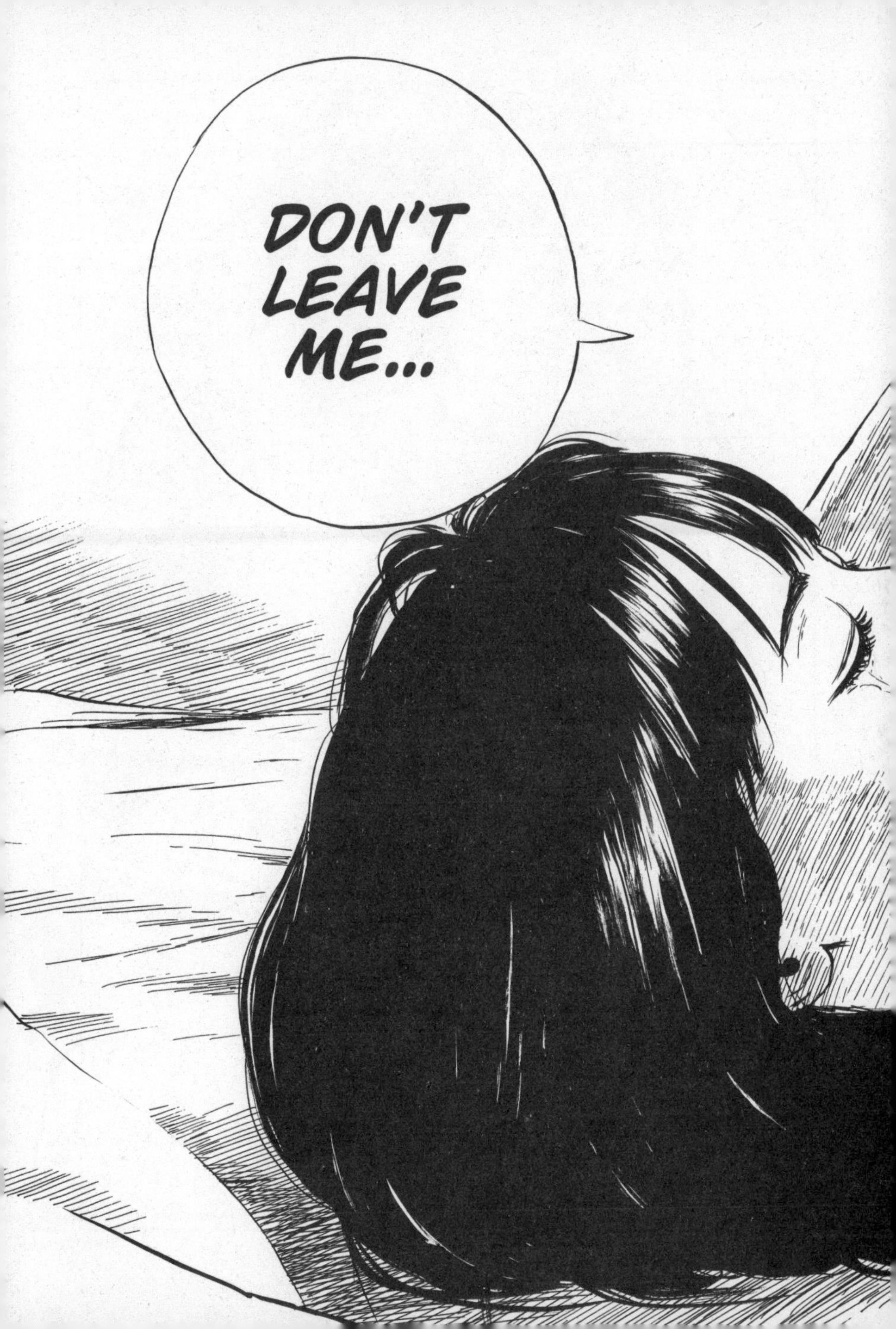
DON'T LEAVE ME...

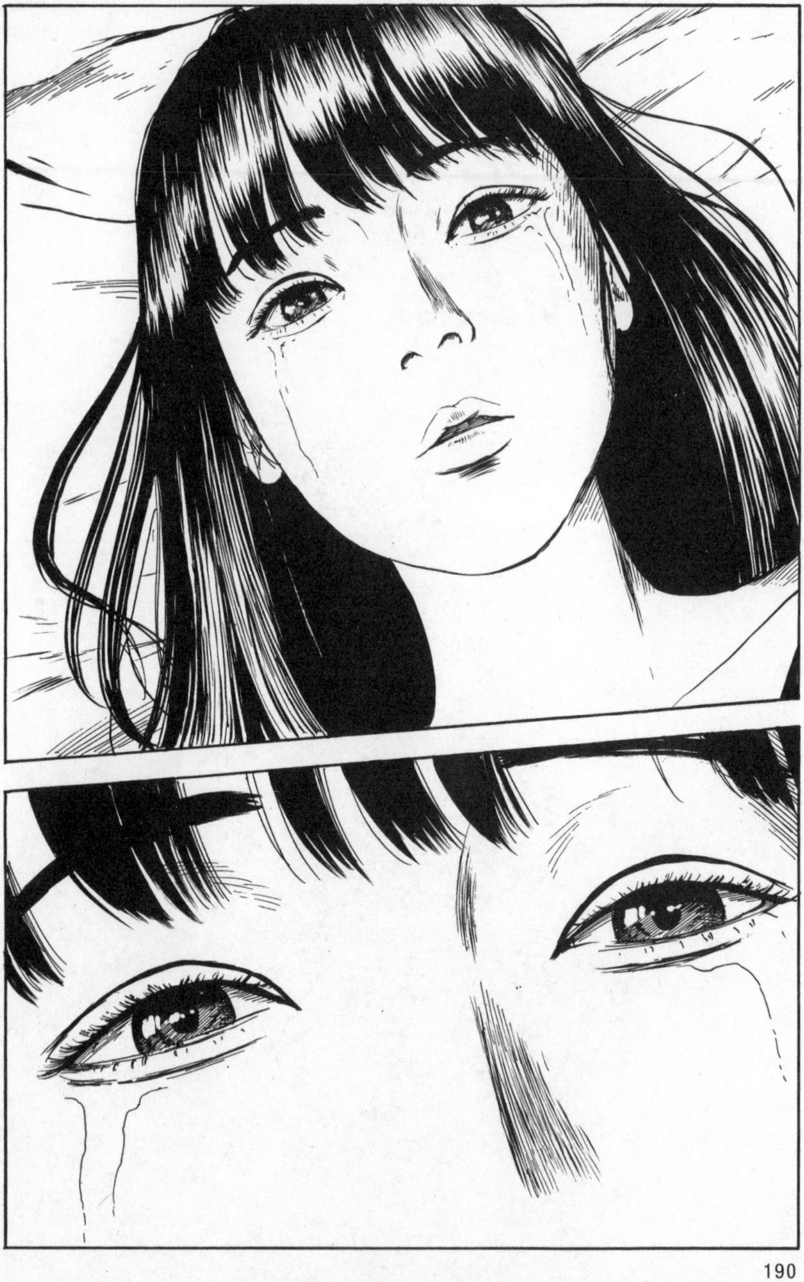

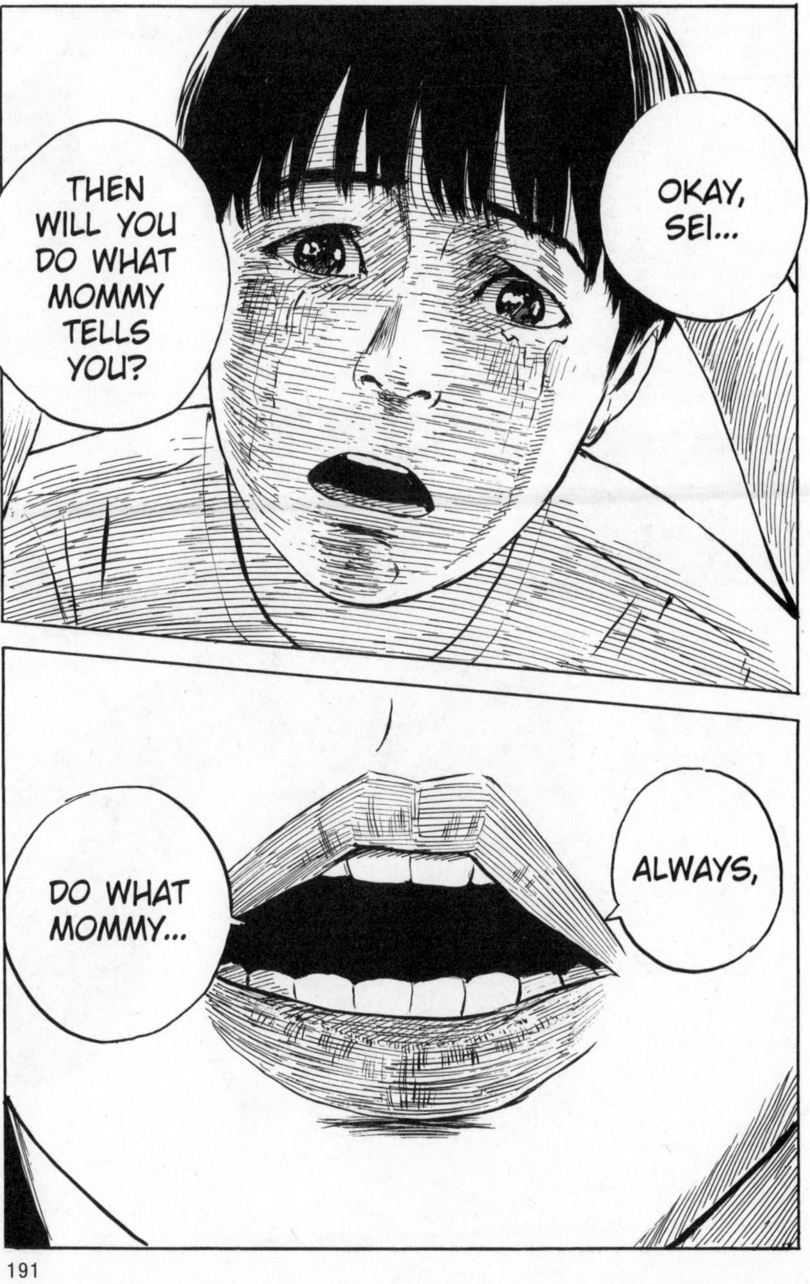
OKAY, SEI...
THEN WILL YOU DO WHAT MOMMY TELLS YOU?
ALWAYS,
DO WHAT MOMMY...

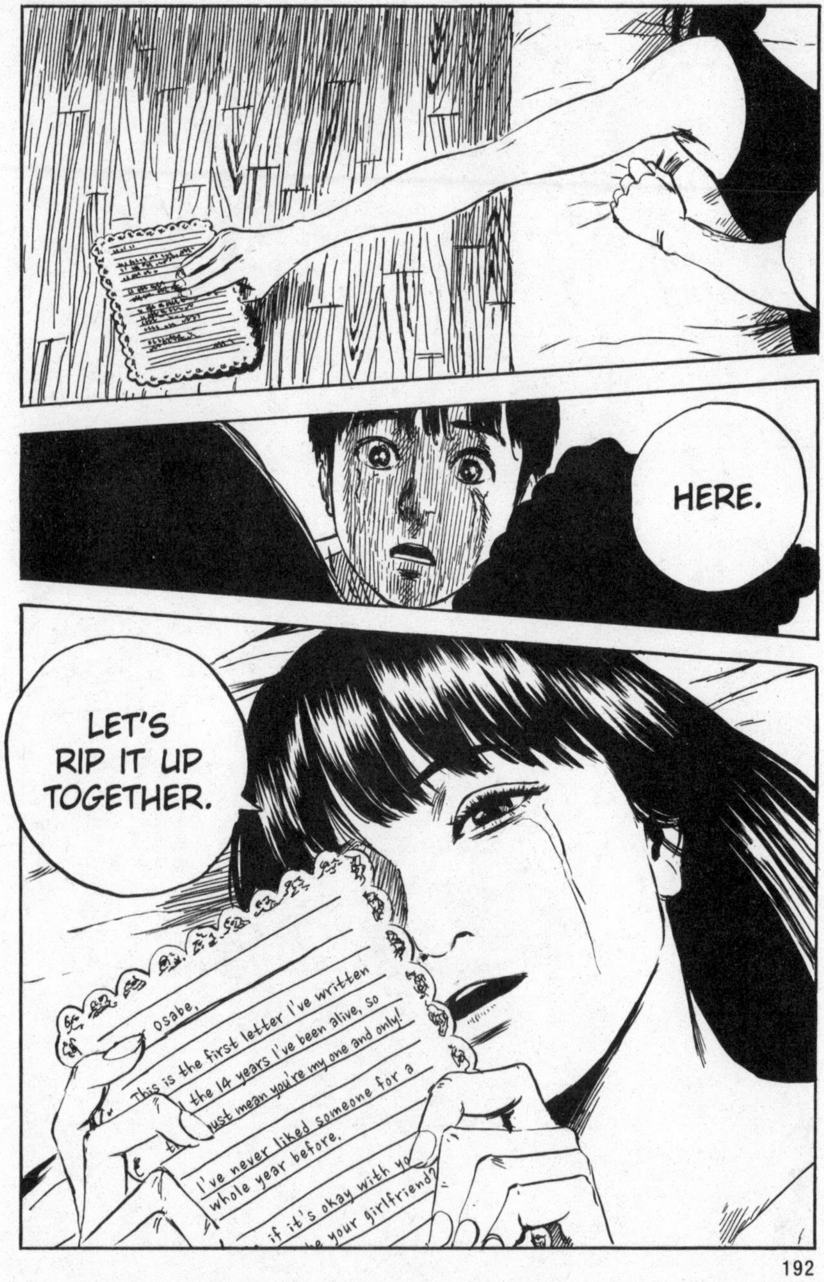
HERE.
LET'S RIP IT UP TOGETHER.
Osabe,
This is the first letter I've written
the 14 years I've been alive, so
just mean you're my one and only!
I've never liked someone for a
whole year before.
if it's okay with yo
be your girlfriend?

COME ON.
COME HERE.
Dear Osabe,
This is the first letter I've written in all the 14 years I've been alive, so that must mean you're my one and only!
I've never liked someone for a whole year before!
So, if it's okay with you, could I be your girlfriend?
Even if the answer is no let me know either way.
But don't tell anyone, okay?
Love, Yuiko

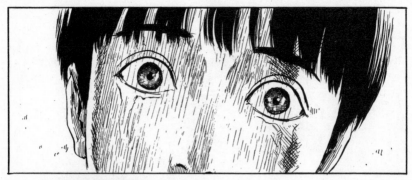

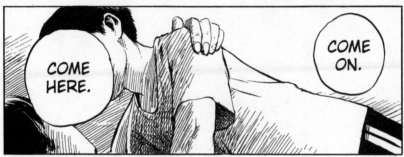

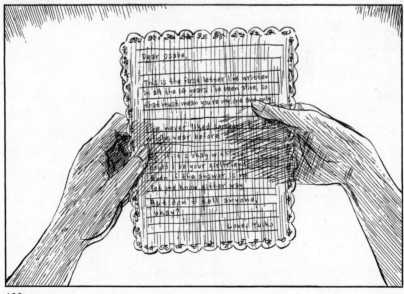

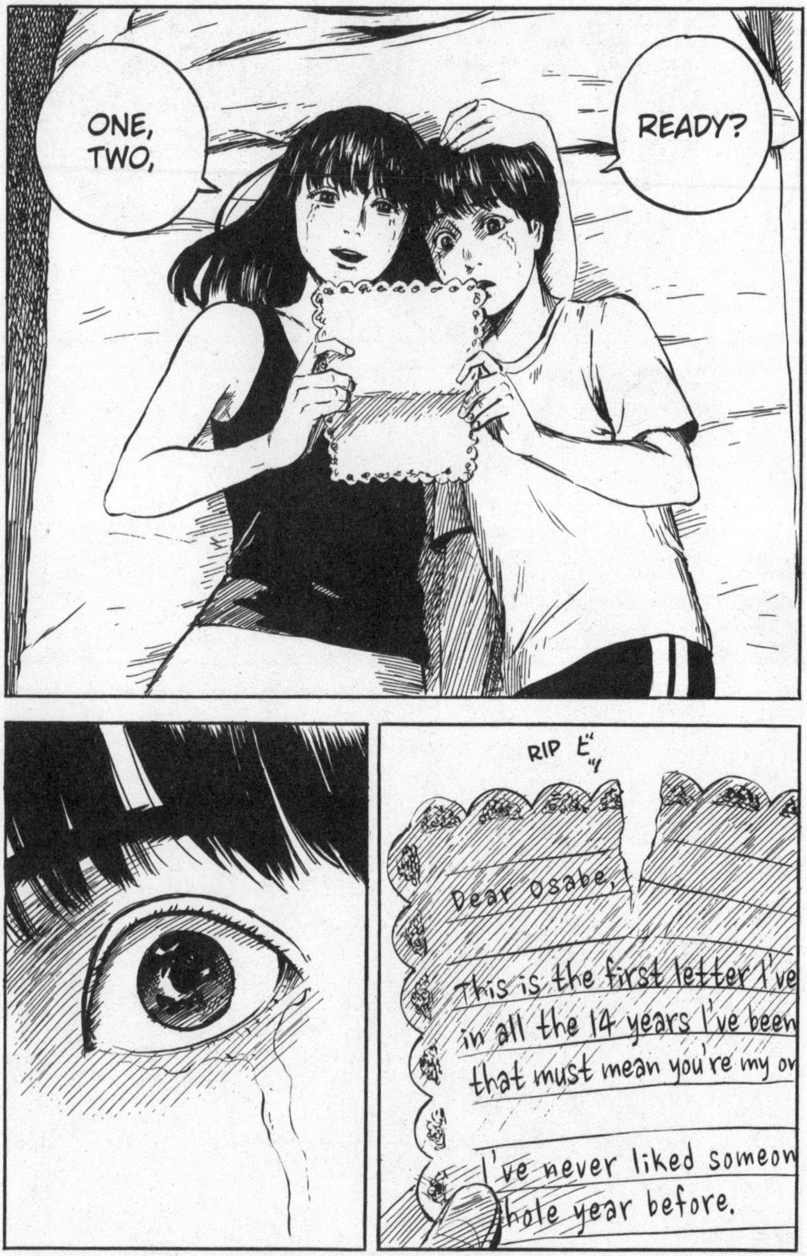
READY?
ONE, TWO,
RIP ビッ
Dear Osabe,
This is the first letter I've
in all the 14 years I've been
that must mean you're my
I've never liked someon
hole year before.

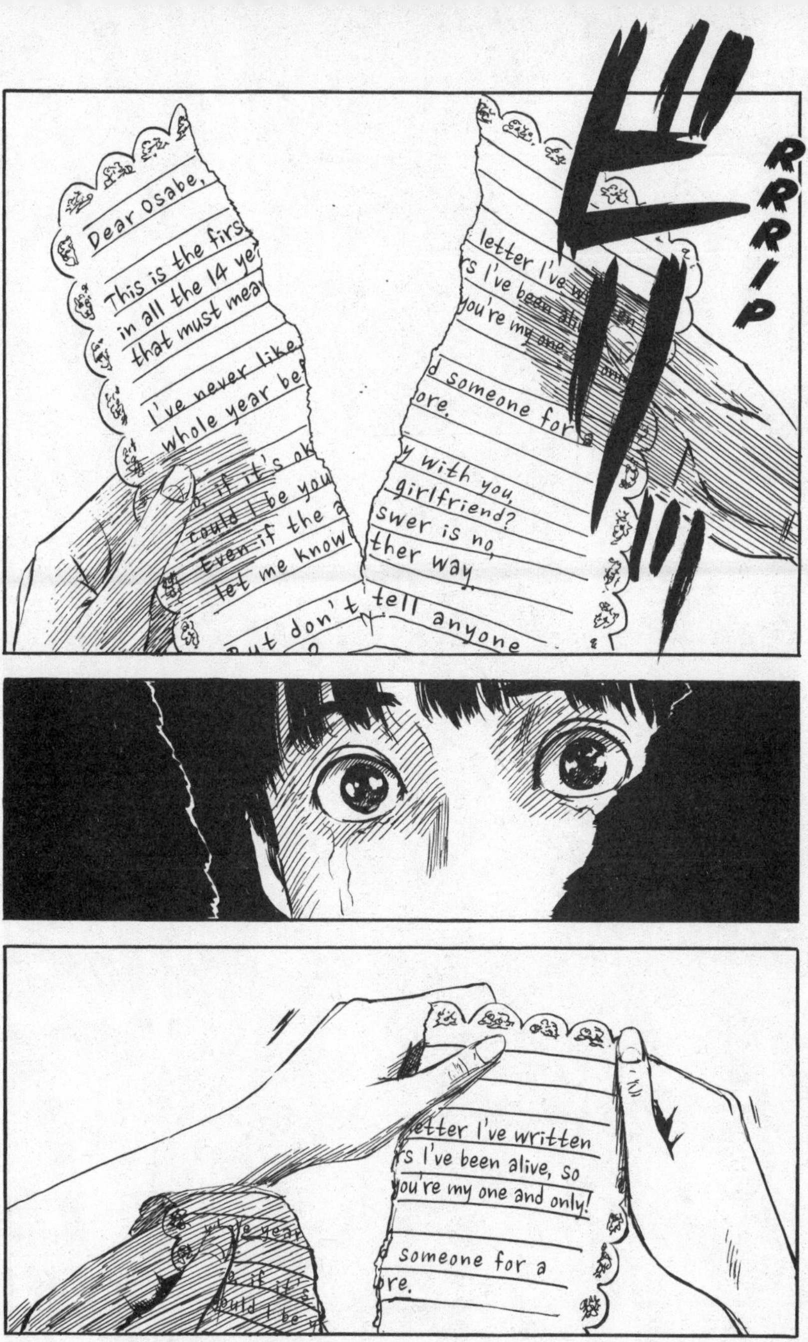
RRRIP
Dear Osabe,
This is the firs
in all the 14 ye
that must mea
I've never like
whole year be
could I be you
Even if the a
let me know
letter I've
rs I've been ali
you're my one
d someone for
ore.
y with you,
girlfriend?
swer is no,
ther way.
But don't tell anyone
etter I've written
rs I've been alive, so
you're my one and only!
someone for a
ore.

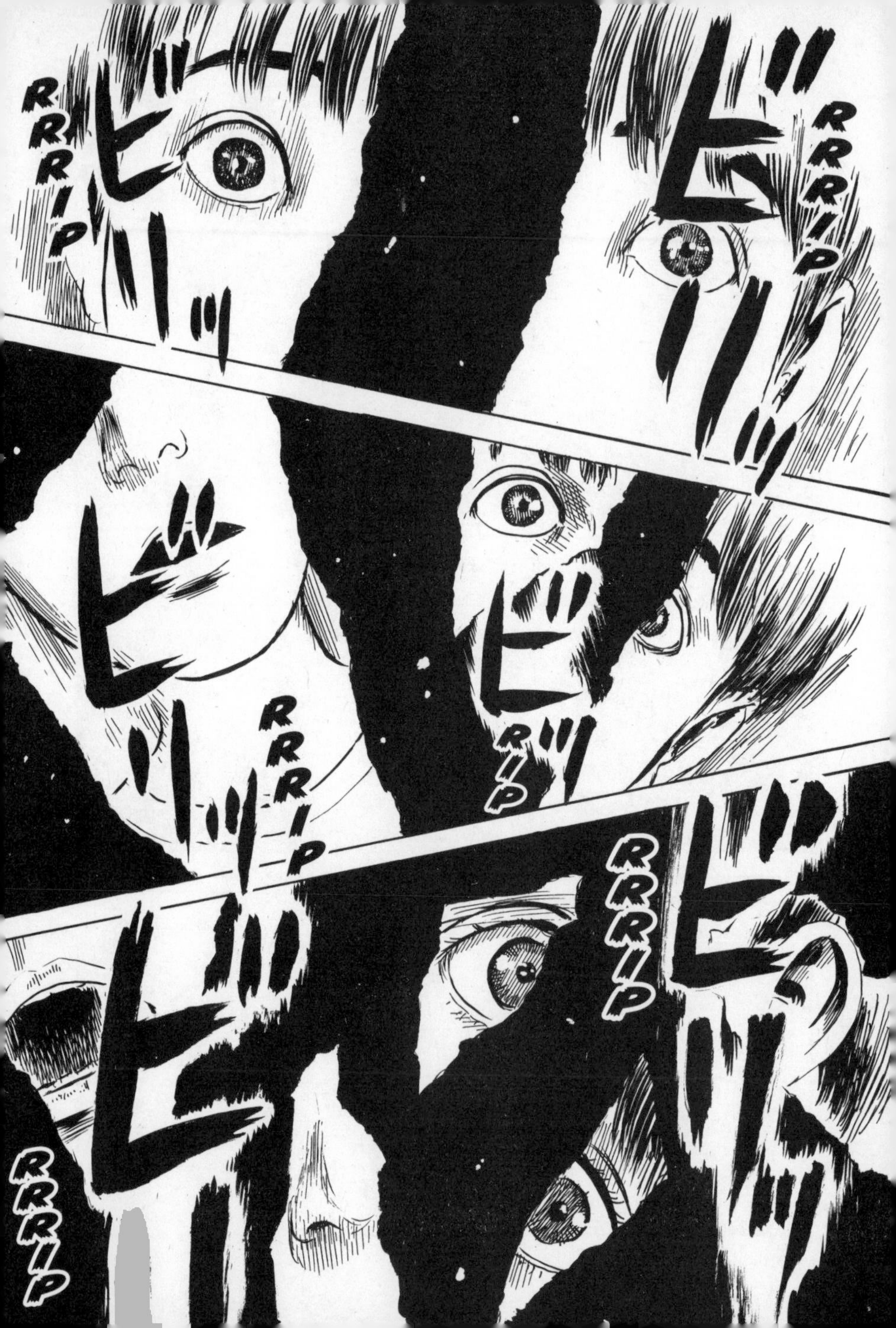
RRRIP
RRRIP
RIP
RRRIP
RRRIP
RRRIP

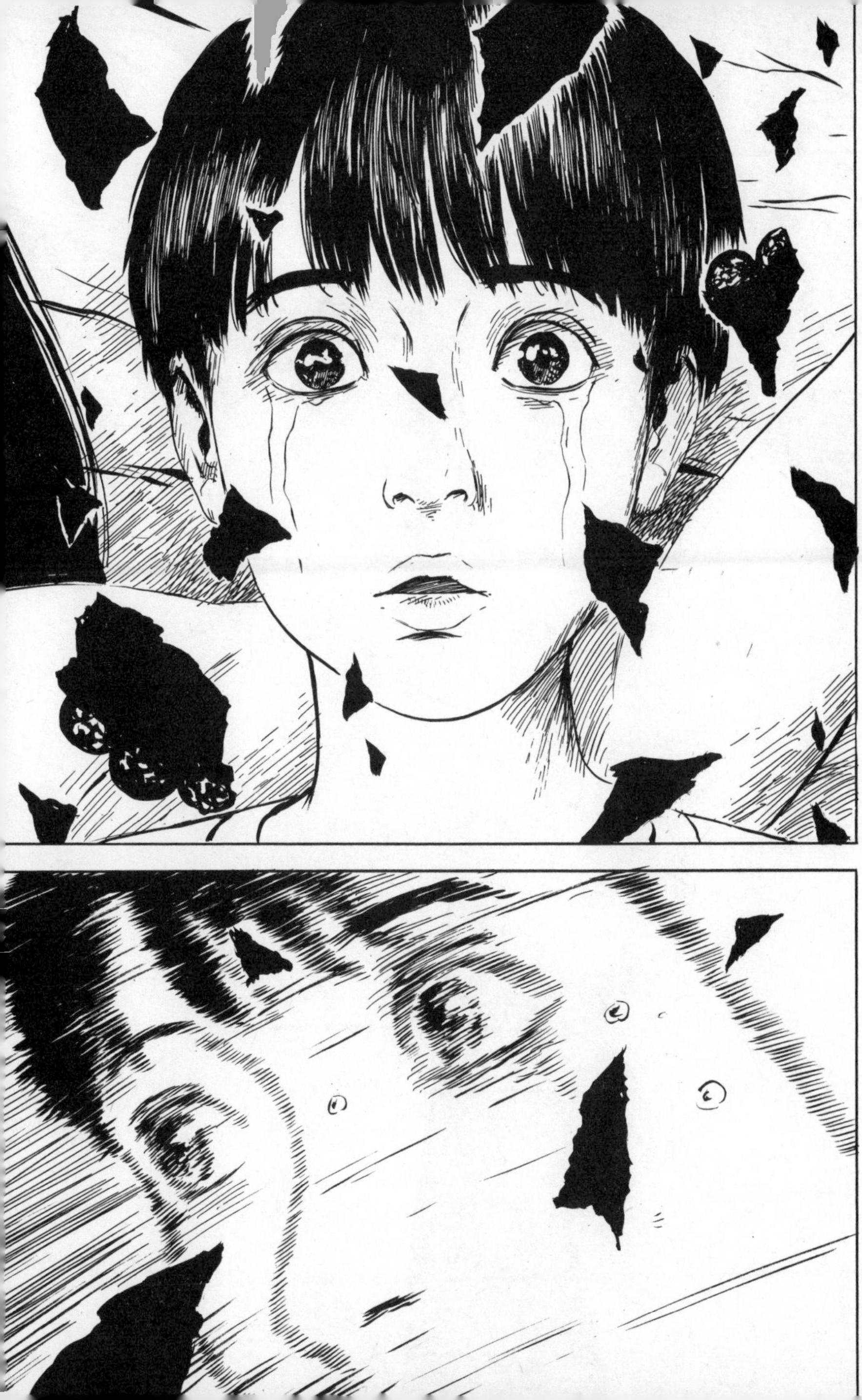

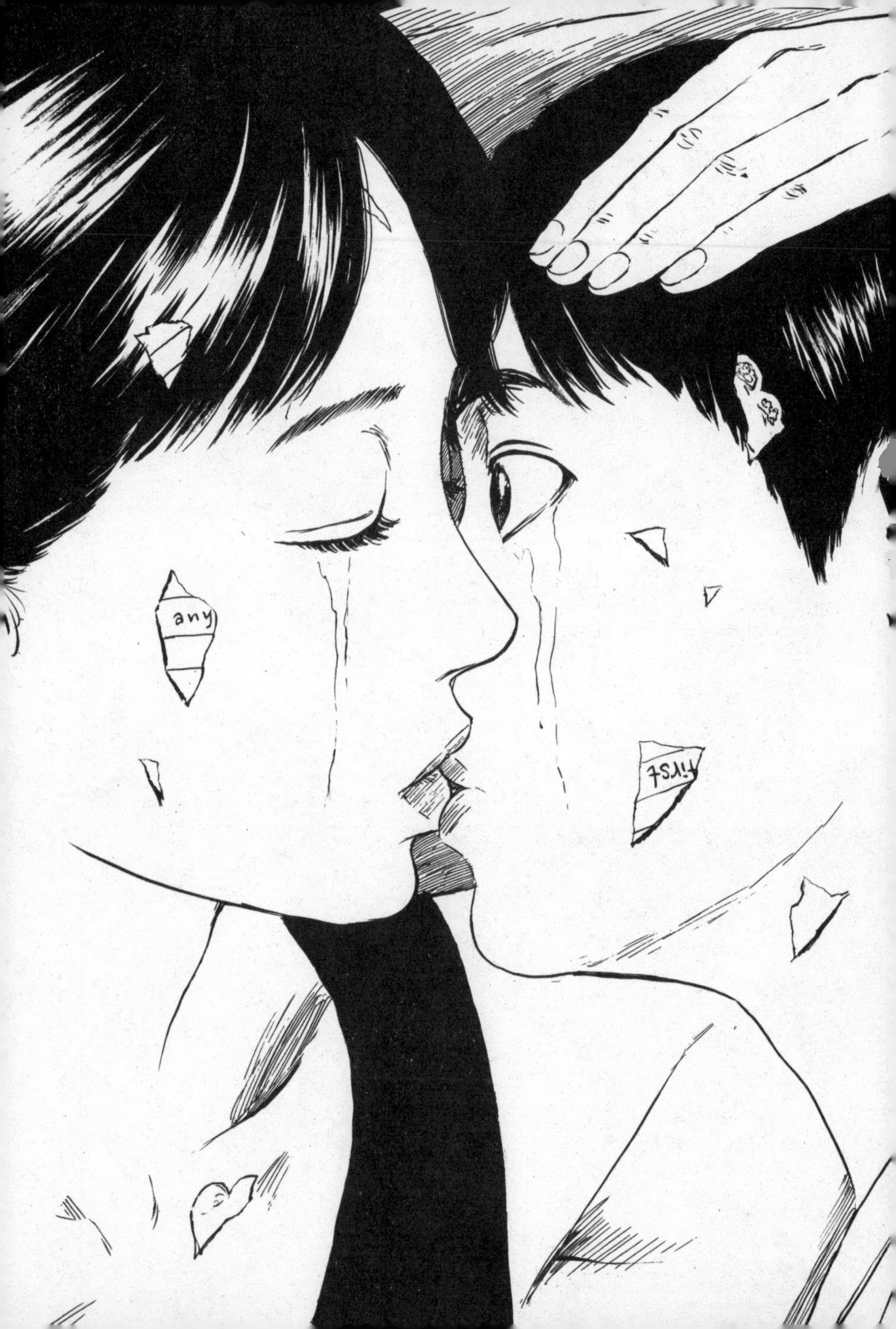
any
first

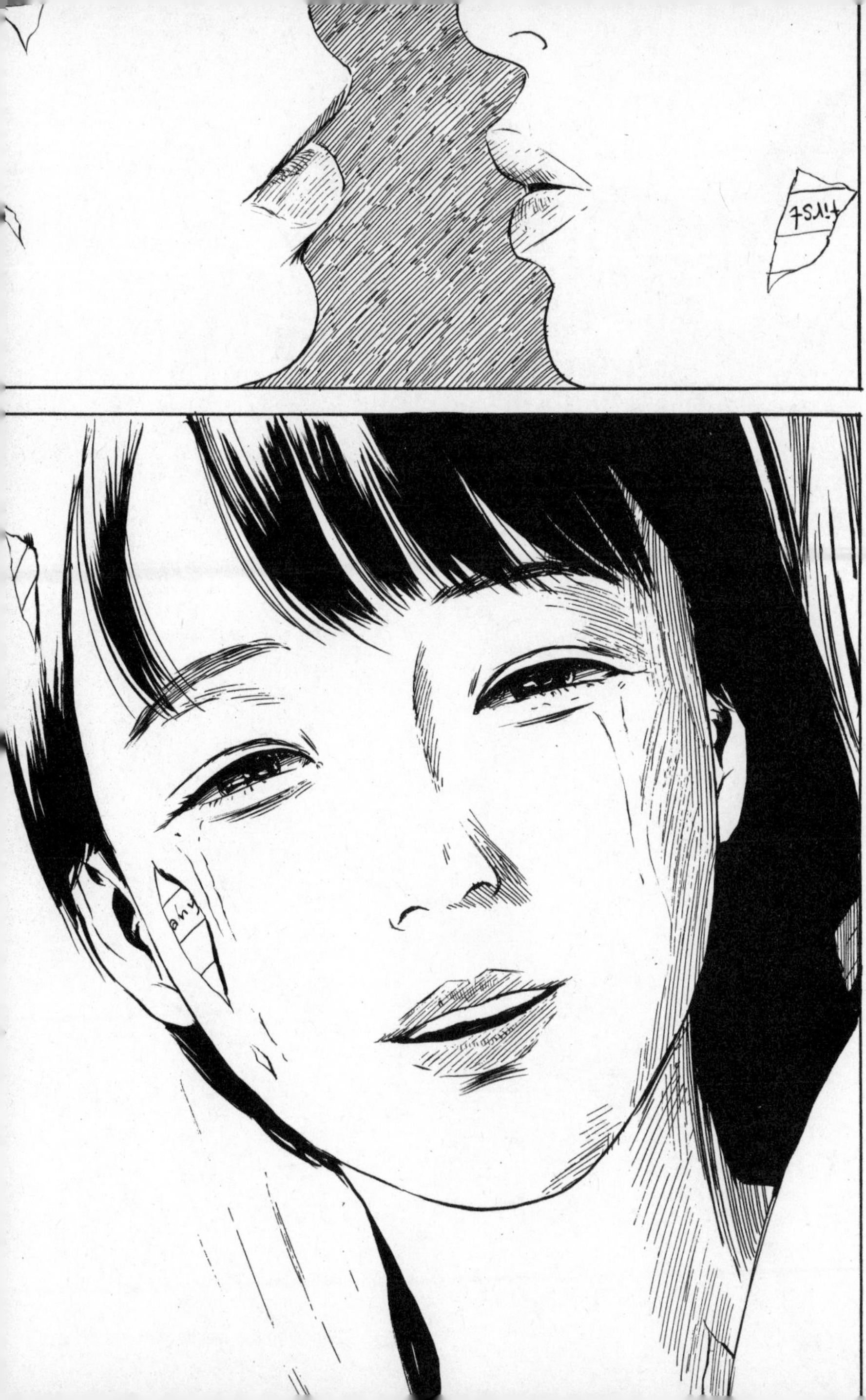
first
any

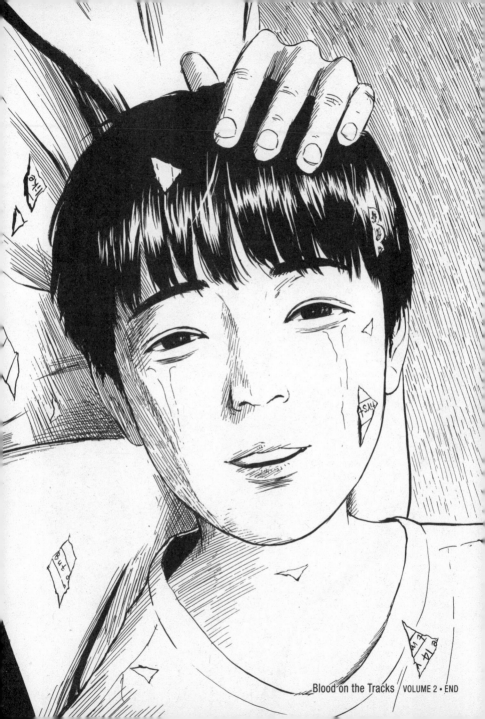

Blood on the Tracks / VOLUME 2 • END

Photo Album

Seiichi
Age 2

First
School
Uniform

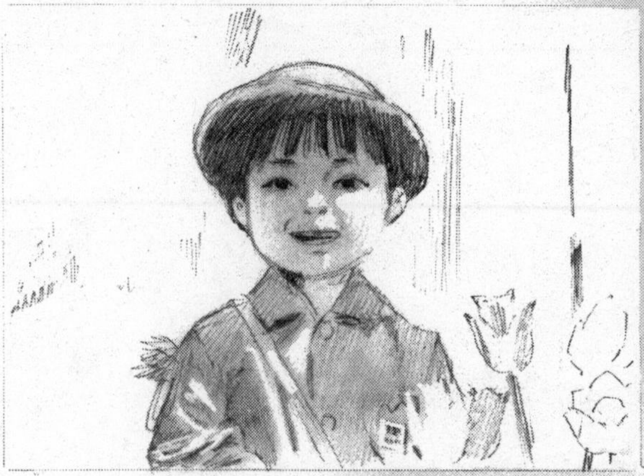

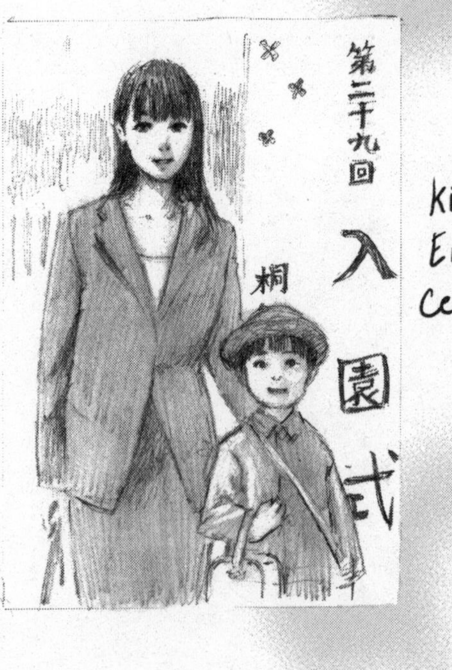
第二十九回
入園式
桐

Kindergarten
Entrance
Ceremony

Loves Picture Books

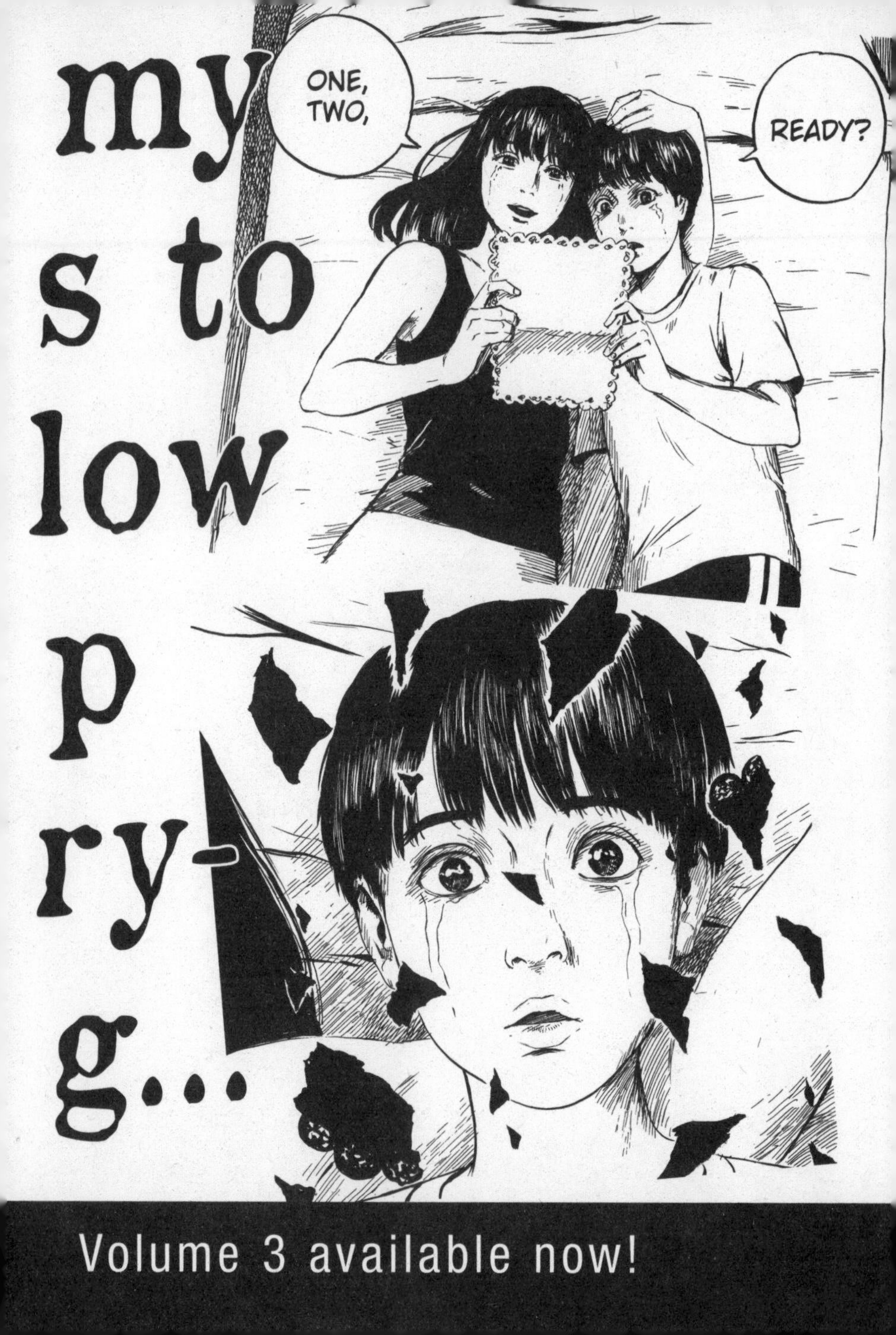
my
s to
low
p
ry-
g...
READY?
ONE, TWO,

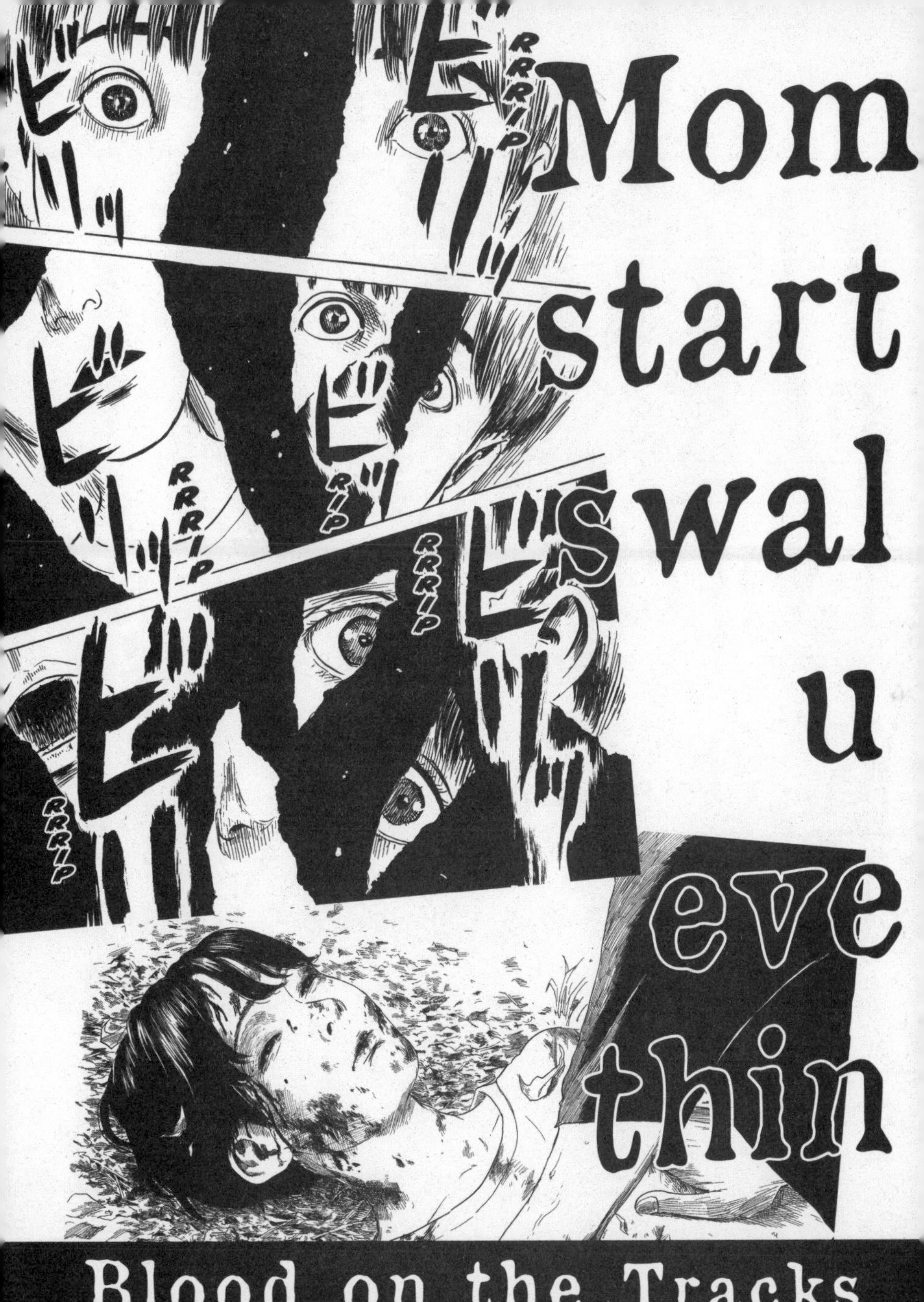
RRRIP
Mom
start
swal
u
eve
thin
RRRIP
RRRIP
RRRIP
RRRIP

Blood on the Tracks